ALPHABETICAL LISTING OF PHILOSOP

Abelard, Peter	1079–1142	Heraclitus	c. 540–480 B.C.
Al-Ghazali	1058–1111	Hobbes, Thomas	1588–1679
Anaxagoras	500–428 B.C.	Hume, David	1711–1776
Anaximander	c. 610–545 B.C.	Husserl, Edmund	1859–1938
Anaximenes	c. 580–500 B.C.	James, William	1842–1910
Anselm, Saint	1033–1109	Kant, Immanuel	1724–1804
Aquinas, Saint Thomas	1225–1274	Kierkegaard, Søren	1813–1855
Aristotle	384–322 B.C.	Leibniz, Gottfried	1646–1716
Augustine, Saint	354–430	Locke, John	1632–1704
Austin, John	1911–1960	Luther, Martin	1483–1546
Averroës	1126–1198	Maimonides, Moses	1135–1204
Avicenna	980–1037	Marx, Karl	1818–1883
Ayer, A. J.	1910–1989	Mill, John Stuart	1806–1873
Bacon, Francis	1561–1626	Newton, Sir Isaac	1642–1727
Beauvoir, Simone de	1908–1986	Nietzsche, Friedrich	1844–1900
Bentham, Jeremy	1748–1832	Ockham, William of	c. 1280–1349
Bergson, Henri	1859–1941	Parmenides	c. 515–450 B.C.
Berkeley, George	1685–1753	Pascal, Blaise	1623–1662
Boethius	c. 480–524	Peirce, Charles S.	1839–1914
Carnap, Rudolph	1891–1970	Plato	c. 428–348 B.C.
Comte, Auguste	1798–1857	Plotinus	205–270
Copernicus, Nicholas	1473–1543	Protagoras	c. 490–420 B.C.
Darwin, Charles	1809–1882	Pyrrho	c. 360–270 B.C.
Democritus	c. 460–360 B.C.	Pythagoras	c. 570–495 B.C.
Derrida, Jacques	1930–	Quine, Willard V. O.	1908–2000
Descartes, René	1596–1650	Rorty, Richard	1931–
Dewey, John	1859–1952	Rousseau, Jean Jacques	1712–1778
Dostoevsky, Fyodor	1821–1881	Russell, Bertrand	1872–1970
Eckhart, Meister	c. 1260–1327	Ryle, Gilbert	1900–1976
Einstein, Albert	1879–1955	Sartre, Jean-Paul	1905–1980
Empedocles	c. 495–435 B.C.	Schopenhauer, Arthur	1788–1860
Engels, Friedrich	1820–1895	Scotus, John Duns	c. 1266–1308
Epictetus	c. 50–138	Socrates	c. 470–399 B.C.
Epicurus	341–270 B.C.	Spinoza, Benedict	
Erasmus, Desiderius	1466–1536	(Baruch)	1632–1677
Erigena, John Scotus	c. 810–877	Thales	624–545 B.C.
Foucault, Michel	1926–1984	Voltaire	1694–1778
Freud, Sigmund	1856–1939	Whitehead, Alfred North	1861–1947
Galileo	1564–1642	Wittgenstein, Ludwig	1889–1951
Gorgias	c. 483–375 B.C.	Xenophanes	c. 570–478 B.C.
Hegel, Georg W. F.	1770–1831	Zeno the Eleatic	c. 490–430 B.C.
Heidegger, Martin	1889–1976	Zeno the Stoic	c. 336–264 B.C.

CHRONOLOGICAL LIST OF PHILOSOPHERS

THE ANCIENT PERIOD

Thales	c. 624–545	B.C.
Anaximander	c. 610–545	B.C.
Anaximenes	c. 580–500	B.C.
Pythagoras	c. 570–495	B.C.
Xenophanes	c. 570–478	B.C.
Heraclitus	c. 540–480	B.C.
Parmenides	c. 515–450	B.C.
Anaxagoras	500–428	B.C.
Empedocles	c. 495–435	B.C.
Zeno the Eleatic	c. 490–430	B.C.
Protagoras	c. 490–420	B.C.
Gorgias	c. 483–375	B.C.
Socrates	c. 470–399	B.C.
Democritus	c. 460–360	B.C.
Plato	c. 428–348	B.C.
Aristotle	384–322	B.C.
Pyrrho	c. 360–270	B.C.
Epicurus	341–270	B.C.
Zeno the Stoic	c. 336–264	B.C.
Epictetus	c. 50–138	
Plotinus	205–270	

THE MIDDLE AGES

Augustine, Saint	354–430	
Boethius	c. 480–524	
Erigena, John Scotus	c. 810–877	
Anselm, Saint	1033–1109	
Avicenna	980–1037	
Al-Ghazali	1058–1111	
Abelard, Peter	1079–1142	
Averroës	1126–1198	
Maimonides, Moses	1135–1204	
Aquinas, Saint Thomas	1225–1274	
Eckhart, Meister	c. 1260–1327	
Scotus, John Duns	c. 1266–1308	
Ockham, William of	c. 1280–1349	

THE MODERN PERIOD

Erasmus, Desiderius	1466–1536
Copernicus, Nicholas	1473–1543
Luther, Martin	1483–1546
Bacon, Francis	1561–1626
Galileo	1564–1642
Hobbes, Thomas	1588–1679
Descartes, René	1596–1650
Pascal, Blaise	1623–1662
Spinoza, Benedict (Baruch)	1632–1677
Locke, John	1632–1704
Newton, Sir Isaac	1642–1727
Leibniz, Gottfried	1646–1716
Berkeley, George	1685–1753
Voltaire	1694–1778
Hume, David	1711–1776
Rousseau, Jean Jacques	1712–1778
Kant, Immanuel	1724–1804
Bentham, Jeremy	1748–1832
Hegel, Georg W. F.	1770–1831
Schopenhauer, Arthur	1788–1860
Comte, Auguste	1798–1857
Mill, John Stuart	1806–1873
Darwin, Charles	1809–1882
Kierkegaard, Søren	1813–1855
Marx, Karl	1818–1883
Engels, Friedrich	1820–1895
Dostoevsky, Fyodor	1821–1881
Nietzsche, Friedrich	1844–1900

THE CONTEMPORARY PERIOD

Peirce, Charles S.	1839–1914
James, William	1842–1910
Freud, Sigmund	1856–1939
Husserl, Edmund	1859–1938
Bergson, Henri	1859–1941
Dewey, John	1859–1952
Whitehead, Alfred North	1861–1947
Russell, Bertrand	1872–1970
Einstein, Albert	1879–1955
Wittgenstein, Ludwig	1889–1951
Heidegger, Martin	1889–1976
Carnap, Rudolph	1891–1970
Ryle, Gilbert	1900–1976
Sartre, Jean-Paul	1905–1980
Beauvoir, Simone de	1908–1986
Quine, Willard V. O.	1908–2000
Ayer, A. J.	1910–1989
Austin, John	1911–1960
Foucault, Michel	1926–1984
Derrida, Jacques	1930–
Rorty, Richard	1931–

1 800 - 423 - 0863

THE VOYAGE OF DISCOVERY
A HISTORICAL INTRODUCTION TO PHILOSOPHY

THE CONTEMPORARY VOYAGE
1900–

SECOND EDITION

William F. Lawhead
University of Mississippi

WADSWORTH

THOMSON LEARNING

Australia • Canada • Mexico • Singapore • Spain
United Kingdom • United States

WADSWORTH

✦ ™

THOMSON LEARNING

Publisher: Eve Howard
Philosophy Editor: Peter Adams
Assistant Editor: Kara Kindstrom
Editorial Assistant: Chalida Anusasananan
Marketing Manager: Dave Garrison
Marketing Assistant: Adam Hofmann
Print/Media Buyer: Barbara Britton
Permissions Editor: Joohee Lee

Production Service: The Book Company
Text Designer: Wendy LaChance
Photo Researcher: Myrna Engler
Copy Editor: Jane Loftus
Cover Designer: Yvo Riezebos
Cover Image: Shinichi Eguchi/Photonica
Compositor: Thompson Type
Cover and Text Printer: R. R. Donnelley, Crawfordsville

For more information about our products, contact us:
Thomson Learning Academic Resource Center
1-800-423-0563
http://www.wadsworth.com

International Headquarters
Thomson Learning
International Division
290 Harbor Drive, 2nd Floor
Stamford, CT 06902-7477
USA

UK/Europe/Middle East/South Africa
Thomson Learning
Berkshire House
168-173 High Holborn
London WC1V 7AA
United Kingdom

Asia
Thomson Learning
60 Albert Street, #15-01
Albert Complex
Singapore 189969

Canada
Nelson Thomson Learning
1120 Birchmount Road
Toronto, Ontario M1K 5G4
Canada

Wadsworth/Thomson Learning
10 Davis Drive
Belmont, CA 94002-3098
USA

Library of Congress Cataloging-in-Publication Data
Lawhead, William F.
　The contemporary voyage / William F. Lawhead.
　　p. cm.
　Includes bibliographical references and index.
　ISBN 0-534-56126-8
　　1. Philosophy, Modern—History.　I. Title.

B791 .L37 2001
190—dc21　　　　　　　　　2001045345

To the memory of my mother, Cecelia Lawhead,
and that of
my father, James Lawhead,
and to Pam, Joel, and Andy

CONTENTS

THE VOYAGE OF DISCOVERY

PREFACE

This current volume belongs to a four-part paperback series that includes *The Ancient Voyage, The Medieval Voyage, The Modern Voyage,* and *The Contemporary Voyage.* Each of these four volumes focuses on one particular period in the history of philosophy and represents one of the parts of the complete one-volume work *The Voyage of Discovery: A Historical Introduction to Philosophy* 2nd ed. It is hoped that publishing the book in multiple formats will make it more flexible and will increase its usefulness for instructors. Those who are teaching a particular historical period can use the appropriate paperback volume or volumes for that time period. This makes it cost effective to use my historical discussions with a collection of primary source readings. On the other hand, some will prefer to use the complete one-volume work for an introduction to philosophy course that covers significant thinkers from the Greeks to the contemporary period. Others (like me) teach a topically organized introduction course and follow that with one or two courses that survey the history of philosophy, using the complete *The Voyage of Discovery.*

This book has grown out of my thirty years of teaching the history of Western philosophy. I love to teach this subject. I have found that the history of philosophy develops students' critical thinking skills. After journeying with the course for awhile and following the point and counterpoint movements of the great historical debates, students begin to show a flare for detecting the assumptions, strengths, problems, and implications of a thinker's position. Furthermore, the history of philosophy provides students with an arsenal of essential terms, distinctions, categories, and critical questions for making sense out of the barrage of ideas they encounter in history, literature, psychology, politics, and even on television.

One reward of teaching philosophy is to see students develop new confidence in themselves on finding a kindred spirit in one or more of the great minds of history, who agree with their own assessment of what is fallacious or sound. By exposing students to unfamiliar viewpoints that are outrageous, fascinating, perplexing, hopeful, dangerous, gripping, troubling, and exhilarating, the history of philosophy helps them gain a renewed sense of childlike wonder, teaching them to look at the world with new eyes. Finally, throughout the history of philosophy, students often find ideas that are liberating and challenging, leading them down exciting paths that were not even on their conceptual maps when they started the course. I hope that this book will be an effective navigator's guide to such intellectual journeys.

GOALS THAT GUIDED THE WRITING OF THIS BOOK

After many years of teaching a course, a professor begins to get a sense of the "ideal" textbook. For me, an effective history of philosophy text should achieve the following goals:

1. Make the ideas of the philosophers as clear and accessible as possible to the average person. A student-friendly philosophy text will not read like an encyclopedia article, which contains dense but terse summaries of factual information.

2. Provide strategies for sorting out the overwhelming mass of contradictory ideas encountered in the history of philosophy.

3. Find the correct balance between the competing concerns of (a) technical accuracy versus accessibility and (b) breadth of scope versus depth of exposition.

4. Communicate the fact that philosophy is more than simply a collection of opinions on basic issues. Understanding a philosopher's arguments is just as important as the philosopher's conclusions.

5. Encourage the reader to evaluate the ideas discussed. The history of philosophy should be more than the intellectual equivalent of a wine-tasting party, where various philosophers are "sampled" simply to enjoy their distinct flavors.

Although that is certainly one of the delights of studying philosophy and should be encouraged, assessing the strengths and weaknesses of a philosopher's ideas is equally important.

6. Make clear the continuity of the centuries-long philosophical conversation. A course in the history of philosophy should not be like a display of different philosophical exhibits in glass cases. For me, the guiding image is philosophy as a big party where new conversations are continually starting up, while the themes of previous conversations are picked up and carried in different directions as new participants join the dialogue.

DISTINCTIVE FEATURES
OF THIS TEXT

• *A consistent structure is used.* For consistency and ease of comparison, the majority of chapters follow the same basic pattern:

1. The life and times of the philosopher

2. The major philosophical task that the philosopher tried to accomplish

3. Theory of knowledge

4. Metaphysics

5. Moral and political philosophy (when relevant)

6. Philosophy of religion (when relevant)

7. Evaluation and significance

• *Analysis of philosophical arguments is provided.* To emphasize that philosophy is a process and not just a set of results, I discuss the intellectual problems that motivated a philosopher's position and the reasons provided in its support. The book analyzes a number of explicitly outlined arguments of various philosophers, providing models of philosophical argumentation and analysis. In addition, I informally discuss numerous other arguments throughout the book.

• *The evaluation of ideas is stressed.* Most of the chapters end with a short evaluation of the philosophy discussed. These evaluations, however, are not presented as decisive "refutations" of the philosopher, which would relieve the reader of any

need to think further. Instead, the evaluations have been posed in terms of problems needing to be addressed and questions requiring an answer. Whenever possible, I have made this section a part of the historical dialogue by expressing the appraisals given by the philosopher's contemporaries and successors.

• *The significance of the ideas is emphasized.* The conclusion of each chapter also indicates the immediate and long-term significance of the philosopher's ideas and prepares the reader for the next turn in the historical dialogue. It makes clear the ways in which philosophical ideas can lead robust lives that continue far beyond their author's time.

• *The continuity between historical periods is emphasized.* Because each of the four paperback volumes represent a slice from the whole of Western philosophy, a special introductory chapter has been written that is specific to each of these four volumes. This chapter will situate the time period of that particular volume in terms of the philosophies that preceded it so that there will be no loss of continuity. Since *The Ancient Voyage* covers the beginnings of Western philosophy, the introductory chapter for that volume discusses the importance of studying the ancient Greeks. The introduction to *The Medieval Voyage* shows how that historical period arose out of the philosophies of the Greeks. In the introduction to *The Modern Voyage,* the shift from medieval thought is outlined in terms of four contrasts between the medieval and the modern outlook. Finally, *The Contemporary Voyage* begins with a brief overview of Immanuel Kant's philosophy and the various responses to it in the nineteenth century in order to set the stage for twentieth-century philosophy.

• *The philosophers are related to their cultural contexts.* In addition to these introductory chapters that emphasize the continuity with the thought that preceded the philosophies in each paperback volume, each major historical period covered by a particular paperback (Greek, early Christian to medieval, Renaissance and Reformation, Enlightenment, the nineteenth century, and the twentieth century) is introduced with a brief chapter discussing the intellectual-social milieu that provides the setting for the philosophies of that era. The questions addressed are: What were the dominant concerns and assumptions that animated each period in history? How did the different philosophers respond to the currents of thought of their time? and How did they influence their culture?

• *Diagrams.* Diagrams and tables provide visual representations of the elements of various philosophers' ideas.

• *Glossary.* A glossary is provided in which key terms used throughout the book are clearly and thoroughly defined. Words appearing in bold-face in the text may be found in the glossary.

• *Questions for review and reflection.* At the end of each chapter are two lists of questions. The questions for understanding are more factual and enable the readers to review their understanding of the important ideas and terms. The questions for reflection require the readers to engage in philosophy by making their own evaluations of the philosopher's ideas, as well as working out their implications.

• *Instructor's manual.* In addition to the usual sections containing test questions and essay questions, this manual provides suggested topics for research papers, tips for introducing and motivating interest in each philosopher, chapter-by-chapter topics for discussion, and the contemporary implications of each philosopher's ideas.

SUGGESTED WAYS TO USE THIS BOOK

This book may be used with students who are already familiar with the leading issues and positions in philosophy and who now need to place these ideas in their historical context. However, since it does not assume any previous acquaintance with the subject, it may also be used to introduce students to philosophy for the first time, through the story of its history. I have tried to make clear that philosophy is an ongoing conversation, in which philosophers respond to the insights and short-comings of their predecessors. Nevertheless, the chapters are self-contained enough that the instructor may put together a course that uses se-

lected chapters. For example, the chapter on Aquinas could be used as representative of medieval philosophy and Descartes used to represent the modern rationalists (skipping Spinoza and Leibniz). In the case of chapters that discuss a number of philosophers, only certain sections could be assigned. For example, to get a quick but partial glimpse of the wide range covered by analytic philosophy, the students could read only the sections on the early and later Wittgenstein. Although skipping over key thinkers is not ideal, teaching is a continual battle between time constraints and the desire to cover as much material in as much depth as possible.

The *Instructor's Manual* contains objective and essay questions that may be used in making up tests. In addition, Part 1 contains more reflective questions for discussion and essay assignments. I would encourage the instructor to make use of these questions in class in order to emphasize that philosophy is not a list of "who said what" but that it also involves the evaluation and application of the great ideas. Furthermore, because the students will have some of these topics and others posed as questions for reflection at the end of each chapter, they can be asked to have thought about their response to these questions prior to their discussion in class.

ABOUT THIS SECOND EDITION

I am gratified by the responses to the first edition of *The Voyage of Discovery* that I have received from professors using the book, from students who have been introduced to philosophy and its history through it, as well as from interested readers around the world who read it for personal enrichment. This second edition continues to have the distinctive features that so many enjoyed in the first edition and that have been highlighted in the previous sections of this preface. The subtitle has been changed to "A Historical Introduction to Philosophy" to communicate the fact that the book is intended to be used to introduce readers to philosophy for the first time as well as providing a comprehensive survey of Western philosophy. Besides some changes that have been made to aid in clarity and ease of reading, this current edition ends each chapter with questions to aid the reader in studying the material and in engaging in philosophical reflection on the ideas. Some of these questions have been taken from the essay and discussion questions in the *Instructor's Manual*. Nevertheless, over fifty percent of the essay questions in the *Instructor's Manual* remain unique to it. This edition is now available in two formats. As before, there is the one-volume edition that covers philosophy from the early Greeks to the contemporary period. New to the second edition is an alternative format that divides the book into four paperback volumes, corresponding to the four parts of the book. This makes it much more economical for the instructor to use parts of the book for courses that emphasize only particular time periods.

I hope that everyone who uses this book will find it both profitable and interesting. I encourage both professors and students to share with me their experience with the book as well as suggestions for improvement. Write to me at: Department of Philosophy, University of Mississippi, University, MS, 38677-1848. You may also send me e-mail at: wlawhead@olemiss.edu.

ACKNOWLEDGMENTS

From the initial, tentative outline of this book to the final chapter revisions, the manuscript has been extensively reviewed both by instructors who measured its suitability for the classroom and by scholars who reviewed its historical accuracy. Their comments have made it a much better book than the original manuscript. I take full responsibility, of course, for any remaining shortcomings. I am indebted to the following reviewers of this second edition: Jim Friel, State University New York—Farmingdale; John Longenay, University of Wisconsin—Riverside; Scott Lowe, Bloomsburg University; Michael Potts, Methodist College; and Blanche Premo-Hopkins, University of South Carolina—Aiken.

I also want to thank the reviewers of the first edition for their contributions: William Brown, Bryan College; Jill Buroker, California State University at San Bernardino; Bessie Chronaki, Central Piedmont Community College; Vincent Colapietro, Fordham University; Teresa Contrell, University of Louisville; Ronald Cox, San Antonio College; Timothy Davis, Essex Community College; Michelle Grier, University of San Diego; Eugene Lockwood, Oakton Community College; Michael Mendelson, University of California at San Diego; William Parent, Santa Clara University; Anthony Preus, State University of New York at Binghamton; Dennis Rothermel, California State University at Chico; James D. Ryan, Bronx Community College; James Spencer, Cuyahoga Community College; K. Sundaram, Lake Michigan College; Ken Stikkers, Seattle University; Robert Sweet, University of Dayton; Howard Tuttle, University of New Mexico; Jerome B. Wichelms, Jefferson Community College.

My thanks to the many people at the Wadsworth Publishing Company who played a role in the book's production. In particular, I appreciate the encouragement and support I received from Peter Adams, my editor.

The acknowledgments would be incomplete if I did not express my thanks to those individuals who have been particularly supportive throughout my career. My first exposure to philosophy was under the instruction of Arthur Holmes, my undergraduate chair, who ignited my love for the history of philosophy. The late Irwin C. Lieb guided me throughout my career as a graduate student, first as my professor, then as my department chair, and finally as graduate dean. Years of team teaching with David Schlafer, my former colleague, provided exciting lecture performances that have influenced what and how I teach. I have benefitted from good philosophical discussions with present and past colleagues, particularly Michael Harrington, Michael Lynch, Louis Pojman, and Robert Westmoreland. I also need to thank the many bright students who taught me how to teach.

This book is dedicated to my parents, James and Cecelia Lawhead, who first introduced me to the two dimensions of philosophy, love and wisdom; to my wife, Pam, who knows that love sometimes means being close and sometimes it means giving space; and to my sons, Joel and Andy, who taught me how much I do not know.

William Lawhead

This volume covers contemporary philosophy and focuses on the philosophies that dominated the greater part of the twentieth century. However, in the last chapter of this volume we will survey some of the recent issues and movements in philosophy that have arisen in the late twentieth century and that continue to be dominant forces in philosophy today.

Just as I could not fully understand you without understanding the hometown in which you grew up and the parents who raised you, so twentieth-century thought did not spring into being out of a vacuum but evolved out of the ideas and movements of the nineteenth century, which itself evolved out of the ideas that preceded it. So, in studying the movements of the twentieth century we are looking at ideas in motion; ideas that received some of their momentum from previous centuries, even though those ideas took directions and spins that could not have been anticipated when they were launched by earlier generations. To provide a minimal amount of background, this brief introduction will merely suggest some of the sources of the ideas and issues that we find in the twentieth century.

As will be mentioned in the next chapter, much of the story of contemporary philosophy goes back to the German philosopher Immanuel Kant (1724–1804). Kant argued that all our knowledge begins with experience, but claimed that it does not follow that it all arises out of experience. What he meant was that while the external world provides us with sense data, our experience and, hence, our knowledge is the result of the mind organizing, categorizing, and providing a form to that sense data. As Kant put it, "sensations without concepts are blind and concepts without sensations are empty." Since we can't jump out of our minds to see how this works, try this thought experiment. Consider what your experience is like when the alarm goes off in the morning. You are bombarded with sense data but, at first, it is pretty confusing until you begin to conceptualize what is happening. The mind has to play a role in giving some form to the sense data. This analogy is only a rough one, however, for Kant would say as soon as you hear the alarm, you are experiencing it as a spatial event and as one that has temporal duration. It is experienced not as a collection of distinct sensory data, but as "that sound" (something that has a location, a length, and a unity). Hence, the mind has already been at work from the beginning of the experience. For Kant, everyone's mind works the

same way, so everyone's experience will have certain universal and necessary features to it, those universal features being the product of reason.

Kant drew several conclusions from this thesis. First, we cannot know reality as it is in itself, but we can only know the world of experience, a world that is shaped by the human mind. This undercut previous philosophers' attempts to reason about reality itself. Second, Kant concluded that the contents of experience are primarily known through science. So, knowledge of the world of experience is identical to scientific knowledge. Third, Kant still believed that though we could not have knowledge (strictly speaking) about what lies outside experience, we still could not resist thinking in terms of that realm and that it was useful to do so. Specifically, he said that there were three things that could not be the objects of knowledge but that still played an important role in human thought. These were God, the cosmos as a whole, and the self that lay behind experience, the self that was more than our passing psychological states. Furthermore, Kant believed that science could never provide the basis for morality, but that morality could be understood on the basis of reason alone. So in our moral experience we are in touch with something that transcends the limits of science.

The important points in Kant's philosophy is that we cannot know what reality is like in itself. (We cannot get the "big picture.") Knowledge about the world is confined to what we can experience and discover scientifically (as well as to the form that the mind imposes upon experience). Yet, we still have concerns about issues that transcend the limits of science and we get a glimpse of this realm in moral experience.

Kant's philosophy was so influential that all philosophy after him is called "post-Kantian philosophy." The nineteenth-century philosophers reacted to Kant in various ways. Some sought to overcome the severe limitations that Kant placed upon reason and tried once again to philosophize about reality as a whole. G. W. F. Hegel (1770–1831) agreed that we could not know what lay outside the mind but theorized that our individual minds are simply limited manifestations of the World Spirit. Thus, in his quasi-theistic metaphysics, he claimed that all reality is rational and has the character of mind. Since our minds participate in the rationality of the world and our experience is a partial but ever-growing manifestation of the whole, we can know reality in itself. What is important to know about Hegel is that he built a grand metaphysical system out of these notions. Many philosophers in the nineteenth and twentieth centuries reacted against Hegel's speculative metaphysics (for various reasons) and tried to bring philosophy back down to earth and give it a more limited task.

Karl Marx (1818–1883) thought that his system told us what reality is like, but he based his thought on a materialistic view of reality and on a scientific study of history. For Marx, reality is not the grand, spiritual system that Hegel outlined, but is matter in motion. Since there is nothing more to reality beyond the material world that we encounter in experience, we can know what reality is like. A distinctive theme in Marx's philosophy is that the material forces in reality manifest themselves in human history through the dynamics of our material, economic life. What is important to know about Marx is that he thought we could know reality as it is and that we can know it through science. Hence, he believed that through science we can get the "big picture" and that reality is the here-and-now material world encountered in concrete, human experience.

The nineteenth-century forerunners of existentialism took a different tack. These were Søren Kierkegaard (1813–1855) and Friedrich Nietzsche (1844–1900). Kierkegaard was a passionate Christian and Nietzsche was a passionate atheist. Nevertheless, both agreed with Kant that reason is limited and that our knowledge begins with experience. But the experience they were talking about was not sense data or the sort of experiences that provide us with scientific observations. Instead, they focused on our subjective, passionate experience as concrete individuals. Hence, they reacted against Hegel's grand, rationalistic, speculative metaphysical system and claimed that it was too ideal, too abstract, and too detached from the human situation. Furthermore, they agreed with Kant that our experience is shaped by us, but claimed that there were multiple ways to shape experience that were relative to each individual. In short, these existential thinkers sought a kind of knowledge that transcends the limits of reason, claimed that science gives us only abstractions and does not speak to our lived-experience, and abandoned the pretensions of reason to reveal reality as it is in itself. (They agreed with Kant that we cannot get the "big picture.") The only reality that matters, they claimed, is reality as we concretely and subjectively encounter it in our individual journeys through life.

Finally, the nineteenth-century empiricists sought to limit our knowledge and discourse to what could be given in experience as it was scientifically known.

Whereas Kant always hinted at a reality that transcended the limits of science and thought that morality was to be found there, these empiricists thought that this was meaningless, unnecessary conceptual baggage. They believed that we could not get the "big picture," but that we could have hard, concrete, and positive but limited knowledge based on sense data. Unlike Kant they also believed that an ethical system could be based on science by examining the consequences of our actions and gauging their practical effects. The nineteenth-century empiricists included the French positivist Auguste Comte (1798–1857) and the British utilitarians Jeremy Bentham (1748–1832) and John Stuart Mill (1806–1873).

In the next chapter, which will be an overview of the early to middle twentieth-century philosophical movements, we will look at three large-scale questions. The different philosophical movements can be organized in terms of how they respond to these three questions. These are: (1) Should philosophy be done by piecemeal analysis or by grasping the big picture? (2) What is the role of science in philosophy? (3) What is the role of language and experience in philosophy? As you can see, much of this agenda arose out of Kant's philosophy and the various reactions to it. Furthermore, how various philosophers respond to these questions depends on how the terms contained within them are understood. For those who claim that philosophy should strive to give us a large-scale picture of things, for example, we still need to ask: Is this an objective picture of what reality in itself is like or is it the world as viewed from within the outlines of our individual or human situation? In asking about the role of experience in philosophy, we need to ask: Does this mean experience as studied in our scientific pursuits or is it subjective experience? In other words, does experience consist of sense data alone, or does it include the experiences of despair, anxiety, moral intuitions, or love? With respect to the third question, Kant did not say much about the role of language in philosophy, for this issue is a result of the "linguistic turn" in twentieth-century philosophy. Nevertheless, what one considers to be the proper domain of philosophical discourse has a lot to do with the stance one takes on Kantian issues about what we can know. As you study the various philosophies of the contemporary period, think about how each one relates to the issues Kant raised and to the various responses of the nineteenth-century philosophers who preceded them.

P | A | R | T

IV

THE CONTEMPORARY PERIOD

29

The Twentieth-Century Cultural Context: Science, Language, and Experience

THE TWENTIETH CENTURY HAS BEEN DESCRIBED in a number of ways. It has been called "the Age of Analysis," "the Age of Technology," and "the Information Age." These titles capture the global impact that science and technology have made on our sensibilities and the way we live. However, the happy notes sounded by these developments must be balanced by the discordant themes of two world wars, continuing threats of nuclear war, economic crises, environmental problems, social unrest, a sense of personal alienation, and . . . the list goes on. Hence another favorite title for the twentieth century has been "the Age of Anxiety."

Although these labels and others like them have their point to make, perhaps the safest generalization to make in terms of the history of philosophy is that this century has been "the Age of Plurality." At the same time that our information technology has turned our world into a global village, the explosion of perspectives has made our culture seem like a ship with multiple rudders and navigators, each trying to set a different course. The effect of this on philosophy was expressed by Edmund Husserl in 1931:

Instead of a unitary living philosophy, we have a philosophical literature growing beyond all bounds and almost without coherence. Instead of a serious discussion among conflicting theories that, in their very conflict, demonstrate the intimacy with which they belong together, the commonness of their underlying convictions, and an unswerving belief in a true philosophy, we have . . . a mere semblance of philosophizing seriously with and for one another. . . . To be sure, we still have philosophical congresses. The philosophers meet but, unfortunately, not the philosophies.[1]

One symptom that an age is in a state of crisis and transition is a recurring obsession with philosophical method and debates over the very nature of philosophy itself. In ancient Greece, we saw this in the conflicts between the Sophists and their culture, which led to Socrates and Plato's attempt at philosophical renewal. During the decline of the Middle Ages, the debate over the roles of faith and reason became a transforming cultural force. Likewise, at the beginning of the modern period the conflict between the rationalists and the empiricists was the manifestation of a culture trying to find its center.

empiricism: a theory that all knowledge originates in experience

453

Part or whole? (jigsaw puzzle) {parts vs whole border}

Whenever there is a crisis in the foundations of culture and thought, there is a concerted effort to find a philosophical method that will put us on the right track. Consequently, all the philosophies in this century are characterized not only by their particular doctrines but by the fact that each one has a distinctive notion of the appropriate philosophical method to be employed. This concern is evident in the four major twentieth-century philosophical movements: pragmatism, process philosophy, analytic philosophy, and the intertwined movements of phenomenology and existentialism.

Living in Kant's Shadow

To set the stage of the twentieth century, it is important to remind ourselves that this is the post-Kantian era in philosophy. The themes and problems introduced by Kant continue to consciously or unconsciously set the agenda for philosophy. To review, Kant sought to set out the limits of knowledge. His conclusion was that what we can know is only the phenomena, or what appears within our spatially and temporally structured experience and can be understood scientifically. The corollary of this was that reality in itself, the noumenon, cannot be comprehended. However, Kant thought that we could not escape thinking in terms of "the big picture." Hence, he thought that "regulative ideas" guide thought, even if they cannot be objects of knowledge. These are the notions of the self, the cosmos as a totality, and God.

From these Kantian materials we can uncover three themes that reappear throughout all the twentieth-century philosophies. First there is the issue of whether philosophy should focus on a detailed analysis of the phenomena or strive for a comprehensive outlook on the self, the cosmos, and God. This includes the question of whether or not the large-scale picture we construct conforms to the nature of reality itself or only traces the outlines of the human situation. Second there are questions concerning the role of science in doing philosophy. Third there are controversies concerning the respective roles that language and experience play in our philosophical investigations. We

will briefly discuss these issues and preview how each philosophical position addresses it.

Philosophy: Piecemeal Analysis or Grasping the Big Picture?

first

To begin with an analogy, there are two ways one can study a particular section of geographical terrain. One can approach it like a chemist, gathering soil samples, analyzing them in the laboratory, and making a detailed list of the elementary chemicals contained within this region of the earth. Or one can get in an airplane and fly high over it, trying to get a feel for the whole, how the region is put together, and the relationships between the different hills and fields within it. Who should the philosopher emulate: the chemist or the aerial surveyor? Should we search for detailed knowledge of the parts or for a comprehensive understanding of the whole? This admittedly rough analogy tries to capture a major divergence within contemporary philosophy: who has a better understanding of the terrain, the person with a knowledge of the parts or of the whole? In the case of the chemist versus the pilot, we would say that which method you should use depends on your goal. For example, do you want to know what crops to plant in the soil, or do you wish to make a map of the terrain? With philosophy, however, the question about the appropriate method cannot be answered by appealing to our goal because the question simply reasserts itself at a more fundamental level: what is the goal of philosophy? Unfortunately, there is no agreement on this question. Philosophy is the one discipline that includes itself within its own domain of questioning so that the question "What is philosophy?" is a central philosophical question.

Those who favor analysis believe that if we get the details right, we can then build up from them to the larger generalities. For want of a better term, we can say that the opposing side is searching for synthesis. They argue that the details have no meaning unless they are interpreted within the larger framework. Think of the two ways people

Something that naturally follows

reviewing Kant

reality or outlines

Part or whole

chemist vs pilot

whole → synthesis ← parts

phenomena: an object or aspect known through the senses rather than by thought or intuition.

Noumenon: affirm object or event as it appears in itself independent of perception by the senses.

The Human Condition I (1933), René Magritte.
In a series of paintings, the French artist Magritte
depicted the epistemological problem of the relationship between the mind and reality that philosophers
from the time of Descartes to the twentieth century
tried to solve. In the above work, our view of the
outside world is obscured by the canvas in front of
the window. However, the images on the painted
canvas (symbolizing the mind and its contents) seem
to represent what is in the outside world. According
to Magritte, this is how we see the world, "we see it
as being outside ourselves even though it is only a
mental representation of it that we experience inside
ourselves."

work a jigsaw puzzle. Some try to find individual
pieces that fit together and continually build isolated collections of pieces, hoping they will all link
up together eventually. Others start with the borders, on the theory that if they can get the main
outline of the picture, they will know where the
individual pieces belong.

Pragmatism represents a compromise position,
because its individual members cover the scale
from the analytic pole to the synthesis pole. The

three pragmatists we will study are C. S. Peirce,
William James, and John Dewey. C. S. Peirce was a
scientifically trained philosopher who sought analytic clarity in our conceptions. Although William
James was also trained in science, he always looked
for the big picture that would make the best sense
out of the details. James did not think that accu-
mulating scientific facts would ever give us the
guidance we needed for life. John Dewey kept
close to the methods and the detailed outcomes of
the sciences, but always wanted to trace out their
implications for the large-scale issues within
human life. Since the pragmatists believed that reason was limited and the world was constantly
changing, they believed any picture of the whole
always had to be tentative and constantly changing
as our experience of the world changed.

Henri Bergson and A. N. Whitehead represent
process philosophy. They thought that a comprehensive understanding of the cosmos and our
place within it was the main goal of philosophy.
Although Bergson appealed to biology for many
of his ideas and Whitehead appealed to both biology and physics, they thought scientific data
were just the grist for the metaphysician's mill.
For Bergson, the method of metaphysics was intuition. For Whitehead, it took a combination of
experience, imagination, and reason.

The *analytic philosophers*, as their very name
suggests, were interested in analyzing the details.
They said that philosophers should give up their
grandiose hopes to know ultimate reality and
should instead stay safely within the bounds of experience. However, the subject of their analysis was
not the facts found through experience, for this en-
deavor can only be carried out by science. Instead,
they believed the primary role of the philosopher is
to analyze language. By getting clear on either the
logical structure of language or how it functions,
we can avoid many of the muddles that have kept
metaphysicians in business. The analysts delegated
the job of dealing with the ultimate meaning of
things to the artists, poets, and novelists. Of course,
the analysts also believed that the vision the artists
give us merely consists of inspiring expressions of
emotion, but nothing that we can sink our cogni-

tive teeth into. Bertrand Russell was always the analysts' best spokesperson. He said he aspired toward the same sort of advance in philosophy that Galileo introduced into physics, which is "the substitution of piecemeal, detailed, and verifiable results for large untested generalities recommended only by a certain appeal to imagination."[2]

In the first two-thirds of the twentieth century, phenomenology and existentialism were the leading movements within Continental philosophy. Edmund Husserl, the founder of *phenomenology*, definitely had an interest in analysis. He proposed phenomenology as a new discipline that would carry out a detailed analysis, not of scientific facts nor of language, but of the structures of consciousness and its objects. Like mountain climbers who will not advance until they have securely anchored themselves and tested the soundness of each foothold, Husserl's method was an agonizingly slow, detailed analysis of the domain of consciousness. The *existentialists* he inspired, however, were not so patient. Compared to Husserl, they moved very quickly to the big issues in human life. However, their "big picture" was much more modest than that of classical metaphysics. Perhaps their one point of agreement with the analysts was that we must accept the Kantian view of the limitations of reason. In contrast to all the other twentieth-century philosophers, they focused on the structures of human existence as it is subjectively lived.

The Role of Science in Philosophy

There is a fundamental divide between twentieth-century philosophers concerning where science should be placed with respect to the appearance–reality distinction. The *pragmatists* saw science as the basis for all our knowledge about the world. However, they had an extremely broad and humanistic view of the scientific method, thinking that it could give us not only the atomic weight of helium (for example), but also values. Hence they saw science as meshing perfectly with our deepest human concerns. In the first half of the twentieth century, the *analytic philosophers* (for the most part) thought that science gives us the last word

on reality and that our prescientific, ordinary ways of viewing the world must be radically revised in the light of the latest discoveries in physics. For these philosophers, however, science was not as generous as the pragmatists supposed. Science could not guide us concerning values. Generally, the analysts believed ethical judgments lacked a factual basis, for they were simply emotive utterances on their view. In contrast, the *process philosophers* (Bergson and Whitehead) and the *phenomenologists* and *existentialists* (such as Husserl and Heidegger) insisted that science arises out of our ordinary ways of experiencing the world, but they claimed it simply gives us the world as viewed through the abstract grid of our quantitative methods.

The Role of Language and Experience in Philosophy

Twentieth-century philosophers can also be divided by the relative weights they give the role of language and experience in the philosophical enterprise. Although many have disagreed concerning the nature of philosophy, few would deny that language is crucial to the enterprise, for philosophy is an attempt to *speak* accurately and coherently about our deepest concerns. With the dawn of the twentieth century, however, many became convinced that all is not well with language. The philosopher and novelist Iris Murdoch expressed it well:

> We can no longer take language for granted as a medium of communication. Its transparency has gone. We are like people who for a long time looked out of a window without noticing the glass—and then one day began to notice this too.[3]

For those attracted to *analytic philosophy*, its methods seemed to provide a fruitful way to clarify our most abstract concepts by looking at the concrete ways in which we speak about them. Although they were empiricists, they believed a mute immersion within experience tells us nothing. Only when experience is described can we get clear on what has been presented. Hence, the propositions we use to make claims about our experience were the focus of their concern. For this reason, analytic philosophy is also called "linguistic philosophy."

Consider how you would answer this age-old philosophical question: What is knowledge? Such questions are likely to provoke a sense of paralysis and uncertainty about how to begin searching for an answer. Now consider these questions:

How do we use the *word* "knowledge"?

In what situations would we *say* that someone has knowledge?

When would we *say* that someone does not have knowledge?

With these sorts of questions, we know where to begin and how to proceed. Promising answers can be supported by examples, and inadequate answers can be rejected by citing counterexamples from our common fund of linguistic usage. Not all the analysts would approach an issue exactly this way. Nevertheless, the example illustrates the way questions of the form "What is *X*?" can be helpfully transformed into questions about language by asking, "What do we mean when we say '*X*'?" The approach of the analytic philosopher was illustrated by Bertrand Russell when he was challenged to explain what meaning life can have to an agnostic. Russell replied, "I feel inclined to answer by another question: What is the meaning of 'the meaning of life'?"[4]

When it came to analyzing statements about experience, the early analytic philosophers such as Bertrand Russell and the logical positivists, worked within the tradition of David Hume and saw experience as a collection of sense data. Hence, they sought an interpretation-free analysis of experience. However, the end result was that the only sort of statements that could be asserted with certainty were statements such as "redness here, now." To say, "I am experiencing a red book," introduces questionable entities such as the self and questionable inferences about the external world. This part of the analysts' program was never successful, for they were either left with totally useless certitudes or had to violate their methodological principles. The later ana-

lysts remedied the situation by developing broader notions of both language and experience.

Although the *pragmatists* did not think the analysis of language was the sole occupation of philosophy, they did think it was a first step to clarifying our concepts. They developed what was known as the "pragmatic theory of meaning," which insisted that the meaning of a term or concept be explicated in terms of the practical effects associated with the object of that conception. For the most part, the pragmatists looked to experience and not to language for the source of philosophical insight. However, their understanding of experience was much broader than that of the early analysts. John Dewey, for example, denied that we ever experience isolated sense data or even single objects and events. Instead, we experience contextual wholes that he called "situations." Experience is not made up of bits of data that bombard a passive mind, but is an arena for action in which we face practical problems, seek solutions, and carry out our projects and aims.

The process philosophers, phenomenologists, and existentialists were the most pessimistic about the insights that language could offer us, and they put the priority on experience, broadly understood. Bergson exemplified the approach that *process philosophy* took. He argued that concepts and the words that carry them are fragmenting, distorting instruments. By putting too much faith in our conceptual and linguistic categories, we try to force a flowing, unified experience into preformed containers that cannot hold it. Likewise, Whitehead complained that language only makes room for those thoughts that have been thought before. An original thought does not already have a home in our language, so our old language must be stretched or a new language created to accommodate novel ideas. He criticized the analytic philosophers for committing "the Fallacy of the Perfect Dictionary" with their assumption that philosophical insights can be gained by analyzing language as it currently stands.[5]

Since Husserl presented his *phenomenology* as a way of breaking free from our ordinary ways of approaching the world, he viewed his philosophical method as a particularly honest "seeing" of the way things are. Language played no role in this process other than to come in at the final phase to articulate and to share what the philosopher has discovered. When Husserl examined our pretheoretical level of experience, he did not find it to consist of a collection of independent sense data as the analysts claimed. Instead, he maintained that in addition to a display of sensory qualities, a faithful reading of experience revealed such contents as universals, meanings, values, moral duties, and aesthetic qualities. Furthermore, according to Husserl, the discrete sense data of the analysts were theoretical abstractions that obscured the rich, multilayered dimensions of experience as it is lived.

The *existentialists* agreed with Husserl in focusing on "lived experience" as opposed to a scientifically interpreted experience. But while Husserl tended to emphasize the way that the contents of experience are cognitively apprehended, the existentialists explored its subjective dimensions. Like their nineteenth-century predecessors Kierkegaard and Nietzsche, the experiences that really mattered to the twentieth-century existentialists were those revelatory of the human situation. These included the experience of our own, unbounded freedom, the experience of the contingency of all existence, and the deep, existential experiences of responsibility, anxiety, guilt, and our confrontation with the possibility of our own death.

Furthermore, the existentialists went much further than Husserl in depicting the role language plays in our intercourse with the world. Martin Heidegger, for example, contrasted ordinary language with the language of poetry. When we are immersed within our daily lives (what he called the mode of "everydayness"), we tend to allow authentic dialogue to degenerate into "idle talk." Idle talk is the detached, unthinking "chit-chat" that characterizes our life when it is lived inauthentically. Taken-for-granted, average points of view become solidified in idle talk and are passed on from one person to another like a worn coin whose distinctive markings have been rubbed smooth. The language of the poets, however, opens us up to reality and uncovers what has been concealed by our mundane, comfortable perspectives.

For Jean-Paul Sartre, another existentialist, the world is intrinsically meaningless in itself. It is simply there. What meaning we find within it is the meaning we create and project onto the world. Hence, language is just one way in which we break the world up into intelligible units and fashion it after our own image. However, it can create the illusion that when we use language to describe something we are really capturing its essence. In his novel *Nausea*, one of his characters, Roquetin, has the horrifying realization while riding a streetcar that words and reality are divorced. Words crystallize the meanings that he has imposed on the world, but the world itself simply exists and is nothing but a mute canvas on which he paints his own, subjective interpretations:

> This thing I'm sitting on, leaning my hand on, is called a seat. . . . I murmur: "It's a seat," a little like an exorcism. But the word stays on my lips: it refuses to go and put itself on the thing. . . . Things are divorced from their names. They are there, grotesque, headstrong, gigantic and it seems ridiculous to call them seats or say anything at all about them: I am in the midst of things, nameless things. Alone, without words, defenceless, they surround me, are beneath me, behind me, above me. They demand nothing, they don't impose themselves: they are there.[6]

Questions for Understanding

1. In what ways did Kant's philosophy influence the agenda of twentieth-century philosophy? What are the three major themes of twentieth-century philosophy?

2. What is the issue of analysis versus synthesis in twentieth-century philosophy? What philosophers or movements are representatives of each stance on this issue?

3. Where do the various philosophical movements stand on the role of science in philosophy?

4. What are the various stances that have been taken on the respective roles of language and experience in twentieth-century philosophy? What philosophers or movements are representatives of each stance?

Questions for Reflection

1. For each of the three issues discussed in this chapter, decide which position you find most plausible. Have you found yourself aligned with the same philosophers or movements in each of the three cases? Argue for one of the following two theses: (a) The three issues are not independent. The choice you make on any one of these issues commits you to a certain position on the other two. (b) The three issues are independent. You could be aligned with, say, the analysts on one issue, but could side with, for example, the process philosophers on another issue.

2. Pick a philosopher from each of the three previous historical periods (ancient, medieval, modern). Try to imagine the stance that each of these philosophers would take on the three issues discussed in this chapter.

Notes

1. Edmund Husserl, *Cartesian Meditations: An Introduction to Phenomenology*, trans. Dorion Cairns (The Hague: Nijhoff, 1960), 5.

2. Bertrand Russell, *Our Knowledge of the External World* (New York: New American Library, 1956), 12.

3. Iris Murdoch, *Sartre* (New Haven, CT: Yale University Press, 1953), 27.

4. Bertrand Russell, "What Is an Agnostic?" *Look Magazine* (1953), reprinted in *The Basic Writings of Bertrand Russell*, ed. R. E. Enger and L. E. Dennon (New York: Simon & Schuster, 1961), 582.

5. Alfred North Whitehead, *Modes of Thought* (New York: The Free Press, 1966), 173.

6. Jean-Paul Sartre, *Nausea*, trans. Lloyd Alexander (New York: New Directions, 1964), 168–169.

Pragmatism:
The Unity of
Thought and Action

The Origins of Pragmatism

The French writer De Tocqueville complained in his 1835 book *Democracy in America* that there was no country in the civilized world in which philosophy was taken less seriously than in America. This is not entirely true, for from the colonial period on, philosophy played an active role in American intellectual life. Throughout the nation's history, a number of American writers made original contributions to philosophy, ranging from political theory to philosophy of religion and metaphysics. It could be argued, however, that up until the latter part of the nineteenth century, a great deal of American philosophy was by and large a reflection of the philosophical movements that arose in Great Britain and Europe. However, with the development of the movement known as **pragmatism**, American thinkers made their most distinctive contribution to the world of philosophy.

People often say that pragmatism reflects the spirit of American culture. It is down-to-earth and shuns abstruse abstractions that have no "cash" value. It is oriented toward experience, action, and practical issues, the sort of characteristics that enabled a fledgling nation to come late onto the scene and shortly become a major cultural force in the world. Pragmatism views ideas as tools for getting a job done and values them only if they are successful when put to work. Furthermore, many people say that pragmatism fits in well with the spirit of science and technology and the enthusiasm for problem solving that Americans exemplify. However, while there is a measure of truth in all this, it is good to keep in mind that not all American philosophers have been pragmatists and not all pragmatists have been American. Furthermore, pragmatism has had a very deep impact not only on American culture but on the whole contemporary world as well. For example, Dewey's lectures in China and Japan were enthusiastically received.

In everyday contexts, people speak of a policy as being a "pragmatic" solution to a problem and politicians love to brag that they are "pragmatists." Thus, pragmatism ranks with cynicism, epicureanism, stoicism, and existentialism as a philosophy that so captured the public imagination that it found its way into popular discourse. However, fame is both a blessing and a curse. With most popular philosophies, such as pragmatism, the original versions propounded by the philosophers are more sophisticated and refined than the fashionable adaptations of them. For example, in popular usage, "pragmatic" is associated with "practical" and this is seen as contrasting with the "theoretical." However, nothing could be further from the teachings of the pragmatic philosophers, for they believed that the best theories will be practical and that nothing can be practical unless it is undergirded by sound theory.

Although typically thought of as a twentieth-century movement, pragmatism actually came to birth in the late nineteenth century. It began with a group of thinkers who met in Cambridge, Massachusetts, in the 1870s to read and debate philosophical papers. With both a sense of irony and defiance, they called themselves the "Metaphysical Club," for most of them were skeptical of the rationalistic and dogmatic metaphysics of the Hegelians. Among the better-known members of this circle were Charles Sanders Peirce, William James, and Oliver Wendell Holmes, a legal theorist who would later become the chief justice of the U.S. Supreme Court. The members of this group were by and large empiricists, and many were influenced by the writings of Bentham and Mill as well as Darwin's theory of evolution.

In 1878 Peirce introduced the term "pragmatism" to apply to this new outlook in philosophy. He derived the term from Kant's notion of *pragmatisch*, which refers to principles that are empirical or experimental, as opposed to *a priori*. Accordingly, Peirce was interested in developing a theory of inquiry and a theory of meaning that would primarily apply to our scientific conceptions. At the end of the nineteenth century, William James popularized the philosophy and expounded it as a theory of truth with applications to psychology, morality, and religion. Consistent with these interests, James traced his own use of the term "pragmatism" back to its roots in a Greek word that means "action," "deed," or "practice." John Dewey developed pragmatism further, making it a comprehensive philosophy with implications for our understanding of nature, knowledge, education, values, art, social issues, religion, and just about every area of human concern.

The pragmatists' ideas arose out of a dissatisfaction with all the other options in philosophy available in their day: rationalism, empiricism, Kantianism, and Hegelianism. They opposed the rationalists' notion that the ultimate truths are eternal and necessary and that there is a certain way the world *must* be that we can discern through pure logic. Instead, the pragmatists approached the world with a sense of openness and in a spirit of experimentalism. The truths that are the most unchanging, they said, are also the most abstract and will not give us knowledge of a concrete and changing world.

Although their rejection of rationalism obviously aligned them with empiricism, the pragmatists did not think the traditional versions of empiricism were any more adequate. Empiricists such as John Locke and David Hume sought to validate our ideas by tracing their origins back to original sensory impressions. Instead, the pragmatists said it was not the origin of our ideas but their future consequences that determine their truth and meaning. In criticizing the classical empiricists, John Dewey says the role of our general ideas is not that of "reporting and registering past experiences" but to serve as "the bases for organizing future observations and experiences."[1] Furthermore, the empiricists treated experience as a collection of isolated sense data. According to the pragmatists, however, sense data are artificial, selective abstractions from the rich, integrated field of experience. Dewey says that we do not first experience sensory impressions nor even objects, but we experience

Rationalists & empiricists viewed as looking at the mind as a kind of container that holds ideas.

"situations" or contextual wholes within which particulars find their meaning.

The pragmatists faulted both the rationalists and the empiricists for conceiving the mind as a kind of container that holds ideas. Instead of viewing the mind as a static entity, they spoke of *mind* as a name for the many cognitive activities by means of which we come to terms with the world. Ideas, as well, are not simply mental furniture, but are tools that we actively employ for solving practical problems. They criticized what they called the "spectator view" of knowledge, which pictures the mind as passively contemplating the world from a distance. Instead, the pragmatists insisted that having a mental life means being actively engaged with the biological and cultural matrix out of which our experience emerges. They agreed with Kant that the mind is active and creative, but rejected his notion that our mental structures are innate and fixed. On the contrary, the pragmatists said, our conceptual categories arise through experience and are changed by it.

The pragmatists agreed with Hegel that our ideas and the world are continually developing, but rejected the notion that this process is simply the unfolding of a set, logical pattern. We are not pawns of history, for our decisions and actions affect the outcome of things. Hence, they emphasized the future and embraced, in the words of John Dewey, "the conception of a universe whose evolution is not finished, of a universe that is still, in James's term, 'in the making,' 'in the process of becoming,' of a universe up to a certain point still plastic" (PC 25).

CHARLES SANDERS PEIRCE

|||

The Obscure Founder of a Famous Philosophy

C. S. Peirce (1839–1914) was the son of Benjamin Peirce, a distinguished Harvard University mathematician.* Graduating from Harvard with a degree in chemistry, C. S. Peirce worked as a scientist for the U.S. Coast and Geodetic Survey from 1861 to 1891. During this time he also taught intermittently at Harvard and Johns Hopkins University. However, his nonconformist personality prevented him from securing a permanent academic position despite his wealthy friend William James's efforts on his behalf. He was forced to devote a great deal of time to writing book reviews and publishing in popular magazines to shore up his dwindling finances. Peirce spent his last years in poverty and was saved from total destitution only by the generosity of James. While Peirce wrote volumes of essays during his life, with the exception of a few articles, his work never saw the light of day until his papers were finally edited and published long after his death. Consequently, he remained a relatively obscure figure to his contemporaries, and his ideas had very little influence during his lifetime. Plagued by ill health, living the life of a recluse with only the care of his faithful French wife, Juliette, C. S. Peirce died in 1914. Relatively unknown during his lifetime, his philosophy has merited a great deal of interest in the latter half of the twentieth century. He has had an impact on the fields of logic, epistemology, and philosophy of science. Furthermore, his highly original contribution to the theory of signs has attracted the attention of those working in the areas of philosophy of language, information theory, and literary interpretation.

The Nature of Inquiry

In the late 1870s Peirce wrote a series of articles in *Popular Science Monthly* in which he presented

*Peirce pronounced his name as *Purse*.

some of his seminal ideas. This may seem a strange place for a philosopher to publish, but it gave his ideas a wide dissemination and illustrated his conviction that philosophy should be brought down out of the clouds and applied to issues of practical science. In one of these articles, "The Fixation of Belief" (1877), Peirce attacks traditional epistemology for construing thought as the detached acquisition of truth. In contrast, Peirce emphasizes that thought has the job of producing beliefs. Beliefs are not just pieces of mental furniture that reside in the mind nor are they momentary psychological states. Instead, "our beliefs guide our desires and shape our actions" (FB §371).[2] They affect action because beliefs are actually habits or dispositions to act in certain ways in certain circumstances. For example, if I believe that a drinking glass is a very expensive piece of fine crystal, I will expect it to be fragile and will treat it gently and even apprehensively. However, if I believe it is cheap, easily replaceable, and unbreakable, I will expect it to be immune from harm and will be much more careless in handling it. Undergirding every action is a series of beliefs. In contrast, a belief that does not have implications for action is empty and dead. For example, I once saw a team of policemen inspecting a classroom building in response to a phone call stating that a bomb was set to go off at 2 P.M. Concluding that it was a false alarm, they radioed to headquarters that the building was safe and its occupants did not need to be evacuated. However, a minute before 2 P.M., the bomb squad came running out of the building and took up a position from a safe distance. Peirce would say that if they genuinely believed the building was safe, their actions would have been quite different.

As long as our beliefs are successful, we do not need to engage in inquiry. The bulk of our daily lives are routine, and we can fall back on habitual beliefs and their corresponding patterns of behavior that have proven themselves. For example, as I casually switch on my computer each morning, I am acting on the implicit belief that since my computer was in good working condition yesterday, it will work for me today. However, suppose I turn on my computer one morning, just as I always do, and the screen remains blank. My routine has been

disrupted. I cannot continue on as I usually do; now I have to search for some solution to this new problem. When a belief is called into question in this way, we are unsettled, we are not sure what to do. Peirce describes this as a state of doubt. Doubt is "an uneasy and dissatisfied state from which we struggle to free ourselves." Doubt stimulates us to action and seeks its own elimination by means of inquiry, which is a process of finding the way to a new and more adequate belief.

Just as there can be empty beliefs, so there can be empty doubts. Peirce has nothing but disdain for the sorts of doubts Descartes rehearsed in his *Meditations*. Inquiry has no purpose unless action is disrupted by real and living doubts. Such doubts must involve an uncertainty as to how to act based on a conflict between old beliefs and new experience. At the beginning of his *Meditations*, Descartes claimed to have doubted whether or not the physical world existed and even whether or not his body existed. Nevertheless, he still got up from his writings to stoke the stove and he avoided touching the flames. Peirce dismisses his doubting as "make-believe" doubt (WPI §416). The goal for Peirce is not to have certainty beyond all possible doubt (something we will never find), but to have beliefs that are free from all actual doubt. "Let us not pretend to doubt in philosophy what we do not doubt in our hearts" (SCFI §265).

There are many ways of escaping doubt and achieving belief. As long as we feel satisfied, does it matter how we arrived at a belief? Peirce says it does, for ends cannot be separated from the means we use to achieve them. He lists four ways to achieve belief of which only one will prove to be satisfactory. The first way of eliminating doubt is what Peirce calls the method of tenacity:

> *If the settlement of opinion is the sole object of inquiry, and if belief is of the nature of a habit, why should we not attain the desired end, by taking as answer to a question any we may fancy, and constantly reiterating it to ourselves, dwelling on all which may conduce to that belief, and learning to turn with contempt and hatred from anything that might disturb it? (FB §377)*

This method involves setting rationality aside and clinging to my opinions with determination and perseverance. This is the approach of someone who says, "I know what I believe, don't confuse me with the facts." Peirce admits that having such unwavering convictions leads to peace of mind. The problem is that it produces tensions with the "social impulse" within us. We will eventually find that reasonable people disagree with us, and this can cause doubt to arise. Although the method of tenacity would work for a hermit who never had to discuss his beliefs with others, for most of us our beliefs must be fixed with reference to the community.

The second way of fixing belief is the *method of authority.* This is the method employed by a community of believers who allow their beliefs to be dictated by an authority or by an institution. It corrects the problem of the first method, for this one will ensure that my beliefs are consistent with my community. Peirce says that great civilizations, such as ancient Egypt and medieval Europe, have been built on this method. It produces a comfortable belief system, but only for those who are content to be "intellectual slaves." In effect, it is the method of tenacity raised to the level of an entire culture. A culture based on this principle cannot tolerate diverse opinions or contact with other belief systems. However, in such a system the specter of doubt lies waiting, for some will realize that their opinions are socially conditioned if they see that other cultures entertain opinions contrary to their own.

Third, there is the *a priori method.* It is better than the first two methods, for the person arrives at beliefs after a process of reflection. By the *a priori* method, Peirce does not mean basing beliefs on logical necessity, but embracing beliefs because they are "agreeable to reason." However, what is "agreeable to reason" is very subjective, for it is based on personal inclinations and sentiments. Peirce thinks there is no settled opinion in metaphysics, because each thinker who uses the *a priori* method has different preferences about what he or she personally considers to be beyond doubt. Hence, a belief system based on this method can end up being nothing but well-entrenched intellectual prejudices.

The problems with the previous three methods illustrate that what is important is not just finding belief but finding it in a certain way. What is needed is a method of fixing belief that does not depend on our human idiosyncrasies but on some "external permanency. . . . The method must be such that the ultimate conclusion of every man shall be the same. Or would be the same if inquiry were sufficiently persisted in" (FB §384). To answer this need, Peirce proposes the fourth and final method, the *method of science.* By this Peirce does not necessarily mean what is done with test tubes, but instead what could be broadly considered an empirical procedure. The fundamental hypothesis underlying this method is

> There are real things, whose characters are entirely independent of our opinions about them; those realities affect our senses according to regular laws, and . . . by taking advantage of the laws of perception, we can ascertain by reasoning how things really and truly are. (FB §384)

Although the method of science cannot prove this hypothesis, Peirce says the method will never lead to doubts about its fundamental principle, as do the other methods. Furthermore, this method has been successful in helping us resolve doubts. Therefore, when applied the method will lead to its own confirmation. Although the other methods make it possible to maintain an internally coherent system, they do so at the expense of being immune from all correction. In contrast, the method of science is error revealing and self-corrective, since it is tested against what is independent of our cherished beliefs or wishes.

The Theory of Meaning

The beliefs we seek through inquiry will only be meaningful and useful if they are clear. Hence, in an 1878 article on "How to Make Our Ideas Clear," Peirce set out a technique for making our ideas clear by making clear the terms in which they are expressed. He begins by criticizing Descartes's account of meaning. Descartes thought we can directly grasp the meaning of a concept within the recesses of the mind in a mental intuition. Other theories have treated meaning as a kind of ghostly "halo" that hovered around a word or idea. But these views make meanings too illusive or private for them to ever be clarified.

In response to this problem, Peirce wants to explain meaning in terms of our interactions with the world and the publicly observable ways the world responds. Accordingly, he offers the following method for clarifying the intellectual content of our ideas:

> Consider what effects, that might conceivably have practical bearings we conceive the object of our conception to have. Then, our conception of these effects is the whole of our conception of the object. (HMIC §402)

Applying his criteria to a concrete case, Peirce examines what we mean when we say something is hard. We say something (such as a diamond) is hard if there are many things that will not scratch it. The meaning of "will not be scratched" refers to a certain operation that may be performed with certain anticipated results. However, we do not have to actually perform the action to understand the meaning of the term, we just have to conceive of what it would be.

If the entire meaning of an idea consists of its conceived effects, then two ideas or theories that cannot be translated into a difference in practice, either of how we expect the world to behave or how we will respond to it, are really not two different concepts at all. To use a well-known example, the claim that "the glass is half full" and the claim that "the glass is half empty" are really the same claim expressed in different words, for each one leads us to expect the same set of conditions with respect to the glass. If we apply Peirce's pragmatic theory of meaning to Bishop Berkeley's idealism and Thomas Hobbes's materialism, we will find no real difference between them, even though they seem to make radically different claims about the world. Berkeley says the objects we perceive are nothing but ideas in our minds whose source is God. Hobbes believes our experiences are caused by material substances. Whether I am an idealist or a materialist, when I experience a moving hammer making contact with my thumb, I will experience pain. To embrace one or the other of opposing metaphysical systems neither adds to

nor subtracts from what is experienced. Thus, if the practical effects of Berkeley's theory are no different from those of the materialist's theory, then there is no disagreement between them. This is because "there is no distinction of meaning so fine as to consist in anything but a possible difference in practice" (HMIC §400).

Truth and Reality

Thus far Peirce has given us a way of arriving at beliefs and a method for clarifying the meaning of our conceptions. However, it would seem that simply having clear and satisfactory beliefs is not enough. We also want to know if our beliefs are true and if they are related to reality. In addressing this issue, it is significant that Peirce talks about beliefs far more than he does knowledge or truth. His reason for emphasizing belief is simple. If we list all our beliefs and then make another list of what we think to be true, they would be the same list. In practical terms, as soon as we reach a satisfactory state of belief, inquiry comes to an end. We can no more jump outside our beliefs than outside our own skin. Not only are the notions of truth and belief inseparable, but the notions of truth and reality are intertwined as well. To think of the true conception of X and to think of X as real is simply to "regard one and the same thing from two different points of view; for the immediate object of thought in a true judgment is the reality" (CP 8.16).

Initially, this view seems problematic. True beliefs are consistent with reality, but we always understand reality in terms of our beliefs about reality. How can we ever escape this circle? In defining reality in terms of the ultimate object of our beliefs, Peirce did not want to embrace the sort of subjectivism that says "reality is whatever I believe it to be." This view makes reality completely dependent on my conceptions and collapses into the method of tenacity. Likewise, Peirce rejects Kantianism, for this makes reality (in the sense of reality-in-itself) so independent of the mind that we could never know it. Peirce's way of avoiding both subjectivism and Kant's position is to say reality is independent of the beliefs of any

(margin note, left:) OS

(margin notes, right:) ?

kant
reality
so
independent
of the
mind

(bottom handwritten note:) If belief is certainty of what I know namely, the truth=reality. Then how is reality independent of the belief?

particular thinker but is not irretrievably beyond the limits of human thought altogether. The notion of "reality" is a kind of ideal located in the future such that it is the object of that "final opinion" the community of inquirers will converge on if the scientific method were applied for an indefinitely long period of time. In this way, Peirce gives us a joint definition of both truth and reality:

> The opinion which is fated to be ultimately agreed to by all who investigate is what we mean by the truth, and the object represented in this opinion is the real. That is the way I would explain reality. (HMIC §407)

By defining truth with reference to community opinion, Peirce is not saying it is all a matter of convention. Instead, he assumes the scientific method is error revealing and self-correcting, so that if continuously applied it successively approximates the perfect truth and the perfect conception of reality. There is no possibility of an error, which in principle could never be detected. Given his theory of meaning, an error that could have no conceivable practical effects, no matter how long inquiry continues, is a meaningless notion. Hence, while you or I can be mistaken in our beliefs, it is inconceivable that in the long run the whole of humanity could not get closer to the truth. In this way, Peirce rejects the Kantian notion of the thing-in-itself that forever eludes our grasp.*

Fallibilism

It follows from Peirce's definition of truth that we have no guarantee that any particular belief will ever be immune from the need to be revised. This position is known as fallibilism. Peirce once made the paradoxical claim that the only infallible statement is that all statements are fallible (CP 2.75). He had to emphasize this point, for if we ever think we have arrived at an infallible truth, this would put an end to inquiry, which is essential to the self-correcting nature of the scientific method. The end result of Peirce's epistemology is not full-blown certainty, but instead the reassurance that at any given time we can find (1) provisional beliefs that work in practice thus far, joined with (2) a method of proceeding on to better beliefs. Thus, instead of searching for the "TRUTH," the cognitive pursuits of humanity need no higher goal than "a state of belief unassailable by doubt" (WPI §416). By "doubt" here, Peirce means real doubt, not Descartes's imaginary doubts. Although we may never reach the destination of perfect knowledge, we can at least know we will be on the right road.

WILLIAM JAMES

|||

From Physician to Philosopher

William James (1842–1910) was born in New York into a family where intellectual and cultural debates were part of the dinner table conversation. His father was an eccentric, mystical theologian and his brother was the famous novelist, Henry James. From the time that he was a teenager, through his university years, James traveled extensively. He studied science, painting, and medicine in England, France, Switzerland, Germany, and the United States, finally earning his medical degree from Harvard in 1869. James started out as an instructor in physiology at Harvard but his interests broadened out into psychol-

---

*Peirce was aware of Hegel's influence on him. Both see thinking as a process of moving from half-truths to fuller truths, and both see the end of inquiry as a convergence on some final totality where truth and reality are one. However, Peirce deviated from Hegel in significant ways. Peirce's method was empirical and not rationalistic. Furthermore, he defines thought in behavioral terms and roots it in a concrete, biological environment.

ogy, a discipline that was still in its infancy as an experimental science. In 1890 he published *Principles of Psychology*, one of the first textbooks in experimental psychology. Eventually he made philosophy his full-time occupation and taught in Harvard's philosophy department alongside such notable figures as Josiah Royce, George Santayana, and, for a brief time, C. S. Peirce.

James and Peirce

Although James and Peirce were committed to the same general approach to philosophy, there were some significant differences between their expressions of pragmatism. In spite of the fact that James shared with Peirce a training in the sciences, the former's interests were primarily oriented around the broader issues of morality and practical living. As John Dewey put it, "Peirce wrote as a logician and James as a humanist."[3] James saw the value of a philosophy almost purely in terms of its contribution to life as it is lived:

> The whole function of philosophy ought to be to find out what definite difference it will make to you and me, at definite instants of our life, if this world-formula or that world-formula be the true one. (P 50)[4]

This practical, humanist emphasis made James in great demand as a speaker. In fact, Peirce's pragmatism never received much attention until James popularized it in a series of lectures. Although James thought he was doing Peirce a service, the originator of pragmatism was appalled at how badly James had distorted his thought. Consequently, Peirce abandoned the term and dubbed his own position "pragmaticism," remarking that this label "is ugly enough to be safe from kidnappers."

The differences between the two pragmatists went much deeper than their style. When Peirce spoke of the "practical consequences" and "usefulness" of our beliefs, he was speaking primarily of the sort of public, empirical observations that would lend themselves to scientific analysis. For James, however, the consequences of a belief were to be understood in terms of the personal and practical impact it has in the life of an individual. This tended toward a much more pluralistic and even relativistic outlook, for the same belief could be "workable" in terms of the needs, interests, and life situation of one person but not to another.

The Cash Value of Truth

At times, James's exposition sticks closely to Peirce's position when he insists that pragmatism is simply a method for clarifying the meaning of our conceptions. However, James deviated radically from Peirce (much to the latter's discomfort) when he additionally presented pragmatism as a theory of truth. James is best known for the extravagant metaphors he uses to define his theory of truth. He says theories are "instruments" that enable us to "handle" reality. True beliefs have the characteristic that "they pay" or have "practical cash value." He defines truth in terms of "what works," what "gives satisfaction," or the "practical consequences" of our beliefs. Many nonpragmatists would accept all this if James were simply setting forth a *pragmatic* test for truth, a way of finding out what propositions are true. But James is not content with saying that "workability" is an indicator that a belief is true. Instead, he seems to be saying "workability" is the *pragmatic definition* of what it means for a belief to be true. Just as a hammer is useful if it enables us to relate to the world in a certain way (driving nails), so a belief is useful (true) if it lets us relate to our experience satisfactorily. Truth is not a fact in the world, but is a quality of satisfactory belief when we put it to work in our interaction with facts. "The 'facts' themselves . . . are not *true*. They simply *are*. Truth is the function of the beliefs that start and terminate among them" (P 225). A crucial aspect of James's view is that the rational and the emotive, knowing and valuing, successful beliefs and successful living cannot be neatly divided. He explicitly links our cognitive and moral endeavors:

> Truth is one species of good, and not, as is usually supposed, a category distinct from good, and coordinate with it. The true is whatever proves itself to be good in the way of belief. (P 75–76)

> "The true" . . . is only the expedient in the way of our thinking, just as "the right" is only the expedient

in the way of our behaving. . . . Expedient . . . in the long run and on the whole. (P 222)

In one of his most startling statements, James says that "Truth *happens* to an idea. It *becomes* true, is *made* true by events" (P 201). He makes a number of applications of this notion. In some cases, a belief is not true unless I act to *make* it true. If I am trying to break an athletic record, rally my political forces to win an election, or win the affections of another person, the hoped-for outcome is not yet true, but can be made true by my acting with confidence. In science, a hypothesis is merely a conjecture until put to the test, which, if successful, makes the hypothesis a verified truth.

James gives his critics ammunition with the vague, constantly shifting way he expounds his doctrines. According to James, we can say of an idea, "It is useful because it is true," or we can say, "It is true because it is useful." What is problematic is his claim that "both these phrases mean exactly the same thing" (P 204). But are these two expressions really equivalent? The first statement seems unobjectionable, for if a belief is true, then usually it will be useful, in the sense of helping us deal with reality. The problem is that the second half of his formula does not seem as plausible. Just because a belief is useful does not mean it is true, contrary to what James supposes. For example, in a grave emergency it may be necessary to reassure a little child that nothing is wrong, that there is no danger, so that he will follow our directions without panicking. If his false belief that everything is under control causes him to calmly make his way to safety, then under the circumstances, his belief was useful though not true.

James was continually assailed by his critics for reducing truth to subjective satisfaction. Certainly in many passages he leaves himself open to this charge. However, he continually complained that these attacks never hit their target, for they misrepresented his point. When James says a true belief is one that "gives satisfaction" or "works," he was not referring simply to immediate, emotional satisfaction in the short run. I may find it emotionally satisfying to believe that my checking account has a positive balance, but this belief will not prove satisfactory when tested in practi-

cal action. Similarly, any false belief that seems to work will eventually be discovered as unworkable. As James puts it, "experience, as we know, has ways of *boiling over*, and making us correct our present formulas" (P 222).

James agrees with Peirce's fallibilism that "absolute truth" doesn't exist except as the ideal goal of inquiry and the most we can hope for are truths that continue to work for the time being until experience causes us to revise them. The anti-pragmatist's notion of truth, James would say, is a truth he does not have and never can have, so it is not a viable alternative to the pragmatist's conception. James says that discarded theories such as Ptolemaic astronomy "worked" in its day, in terms of the problems to be solved then. In our present situation, we now consider the theory false, although we could say it was "relatively true" or "true within those borders of experience" defined by its own time (P 223).

In response to charges that his view is too subjective, James tries to provide objective criteria for truth. "True ideas are those that we can assimilate, validate, corroborate, and verify. False ideas are those that we cannot" (MT v–vi). Furthermore, although James is much more subjective than Peirce when he speaks of the search for true ideas as a personal quest for ideas that work in an individual's life, he never neglects the larger context in which our beliefs and our lives are rooted. "As we humans are constituted in point of fact, we find that to believe in other men's minds, in independent physical realities, in past events, in eternal logical relations, is satisfactory" (MT 192).

The Subjective Justification of Beliefs

There is a significant contrast between Peirce and James concerning the issues to which they applied the pragmatic method. Peirce was interested in clarifying scientific language by providing operational definitions of such terms as "hardness" and "solubility." But James was interested in wide-ranging questions that penetrated to the core of human life as subjectively lived. We can get an in-

Vida devería ser construida en el hacer, el sufrimiento y la creación

sight into James's thought concerning the personal and practical character of philosophical ideas by examining how he resolved a personal crisis early in his life. As a result of his years of studying science and medicine, James became morbidly depressed by the thought that human beings might be nothing more than determined mechanisms doomed to live in a closed universe where nothing escapes the domination of physical laws.

James recorded his struggles in a diary entry written in 1870, when he was twenty-eight and one year out of medical school. He apparently found relief from his torments in the form of a decisive philosophic commitment of the sort that Kierkegaard, Nietzsche, and Dostoevsky would have appreciated. James resolved that if he was to go on living and find any sort of meaning at all in life, he would have to commit himself to the thesis that free will is not an illusion and base his actions on that conviction:

> My first act of free will shall be to believe in free will. . . . I will go a step further with my will, not only act with it, but believe as well; believe in my individual reality and creative power. . . . Life shall be built in doing and suffering and creating.[5]

Although this was a turning point in his life, it would be a mistake (and some have made this mistake) to suppose James is simply saying, "Believe what you find it pleasant to believe," without any further qualifications. Certainly, when logical or empirical considerations can decisively resolve an issue, James would say our beliefs must be subservient to reason and the facts. However, he says that in some issues of vital importance logic and science do not clearly guide us one way or another, because the objective facts are consistent with different interpretations. In these cases, James offers us the following rule:

> Of two competing views of the universe which in all other respects are equal, but of which the first denies some vital human need while the second satisfies it, the second will be favored by sane men for the simple reason that it makes the world seem more rational. (MT preface)

The general argument that James uses throughout his works may be formalized as follows:

(1) *The impossibility of the neutral standpoint:* There are significant issues in life about which we are forced to make a decision for one hypothesis or another.

(2) *The insufficiency of reason:* Most of the important decisions in life are ones in which none of the competing alternatives can be conclusively proven on rational grounds.

(3) *The reasonableness of subjective justifications:* Since we cannot avoid making a decision about ultimate issues, and are left without the guidance of objective criteria, it follows that we are justified in making the decision on the basis of subjective considerations.

This sort of reasoning is the basis of most of James's discussions on issues such as freedom of the will, morality, and religious belief.

Freedom and Determinism

As apparent from the diary entry, one philosophical issue that concerned James was that of freedom of the will. In his essay "The Dilemma of Determinism" (1884), James presents the issue as the choice between two large-scale conceptions of the universe: determinism and indeterminism:

> What does determinism profess? It professes that those parts of the universe already laid down absolutely appoint and decree what the other parts shall be. . . .

> Indeterminism, on the contrary, says that the parts have a certain amount of loose play on one another, so that the laying down of one of them does not necessarily determine what the others shall be. (DD 40–41)

Having set out the alternatives, James first argues for the impossibility of the neutral standpoint. The two possibilities are clear contradictories: "The truth *must* lie with one side or the other, and its lying with one side makes the other false" (DD 41). Hence, because the issue is a fundamental one, we find ourselves living as though one or the other of the beliefs is true. Second, he argues for the insufficiency of reason on this issue. Concerning a particular decision, for example, science only deals with facts, with what has happened—it cannot tell us whether the decision necessarily had to be this way or whether another decision would have been possible (DD 42).

Finally, James indicates reasons why determinism is subjectively unsatisfactory. His lengthy discussion may be distilled into this argument:

(1) There are many actions in this world, performed by ourselves or by others, that we *regret* (such as acts of murder or wanton cruelty).

(2) Determinism defines the universe as a place in which it is impossible for anything to be otherwise than it is.

(3) If everything is the inevitable result of previous causes, then determinism implies that judgments of regret are in error, for regret suggests that things could have been different from the way they are.

(4) However, this leads to the totally pessimistic position that evil actions, such as murders, are necessary and unavoidable and should not be regretted but accepted.

(5) A determinist can avoid this total pessimism by saying that acts of murder are actually good (because they were rationally necessary from all eternity and serve some greater good). But we can only avoid pessimism at the price of saying that regret is bad (because it is irrational). On the other hand, if regret is good, then murder is bad. But both types of events are supposed to have been determined. So, the world "must be a place of which either sin or error forms a necessary part."

(6) Therefore, if determinism is true, then "something must be fatally unreasonable, absurd, and wrong in the world" (DD 50).

Having set out the consequences of believing in determinism, James does the same for indeterminism. If we choose to believe there is freedom or indeterminism in the universe, then there are real possibilities and our actions can make a decisive difference as to whether good or evil will triumph:

That is what gives the palpitating reality to our moral life and makes it tingle . . . with so strange and elaborate an excitement. This reality, this excitement, are what the determinisms [of all varieties] . . . suppress by their denial that anything is decided here and now, and their dogma that all things were foredoomed and settled long ago. (DD 64)

It is important to realize that James never claims he has refuted determinism or proven indeterminism. He has simply set out the practical consequences of believing in one or the other. As was true in his own life, we have the option to choose which vision of the universe we find the most reasonable and fulfilling to assume.

The Will to Believe (religious belief)

James applies this same reasoning to the issue of religious belief in his essay "The Will to Believe" (1896). Many wrongly thought that in talking of "the will to believe" James meant we could believe anything we wanted to. He later said he should have expressed his principle as "the right to believe." James was responding to an article by W. K. Clifford titled "The Ethics of Belief," in which this philosopher discussed the conditions that give us the right to believe something and when it would be immoral to do so. Clifford argued that "it is wrong always, everywhere, and for every one, to believe anything upon insufficient evidence."[6] James's account of religious belief rests on the assumption that no compelling evidence either proves or disproves the religious hypothesis. Thus, whatever position we take will not be based on hard evidence. James attempts to counter Clifford's conclusions by arguing that even without sufficient evidence we must make a choice one way or another on this issue, and it is reasonable to choose religious faith.

James writes, "Let us call the decision between two hypotheses an *option*." Options may be living or dead, forced or avoidable, momentous or trivial. A live option is one in which each of the opposing alternatives "makes some appeal, however, small, to your belief." A forced option is one "based on a complete logical disjunction, with no possibility of not choosing." A momentous option is one where the choice has important consequences for the conduct of life as opposed to a trivial one where the stakes are insignificant or when the decision is reversible. For most people, the question of whether or not beings from another planet built the pyramids is a dead option. I do not need to consider this hypothesis seriously, because nothing about it seems plausible. It is not a forced option, because I can suspend judgment on the issue, refusing to commit myself one way or another. Finally, it is not a momentous option, because whether I believe one alternative or another would not seem to make much difference to my life.

Example

In the religious option, however, subjective justification is appropriate. Since philosophers continue to debate the existence of God, it is clearly a live option for many people. Second, I will either live my life with a religious perspective on the world, or by default I will live as though there is no God. Hence it is a forced option. Finally, it is a momentous option, because which way I choose will influence how I approach my life. When an option meets these three criteria, then it is a *genuine* option. Contrary to Clifford, I have a right to believe what is subjectively and pragmatically appealing concerning a genuine option when the evidence is insufficient. "Our passional nature not only lawfully may, but must, decide an option be-

tween propositions, whenever it is a genuine option that cannot be decided on intellectual grounds" (WB 95). Since James, like David Hume, does not think that rational arguments for or against God's existence are persuasive, the grounds for belief are to be found in practical considerations. "On pragmatistic principles, if the hypothesis of God works satisfactorily in the widest sense of the word, it is 'true' " (P 299).

Despite his impassioned defense of religious belief, James never argued for any specific religious view. He was content to say that the evidence points toward "some form of superhuman life with which we may, unknown to ourselves, be co-conscious" (APU 309). However, when it came to the nature of this superhuman life, he took the unorthodox position that the amount of evil and imperfection in the world suggests that "there is a God, but that he is finite, either in power or in knowledge, or in both at once" (APU 311). Concerning the question of whether or not good will triumph over evil in the world, James was neither an optimist nor a pessimist. Instead, he took the middle position of *meliorism*. This position views the "salvation" of the world as neither necessary nor impossible but as a possibility to be achieved by the combination of divine and human efforts (P 285–286). Hence, we are not pawns in a vast, predetermined scheme, but how the world turns out may, in part, be up to us.

JOHN DEWEY

The Ambassador-at-Large of Pragmatism

John Dewey (1859–1952) was born in 1859 in Burlington, Vermont. He received his undergraduate education at the University of Vermont and went on to complete a doctorate in philosophy at the newly organized Johns Hopkins University (where Peirce was one of his professors). After teaching philosophy at the University of Michigan for ten years, he accepted a position at the University of Chicago

as the head of the department of philosophy, psychology, and education. At Chicago he developed his ideas into a theory of progressive education and created an experimental elementary school to serve as a laboratory for testing his educational theories. His theory of education was widely adopted and transformed American school systems. In 1904 Dewey ran into conflicts with the university administration over the laboratory school. As a result he resigned and went to Columbia University, where he remained until his retirement in 1929. He was not content to simply express his ideas in books, but was an evangelist of liberal approaches to education, going all over the world to gain the largest possible audience. He lectured in Japan, China, Turkey, Mexico, and the Soviet Union. Furthermore, his works have been translated into every major language.

Dewey's Task

A glance at the multitude of Dewey's writings would make it appear as though there were two Deweys. The first Dewey was interested in technical issues in the theory of knowledge, which were addressed by his theory of instrumentalism. The second Dewey was interested in the humanities and dealt with questions concerned with education, art, value theory, and social philosophy. However, in Dewey's mind these diverse areas were linked together in that the theory of pragmatism deals with the consequences of our ideas, which have implications for every area of human concern. In this way, Dewey's philosophy synthesized the logical and scientific concerns of Peirce with the moral and humanistic ideals of James. Throughout his life, Dewey believed the split between science and human values was "the greatest dualism which now weighs humanity down" (RP 173).[7] For this reason, he wrote the book *Reconstruction in Philosophy*, which proposed a new approach to old philosophical problems. His ability to synthesize the best in his predecessors, as well as the broad range of the issues he addressed, made Dewey the most influential of all the pragmatists.

Influences on Dewey's Thought

Dewey began his career under the influence of Hegelian idealism and neo-Kantianism. Although he eventually abandoned the explicit doctrines of both philosophies, some of their spirit remained throughout all his writings. The most important influence on Dewey's thought was the theory of biological evolution. He was born in 1859, the year Charles Darwin published his theory of evolution. Dewey built his philosophy on the notions

that we are rooted in our biological environment and our intellectual life is the result of our attempts to adapt to the changing world around us. Darwin's evolutionary model enabled Dewey to retain Hegel's developmental perspective while discarding its metaphysical shell. Likewise, just as evolution never reaches a finished state of perfection, so Dewey taught that we continuously modify our ideas as they prove inadequate and replace them with fuller, richer conceptions—without, however, ending in any sort of Hegelian absolute knowledge. After going beyond neo-Kantianism, Dewey still maintained that cognition is not simply a passive mirroring of the world, but is a matter of actively constructing concepts that will make our experience intelligible.

Instrumentalism

Dewey called his theory of knowledge "instrumentalism," to distinguish it from the other versions of pragmatism. The term captures Dewey's emphasis that ideas are tools for solving problems and for shaping our environment to our ends. Throughout his works he battled the spectator view of knowledge, which presents the mind as a closed room detached from the world, containing ideas the way a museum contains pictures. This image of the mind and its contents existing in isolation from the external world led philosophers such as Descartes to wonder whether these pictures (ideas) correctly represented what was outside or even whether anything was outside the mind at all.

According to Dewey, the Cartesian kind of account completely misconstrues our situation. In the historical evolution of the species as well as in a person's development from infancy to adulthood, our cognitive skills develop in response to a world that makes demands on us. Hence, when we begin to reason we do so as biological organisms that have already wrestled with our environment:

The function of intelligence is therefore not that of copying the objects of the environment, but rather a taking account of the way in which more effective and more profitable relations with these objects may be established in the future. (DAP 30)

Note that Dewey is very cautious with the term "mind." Much of the time he uses it in reference to positions he rejects, such as Descartes's. When discussing the issues in epistemology where the word *mind* would usually occur, Dewey prefers to use "intelligence," because this term refers to a capacity that manifests itself in interactions with concrete problems rather than a metaphysical substance.

The core of Dewey's instrumentalism is found in his theory of inquiry. According to Dewey, all inquiry takes place within a specific situation in which our ability to successfully interact with our environment has broken down. Inquiry is a transitional process between two stages: "a perplexed, troubled, or confused situation at the beginning and a cleared-up, unified, resolved situation at the close" (HWT 106). This account is very similar to Peirce's view that reasoning takes us from doubt to belief. However, whereas Peirce tended to treat doubt as a psychological state, Dewey was much more influenced by theories of biological evolution and so gave the environment a much larger role. It is not just our state of mind that is indeterminate, uncertain, unsettled, or disturbed, he says, but also the *situation* has these qualities. "We are doubtful because the situation is inherently doubtful" (LTI 105–106).

Dewey gives a rather simple example of how a perplexing situation leads to inquiry and experimentation, which is worth quoting in full:

Suppose you are walking where there is no regular path. As long as everything goes smoothly, you do not have to think about your walking; your already formed habit takes care of it. Suddenly you find a ditch in your way. You think you will jump it (supposition, plan); but to make sure, you survey it with your eyes (observation), and you find that it is pretty wide and that the bank on the other side is slippery (facts, data). You then wonder if the ditch may not be narrower somewhere else (idea), and you look up and down the stream (observation) to see how matters stand (test of idea by observation). You do not find any good place and so are thrown back upon forming a new plan. As you are casting about, you discover a log (fact again). You ask yourself whether you could not haul that to the ditch and get it across

the ditch to use as a bridge (idea again). You judge that idea is worth trying, and so you get the log and manage to put it in place and walk across (test and confirmation by overt action). (HWT 105)

All of this sounds pretty obvious and simplistic. However, Dewey's story is used to support an enormous philosophical claim. He believes *all* human inquiry follows this same model. This claim includes not only the most advanced theories of modern physics but all our wrestling with ethical and political problems as well. Hence, all thinking is problem solving and there is no absolute division between the pattern of inquiry in the sciences, common sense, and morality. In every case, thinking involves a problem, hypotheses, plans of action, observations, facts, testing, and confirmation.

The Concept of Truth

Thus far, Dewey has shown that reason is an instrument or an activity for solving problems. The question is, How does the notion of *truth* fit in here? Dewey makes a considerable effort to avoid using the word *truth* in discussing his theory of knowledge. For example, contrary to what we might expect, in an entire book on the nature of inquiry (*Logic: The Theory of Inquiry*) the word *truth* only occurs in a footnote. His avoidance of the term can be explained by the fact that the notion of truth is burdened with its history, in which it has traditionally been used to refer to a static property of a proposition. However, this approach to knowledge is a long way from Dewey's notion of the active, dynamic relationship between the knower and a changing, problematic world. When he does speak about truth, he often falls back on Peirce's and James's notions of "successfully guiding action," "satisfying the needs and conditions evoked by a problem," "working in action," and so on (RP 156–157).

Dewey typically explains the idea of knowledge in terms of the notion of "warranted assertibility" (LTI 9). This notion captures Dewey's conviction that there is no final end of inquiry where our ideas will be perfectly adequate and immune from the need for revision. Whether our knowledge is complete or adequate is always a relative matter. We can always ask, "Our knowledge is complete or adequate with respect to what goals?" To ask, "Is a hammer adequate?" is meaningless, because a hammer is adequate for some tasks but not for others. Similarly, Newton's physics was thought adequate and almost complete until the end of the nineteenth century. It was an adequate tool for calculating the paths of pendulums, cannon balls, and planets. It proved not to work for other situations, such as predicting certain kinds of subatomic and astronomical events. Inquiry is a continual process of adjusting means to ends. But as new ends arise within a changing world, we need new means, new ideas, and new theories. Theories, like instruments such as the slide rule, are not so much refuted as abandoned when we require new and more adequate instruments to meet our needs.

Ethics as Problem Solving

One problem that has haunted modern philosophy is the dichotomy between facts and values. One position often taken states that science studies facts while ethics studies values. But if facts are located in the spatiotemporal world, where are values located? One answer has been that they are simply subjective preferences located in our sentiments or existential choices. Those who reject this subjectivism often think the only other alternative is to assign some sort of mysterious, transcendent status to values such that they float far above the world of empirical facts (in the mind of God for the medieval or in pure reason for Kant). However, Dewey believes this "two worlds" view of facts and values will not do:

> The problem of restoring integration and cooperation between man's beliefs about the world in which he lives and his beliefs about values and purposes that should direct his conduct is the deepest problem of any philosophy that is not isolated from that life. (QC 255)

If we analyze our experience, we will find that facts and values appear separate only because we ourselves have ripped them apart through a process of abstraction, creating an artificial gulf between them. The truth is, we initially begin with a world we value before we make it an object of inquiry:

> Things are objects to be treated, used, acted upon and with, enjoyed and endured, even more than things to be known. They are things had before they are things cognized. (EN 21)

If we cannot separate facts and values, then it is a mistake to employ one method in the natural sciences and another in morality, for human life is a single project of adapting successfully to the environment. "Morals is as much a matter of interaction of a person with his social environment as walking is an interaction of legs with a physical environment" (HNC 318). Ethical reasoning both begins and is carried out in the same way as any inquiry:

> A moral situation is one in which judgment and choice are required antecedently to overt action. . . . There are conflicting desires and alternative apparent goods. What is needed is to find the right course of action, the right good. Hence inquiry is exacted. (RP 163–164)

Although insisting on the necessity of an empirical theory of value, Dewey criticizes the naivete of the utilitarians' approach. Mill believed that the fact something is *desired* is what we mean by calling it *desirable*. However, Dewey questions this glib identification, for he says that "the fact that something is desired only raises the *question* of its desirability; it does not settle it" (QC 260). For this reason, he distinguishes sharply between "the enjoyed and the enjoyable, the desired and the desirable, the satis*fying* and the satis*factory*" (QC 260).

How then do we distinguish between what is merely satisfying (a subjective fact) and what is satisfactory (the genuinely valuable)? Taking his usual approach, Dewey compares the task of making value judgments with that of making scientific judgments. First, while science begins with observations it is not content to rest on what is initially given in naive perception. Without further inquiry, the earth seems to be flat and moving objects always seem to come to rest. However, science seeks to develop coherent connections between one set of observations and the entire fabric of observations. Similarly, the process of moral reasoning is one of moving beyond what initially seems good to judgments of value that fit the whole of human experience.

Second, scientists accomplish their goals by proposing experimental hypotheses that guide future actions and let us make predictions. Hypotheses that prove successful in all situations to which they are applied are those we will continue to use. Similarly, Dewey says, mere enjoyments become values when intelligent inquiry identifies those attitudes and ways of acting that help humans flourish in the long run. If we took an experimental approach to values, then

> all tenets and creeds about good and goods, would be recognized to be hypotheses. Instead of being rigidly fixed, they would be treated as intellectual instruments to be tested and confirmed—and altered—through consequences effected by acting upon them. (QC 277)

Hence, in one sense we can test moral beliefs in the crucible of experience. In making moral decisions, we proceed just as we would when trying to cross a ditch in the woods. We analyze the situation, imaginatively project possible courses of action, and evaluate the consequences of these actions.

If value judgments are like well-confirmed but always tentative and revisable scientific hypotheses, then moral dogmatism and the search for fixed, eternal, and *a priori* ethical principles are mistaken:

> A moral law, like a law in physics, is not something to swear by and stick to at all hazards; it is a formula of the way to respond when specified conditions present themselves. (QC 278)

Significantly, one of Dewey's most important statements of his moral philosophy appears in a chapter titled "The Construction of Good" (QC chap. 10). He says the "good" is not an autonomous entity, existing independently of the human situation, like an undiscovered planet waiting for us to find it. Instead, to say that "*X* is good" or "one

ought to do *X*" is a constructive proposal for dealing with specific situations to achieve certain ends.

With this topic we return to Dewey's evolutionary theory. Values are just one of the adjustment mechanisms in our lives that let us direct our behavior to achieve the best consequences. Furthermore, just as the theory of evolution showed that all patterns in organic life are changeable, so there are no fixed ends that have unending value beyond the way they fulfill the concrete needs we happen to have. Since we live in a changing world and are changing along with it, there is always the open possibility that we will have to revise our value assessments at a future time.

This leads to Dewey's notion of the *means ends continuum.* Any means can itself come to be valued as an end, and any end we achieve may become a means to further ends. In the final analysis, there are no ends-in-themselves; nothing has intrinsic value except for the ongoing process of seeking better means to ever-increasing ends:

> Honesty, industry, temperance, justice, like health, wealth and learning, are not goods to be possessed as they would be if they expressed fixed ends to be attained. They are directions of change in the quality of experience. Growth itself is the only moral "end." (RP 177)

Education, Social Philosophy, and Religion

Like all the great systems of thought (Plato's, Aristotle's, and Hegel's, for example), Dewey's philosophy is attractive because of its power to illuminate all areas of human experience. For example, Dewey's perspective has had an enormous influence on American education. In his day, education consisted of the rote memorization of a mass of factual information and historical classics. Dewey, however, says the goal of education should be to help students develop effective problem-solving methods and skills for social interaction. Hence, the emphasis is on process and not content, on learning by doing. With Socrates, Dewey says that the role of the teacher is not to provide information but to bring the students to the point of discovering truths for themselves.

Dewey's pragmatism also has many implications for social philosophy. With Peirce he believes inquiry cannot be an individual, subjective project, but will succeed most as a community effort. Science can only succeed in the context of free communication, free action, and mutual dialogue that includes as many points of view as possible. Thus this sort of structure will be valued in a society founded on scientific principles in the broadest sense. Accordingly, Dewey gives a pragmatic defense of the American ideal of a democracy dominated by the values of freedom, participation, and inclusiveness. Furthermore, the biological, organic model that guides all his thought implies that the health of the whole organism is a function of the health of its parts. Hence, his educational philosophy supports his social philosophy, for society has the need as well as the responsibility to help each member become an effective decision maker in a changing world.

Finally, Dewey developed a pragmatic approach to the religious dimension in human experience in a 1934 book titled *A Common Faith*. He says our age consists of two warring camps—those who embrace some sort of traditional religion (each claiming that theirs is the "true" one), and those who are antireligion secularists. Both share the belief that the religious is identified with supernaturalism. Dewey, however, argues for the importance of the religious quality of experience, while claiming it can be freed of all supernaturalistic baggage. The adjective *religious* can apply to any experience in which the self is directed toward an ideal that transcends a person's narrow concerns. Thus, we can encounter the religious dimension of life in aesthetic, scientific, or moral experience, as well as in relationships of friendship and love. Dewey's naturalistic faith retains the word *God* to refer to the active relation between the actual world and the ideals we seek to embody in it. In this way he hoped to move beyond the divisiveness of narrow sectarianism toward a perspective that would retain the religious spirit, harmonize with science, and be a "common faith" shared by all.

The Significance of Pragmatism

True to the spirit of pragmatism, Peirce, James, and Dewey would not claim their writings have completed the task of philosophy, but they would claim they have provided the only method for moving toward that goal. What is the goal of philosophy, according to pragmatism? Dewey summed it up nicely in expressing the crucial test for evaluating his and any other philosophy:

> There is . . . a first rate test of the value of any philosophy which is offered us: Does it end in conclusions which, when they are referred back to ordinary life-experiences and their predicaments, render them more significant, more luminous to us, and make our dealings with them more fruitful? (EN 9–10)

Few philosophers call themselves "pragmatists" today. But this is not because the essential features of pragmatism have been abandoned or discredited. Instead, its major insights have become integrated into most of twentieth-century philosophy, particularly in North America and Britain.

Questions for Understanding

1. What were the points of disagreement between the pragmatists and the rationalists? How did the pragmatists differ from traditional empiricism?

2. In what ways did the pragmatists both agree and disagree with Kant? On what points did they agree and disagree with Hegel?

3. According to Peirce, what is the relationship between beliefs and action?

4. Why does Peirce reject Descartes's method of doubt?

5. According to Peirce, what are the four methods of arriving at belief? Which one does he think we should use? Why? What are his criticisms of each of the other three methods?

6. What is Peirce's theory of meaning?

7. How is Peirce's theory of truth? In what way does it also provide a theory of reality?

8. What is fallibilism? Why does Peirce think it is important that we believe in it?

9. What are the differences between James's pragmatism and Peirce's?

10. What is the difference between a pragmatic test of truth and a pragmatic definition of truth? What is James's theory of truth?

11. What is James's argument for the acceptability of subjective justifications for one's beliefs?

12. How does James argue against pragmatism?

13. What is James's quarrel with W. K. Clifford's approach to belief?

14. According to James, under what conditions is a person's religious belief justified?

15. What did Dewey take as his philosophical task?

16. Why did Dewey label his philosophy "instrumentalism"?

17. What is Dewey's theory of inquiry?

18. Why does Dewey avoid the term "truth"? What phrase does he use in its place?

19. According to Dewey, what is the relation between facts and values? What implications does this have for ethics?

20. In Dewey's philosophy, what are the implications of pragmatism for education, social philosophy, and religion, respectively?

21. According to Dewey what is the criterion for evaluating a philosophy?

Questions for Reflection

1. Given Peirce's theory of reality, why would he reject the following two claims? (a) "Reality is whatever I believe it to be" and (b) "We can never know reality."

2. What are the similarities and differences between Peirce's notion of the "practical bearings" of our concepts and what James refers to as the "practical consequences" of our beliefs?

3. Descartes claimed that we should not accept a belief unless it is free of all possible doubts. How would James respond to this criterion for the acceptability of a belief? What reasons would he give for his position?

4. Some suppose that James claimed that we have a right to believe whatever we find it pleasant to believe. Do you think this is correct? What would James think of this statement of his position?

5. In what way does Dewey consider making an ethical decision to be similar to the approach that a scientist takes in testing a hypothesis? What are the strengths and weaknesses of this sort of approach to ethics?

Notes

1. John Dewey, "The Development of American Pragmatism," in *Philosophy and Civilization* (New York: Putnam's, 1931), 24–25.

2. References to C. S. Peirce's works are in terms of section numbers of the following editions:

   CP   *The Collected Papers of Charles Sanders Peirce*, 8 vols., vols. 1–6, ed. Charles Hartshorne and Paul Weiss, vols. 7 and 8, ed. Arthur W. Burks (Cambridge, MA: Harvard University Press, 1931–1958).

   FB   "The Fixation of Belief," in *Collected Papers*, vol. 5.

   HMIC "How to Make Our Ideas Clear," in *Collected Papers*, vol. 5.

   SCFI "Some Consequences of Four Incapacities," in *Collected Papers*, vol. 5.

   WPI   "What Pragmatism Is," in *Collected Papers*, vol. 5.

3. Dewey, "The Development of American Pragmatism," 21.

4. References to the works of William James are made in terms of page numbers. The following abbreviations are used in the text:

   APU   *A Pluralistic Universe* (New York: Longmans, Green, 1916).

   DD   "The Dilemma of Determinism," in William James, *Essays in Pragmatism*, ed. Alburey Castell (New York: Hafner Press, Macmillan, 1948).

   MT   *Meaning and Truth: A Sequel to "Pragmatism"* (New York: McKay, 1909; reprint, Westport, CT: Greenwood Press, 1968).

   P   *Pragmatism: A New Name for Son Thinking* (New York: Longmans, (

   WB   "The Will to Believe," in William in *Pragmatism*.

5. *The Letters of William James*, ed. Henry James (Boston: Atlantic Monthly Press, 1920), 1:147–148.

6. W. K. Clifford, "The Ethics of Belief," quoted in William James, "The Will to Believe," 93.

7. References to John Dewey's books are in terms of their page numbers using the following abbreviations:

DAP "The Development of American Pragmatism," chap. in *Philosophy and Civilization* (New York: Putnam's, 1931).

EN *Experience and Nature*, 2d ed. (LaSalle, IL: Open Court, 1929).

HNC *Human Nature and Conduct* (New York: The Modern Library, 1922).

HWT *How We Think* (Boston: Heath, 1933).

LTI *Logic: The Theory of Inquiry* (New York: Holt, Rinehart & Winston, 1938).

QC *The Quest for Certainty* (New York: Capricorn Books, 1929).

RP *Reconstruction in Philosophy*, enlarged ed. (Boston: Beacon Press, 1948).

31

Process Philosophy:
Bergson and Whitehead

IF WE POLLED THE KEY FIGURES IN PHILOSOPHY, from its very beginning up to the twentieth century, the majority opinion would be that reality consists of fundamental substances that remain identical throughout their temporal existence. There are many varieties of this basic theme; the general approach can be tagged with the generic label of "substance metaphysics." However, the nature of philosophy is to question all taken-for-granted assumptions and settled opinions. Consequently, critics who advocate a "process metaphysics" have opposed this prevailing tradition. This viewpoint stresses that reality is dynamic and consists of a series of processes or events. "Process" here means more than simply that reality consists of a succession of events. It also includes the claim that creativity is fundamental to the nature of things and that genuine novelties emerge within the process.

Heraclitus, Hegel, and Nietzsche are examples of philosophers covered in previous chapters who emphasized the priority of change and temporality over substances and essences. In the twentieth century, Henri Bergson succinctly stated the core of

process philosophy as follows: "There is change, but there are not things which change" (CM 177).[1] Similarly, Alfred North Whitehead proclaimed, "The flux of things is one ultimate generalization around which we must weave our philosophical system" (PR 317).[2]

Our language is stacked against process philosophy, for the subject of most sentences is a noun to which we attach properties or activities. This reflects Aristotle's metaphysical view that the subjects of discourse are substances in which qualities inhere and that maintain their identity through time, even while undergoing change. For example, we say, "The carpet is blue," or "The carpet is fading," suggesting that the carpet is a fundamental reality that exhibits a color or loses it.

But maybe things are not quite as simple as they seem. Consider these examples: "The weather is becoming humid," "Public opinion is changing," and "Their friendship is solid." Despite our grammar, "the weather," "public opinion," and a "friendship" really are not "things." Rather, they are shorthand and abstract ways of speaking about a collection of more primary and concrete events and activities.

Humidity does not inhere within the weather—the weather is an outcome of those events that create humidity. When one of these "entities" is changing, a set of dynamic conditions exhibiting one sort of pattern is giving way to another set of events with a different pattern. When these "entities" manifest ongoing properties, this is because the changing events exhibit repetitive patterns and similarities.

Perhaps we will better understand the objects in our experience (rocks, trees, people) when we see them as having a status similar to the weather than when we view them as Aristotelian substances. We say, "He is in love," not "Love is in him," suggesting that we find our identity within a larger complex of relationships and events rather than the other way around. Turning to nuclear physics, scientists tell us that material objects are really dynamic collections of subatomic events. This has certainly given new insight to Heraclitus's claim that "All things come into being through opposition and all are in flux, like a river."

If this makes any sense at all, then it is worth considering how Henri Bergson and Alfred North Whitehead, two of the leading process philosophers in the twentieth century, sought to parlay these insights into full-scale visions of the universe. Bergson and Whitehead swam against the stream of the history of philosophy by emphasizing a process view over a substance view. However, they also stood out among their contemporaries for trying to do speculative metaphysics in a time when not only was interest in it decreasing, but also many claimed that achieving a grand vision of reality was impossible. Nevertheless, they were both convinced the human mind could arrive at a coherent synthesis that pulled together our best understanding of knowledge, reality, and values. Both had a spiritual affinity with the romantic poets in sensing a unity between human experience and nature. At the same time, they also looked to the sciences of biology, psychology, and physics for clues to an adequate metaphysics.

HENRI BERGSON

The Philosopher of Creativity

Henri Bergson (1859–1941) was born in Paris on October 18, 1859, into a cosmopolitan Jewish family. It was a good year for producing philosophers: this year also saw the birth of John Dewey, the great American pragmatist, and Edmund Husserl, the founder of phenomenology. As a student Bergson distinguished himself in science, mathematics, and literature. He first received public attention at age eighteen when he won a mathematics competition with a solution good enough to be published in a professional mathematics journal. When the time came to decide on his goals for advanced education, he wavered between science and literature. In the end, he compromised by pursuing a degree in philosophy at the École Normale Supérieure, one of France's most famous schools.

After receiving his degree, Bergson taught at a series of schools and quickly gained a reputation for being an exciting teacher whose passion for ideas was contagious. For Bergson, philosophy was not a narrow academic discipline, but a way of illuminating every area of human experience. This is indicated by the fact that in 1900 he published one of the few philosophical works devoted to the topic of the meaning of laughter in human experience. His philosophical articles and books began to attract attention, leading to his appointment in 1900 to the chair of modern philosophy at the Collège de France, one of the most prestigious positions in the nation. Bergson remained there for the rest of his academic career.

With the appearance of *Creative Evolution* in 1907, he achieved international fame. His reputation brought academics and laypeople to Paris from all over the world to hear him lecture. Before long, he had even become the darling of the social set and his audiences were packed with those who snapped up the latest daring fashions—even in the world of ideas. He appealed to those who felt alienated from institutionalized religion and yet who had no appetite for the chilly materialism that had been offered as the only alternative. As science continued to reduce nature to lifeless particles in motion, Bergson responded with the vision of a rich and value-laden world. The human spirit, for so long alienated from a nature stripped of its enchantment, could now return home and find the world was still as the poets had described it. Over the next fourteen years, Bergson had lecture engagements in New York and throughout England and Europe. Yet this adulation did not seem to affect his naturally modest and unassuming personality.

In 1921, at the height of his career, exhausted by the demands of fame, and suffering from ill health, he resigned his position at the Collège de France. Even in his retirement, the public continued to bestow honors on him, including the Nobel Prize for literature in 1927. For a number of years, the public saw no evidence that he was still actively working. Most assumed he had made his last contribution to philosophy. However, during this period of retreat he was engaging in an intensive study of history, anthropology, and theology. This bore fruit in 1932 with the release of his final book, *The Two Sources of Religion and Morality*.

In the following years he meditated in seclusion, constantly in pain from arthritis, but continuing to follow through on the ideas introduced in his last work. Although of Jewish descent, Bergson became attracted to the Catholic religion and might have become a convert if it hadn't been for the growing wave of anti-Semitism that was sweeping Europe. In the face of this development, he felt obliged to remain identified with the suffering of his people.

When France was taken over by the Nazis in 1940, the new government imposed a series of restrictions on its Jewish citizens. Although Bergson was granted an exemption because of his international reputation, he refused any special treatment. Furthermore, he renounced all state honors

he had achieved, to disassociate himself from the current government. When all Jews were required to be registered with the government, Bergson was again exempted. But although he was now an eighty-one-year-old invalid, he left his bed and waited his turn in the registration line, held up by two attendants throughout the inclement weather. This silent protest turned out to be his last, eloquent message to the world. Bergson died a few days later, on January 4, 1941.

Two Ways of Knowing: Intellect and Intuition

According to Bergson, there are two fundamental ways of knowing the world: intellect and intuition. His entire philosophy is permeated by the division between these two, competing approaches to epistemology. When we approach reality from one side (intuition), reality is opened up to us in all its purity and richness. When we approach it from the other standpoint (intellect), we are left with the dry dust of empty abstractions and fragmentary images. Bergson says that in seeking to know something the intellect moves around the outside of the object, captures it in symbols, and only achieves a relative perspective. However, intuition enters into the object of knowledge, does not depend on symbols, and attains the absolute (IM 21). The difference between knowing something through the intellect versus knowing it intuitively is like the difference between trying to know Paris through a series of photographs as opposed to walking its streets, smelling its smells, feeling its textures, reveling in its spirit, and dwelling within it.

Intuition is a simple act of sympathy that directly grasps what is unique and inexpressible in its object. However, the intellect, which proceeds by means of analysis, must understand things in terms of concepts, categories, and symbols. There is a twofold problem with analysis. First, when it represents its object in terms of concepts and their associated symbols, it is translating the reality, or even worse, replacing it with a representation. Hence, thought and language stand as intermediaries and, therefore, barriers between us and reality. Second, by seeking to capture the object in concepts and language, the method of analysis must reduce it to those qualities that are universal. In this way it falsifies the reality and turns it into a barren abstraction by stripping it of its concrete, unique features.

Although he frequently speaks very harshly of the intellect, Bergson does not wish to discard it, but only to put it in perspective. He explains that the distinction between intuition and the intellect arose as a product of evolutionary processes. Historically, the intellect developed to enhance our ability to cope with the environment. In the history of the species, the instincts were originally our fundamental mode of dealing with the world. As the instincts became self-conscious and reflective, they developed into intuition. The intellect is only a very late development in our history. It is a tool that arose to meet practical needs:

> We do not aim generally at knowledge for the sake of knowledge, but in order to take sides, to draw profit—in short, to satisfy an interest. . . . To try to fit a concept on an object is simply to ask what we can do with object, and what it can do for us. To label an object with a certain concept is to mark in precise terms the kind of action or attitude the object should suggest to us. (IM 38 39)

Hence, to serve our practical needs, the intellect needs to divide reality into a series of static moments in order to create conceptually manageable units. We assign names and labels to these moments such as "the weather" or "my headache," ignoring for practical purposes the fact that these are really abstractions from a dynamic and seamless flow of experience.

Kant claimed the mind imposes its order on reality. From this he concluded that we can never know reality in itself. However, Bergson says that this conclusion is wrong. "But because we fail to reconstruct the living reality with stiff and ready-made concepts, it does not follow that we cannot grasp it in some other way" (IM 51). This other way, of course, is intuition. Bergson agrees with Kant that the mind pours experience into its categories. However, unlike Kant, he does not think

this is an *a priori* necessity. Instead, we can reverse the natural tendency of the intellect and enter into the fluid stream of reality, allowing the mind's categories to be shaped by this process. "In this way it will attain to fluid concepts, capable of following reality in all its sinuosities and of adopting the very movement of the inward life of things" (IM 51). Bergson consistently follows his own advice, expressing his philosophy in rich pictorial metaphors. This feature of his philosophy held his audiences spellbound, while exasperating his more logically inclined critics.

Bergson has such an extraordinary faith in the openness of intuition to reality itself, he says that if intuition could be prolonged beyond a few instants, philosophers would agree (CE 252). The problem is, philosophy cannot function by means of a mute immersion in reality. Instead, it must base itself within language while carrying out a never-ending "raid on the inarticulate / With shabby equipment always deteriorating" (as T. S. Eliot described the task of speaking). Nevertheless, although the imperfections of language necessarily burden the philosopher, Bergson insists that philosophical discourse can have no other source of confirmation than what we read from the experience of intuition.

Bergson was continually charged with "anti-intellectualism" and "irrationalism." This was due to the fact that his propensity toward vivid speech led him to make some rather extreme statements. However, although he frequently seems to be opposed to science, his more moderate passages make clear that only certain approaches to science bother him. He remarks, for example, that the development of the infinitesimal calculus represented the triumph of continuity and becoming over disconnected and static approaches (IM 52). Likewise, Galileo's principles of motion overcame the fixed categories of Aristotelian science (IM 54). Bergson attributes the greatest feats of science to intuitive insights into the continuity and mobility of reality. His own metaphysics sought to integrate philosophy with the current biology of his day. Rather than dismissing science altogether, he says that in their maturest forms, "science and meta-

Giacomo Balla, Street Light *(1909). Influenced, in part, by the theories of Henri Bergson concerning the dynamic nature of reality, a group of Italian artists developed a movement known as Futurism. The Futurists' works were alive with motion and emphasized the dynamic relationship between objects and the environment and between the spectator and the work of art. In this painting, the artist Balla used multiple strokes of intense color to depict a dazzling shower of light rays, creating the illusion of pulsating energy.*

physics therefore come together in intuition" (IM 53–54).

Lurking in the background of Bergson's judgments about the adequate and inadequate ways of obtaining knowledge is a vision of the reality each method is trying to know. If philosophy can succeed only if it develops "flexible, mobile, almost fluid representations," this can only mean that re-

ality itself must be closer to a fluid than to a series of discrete units. Thus, Bergson's epistemology leads quite naturally into his metaphysics.

Metaphysics: Mechanism Versus Vitalism

The fundamental argument of all process philosophers is that if the basic units of reality are "things," we will never be able to explain how motion, much less novelty, are possible. Yet if process, spontaneity, and creativity are fundamental, then stability, order, and continuously existing objects can be understood as abstractions from this flux or repeated patterns within the dynamic flow.

If metaphysics is the study of reality, then it makes sense to begin with a look at that reality we know best. "There is one reality, at least, which we all seize from within, by intuition and not by simple analysis. It is our personality in its flowing—through time—our self which endures" (IM 24). If our own experience gives us a window to reality, then what sort of reality does it reveal to us?

> This reality is mobility. Not things *made, but things in the making, not self-maintaining states, but only changing states, exist. Rest is never more than apparent, or, rather, relative. The consciousness we have of our own self in its continual flux introduces us to the interior of reality, on the model of which we must represent other realities.* (IM 49–50)

Since Descartes, modern philosophy has wrestled with the problem of how we can know that our inner experience tells us about the outer world. Bergson believes that this problem gets off the ground by first assuming that we are islands of consciousness that are somehow isolated from the world at large. Obviously, however, we are a part of reality and there is a constant two-way flow between the inner and the outer. Contrary to the fragmenting perspective of the intellect, we find within our experience a *durée réelle* (real duration). When we intuitively make contact with our own duration, we are in touch with the larger stream of duration:

The matter and life which fill the world are equally within us; the forces which work in all things we feel within ourselves; whatever may be the inner essence of what is and what is done, we are of that essence. (CM 147)

Hence, contrary to Kant, Bergson thinks that there is no ultimate dichotomy between reality as we experience it and reality as it is in itself.

TIME AND DURATION

Bergson's theory of time and its implications for metaphysics was developed in his first work, *Time and Free Will* (French 1889, English version 1910). The phenomenon of time is the central thread throughout all Bergson's philosophy, for time seems to be the bridge that overcomes the dichotomy between the internal mind and the external world. In one sense, time is out there in the world, characterizing the existence of external objects, but it is also something we experience internally as characterizing our subjective experience. Ever alert to polar tensions within human experience, Bergson distinguishes two approaches to time: *scientific time* (also called "clock time"), and what he called *duration* (or "real time"). The first is time as an intellectual, scientific concept, and the second is time as we experience it and live it.

The abstract time of the sciences is thought of in spatial terms, as though it were an unbounded straight line whose points are temporal moments. When we try to appropriate time in language, we talk about "a point in time," "a length of time," "a short time." A future event is spoken of as something that will happen "further on down the line." In contrast, duration is lived time, it is known through intuition as an immediate datum of consciousness. Duration is not a succession of discrete moments but a flowing, indivisible continuum. Its phases "melt into one another and form an organic whole." For practical purposes, our intellect divides this flowing unity into distinct, measurable, conceptualized entities. Although this is useful, it becomes harmful when the artificially constructed, intellectualized world is confused with reality it-

self. The attempt to reduce the world to concepts is like filling buckets with water from the tumultuous, roaring ocean and supposing that if we just had enough buckets, we could capture and recreate the reality of the ocean.

THE EXPERIENCE OF BEING A SELF

Corresponding to these two ways of viewing time are two aspects of the self. There is the superficial self, a succession of psychological states, and there is the real self, which is an enduring and continuous self. These correlate loosely with Kant's empirical self and the noumenal self, but with one difference. Since Kant thought knowledge had to have sensory content and a conceptual form, he did not think it was possible to know the real self. We could only postulate it. However, Bergson does think we can know the real self through intuition by living in it, and thus we can apprehend it by a form of knowledge that eludes the senses as well as the intellect.

The behavioral sciences can study the self as a collection of discrete psychological states like an external object. The problem is that if we think the self is nothing but a series of distinct states, then we will think of the preceding state as causing the state that follows it, as though the moments within experience were like billiard balls setting each other in motion. In this way determinism follows from a faulty psychology. In contrast, if we view the self as a seamless totality, which is the way we experience it, then acts that flow from our whole personality are free actions. It is true that our actions emerge from what preceded them, for where else would they come from? However, each new moment synthesizes the past elements and adds to them, creating a novel unity that could not have been predicted:

Thus our personality shoots, grows and ripens without ceasing. Each of its moments is something new added to what was before. We may go further: it is not only something new, but something unforeseeable. Doubtless, my present state is explained by what was in me and by what was acting on me a moment ago.

In analyzing it I should find no other elements. But even a superhuman intelligence would not have been able to foresee the simple indivisible form which gives to these purely abstract elements their concrete organization. (CE 8–9)

Bergson acknowledges that freedom can't be proven because this would require analysis, a fragmenting process that would obscure the phenomenon of freedom. However, he thinks we will discover freedom in our own experience. When you study psychology, for example, it is easy to view *other people* as objects whose behavior is the product of causes operating on them. However, you cannot view yourself as a deterministic mechanism, because you experience yourself as a free, spontaneous agent who creatively responds to your experience of the external world. Having said this, however, it is possible to live at the level of the superficial self, passively allowing yourself to be acted on by social pressures or other determinants within your environment. But one can only become like an object by refusing to live out of the deepest, most authentic center of one's being.

EVOLUTION IN A NEW LIGHT

The year of Bergson's birth (1859) was the year that Charles Darwin published his theory of evolution in *The Origin of Species*. Obviously, Bergson's perspective has much in common with Darwin's notion that nature does not consist of fixed, static biological categories but is a continuous process in which one form of life evolves into another type of species. Bergson's 1907 book, *Creative Evolution*, was an attempt to build a theory of reality on the evolutionary model. However, he has a number of critical remarks to make regarding Darwin's approach. For example, Darwin's principle of natural selection claimed that random variations would produce changes in a species if they helped it adapt better to its environment. But any increase in complexity creates a greater degree of risk. If survival value were the only force at work, evolution would have stopped with the simplest of organisms (such

as the ant, perhaps). Furthermore, an integrated whole, such as the eye, could not have been produced by partial, random changes.

Although he rejected the mechanistic version of evolution, Bergson also rejected a teleological view that said species develop according to some predetermined plan, whether this is the plan of a Leibnizian God or a Hegelian Absolute Spirit. Evolution, Bergson argues, is neither mechanistic, in which events are pushed by deterministic causes from behind, nor is it teleological, in which events are pulled toward some future goal along tracks laid down in advance. Neither case accounts for the restless, creative striving of nature and the emergence of novelty. What harmony there is in the world is a harmony created on the run. It is a harmony continually in the making with the emergence of each new novelty.

To understand the process of evolution in nature, we can once again look to our inner experience for the key to reality. We find an *élan vital* (vital force) that is manifested in the self's continuous experience of duration. This vital impetus is present in all nature and is the cause of the emergence of novelty. Although the *élan vital* is ever surging and expressing its creative force, it encounters resistance from stable, inert matter and so must find new outlets through which to express itself. Like a vine that forces a crack in a wall to yield to its striving, the *élan vital* breaks through its limits and transcends the present stage of organization in which it finds itself.

As always, when he has done as much as possible to show that his theory corresponds to the facts, Bergson resorts to a metaphor to spark our intuitions. Bergson suggests we imagine a vessel full of steam at a high pressure in which some of the steam is escaping through a crack:

The steam thrown into the air is nearly all condensed into little drops which fall back, and this condensation and this fall represent simply the loss of something, an interruption, a deficit. But a small part of the jet of steam subsists, uncondensed, for some seconds; it is making an effort to raise the drops which are falling; it succeeds at most in retarding their fall.

So, from an immense reservoir of life, jets must be gushing out unceasingly, of which each, falling back, is a world. (CE 269)

Thus, reality is a dynamic process in which the inner spiritual core is the gushing, spontaneous, creative *élan vital* that provides novelty to the world. At the same time, a portion of this vital force "condenses" and leaves behind the world of order, stability, and matter as a residue. With respect to evolution, the emergence of novelties and new species are due to the creative, spiritual core of nature, while the perpetuation of ongoing species is the "falling back" process that results in continuity.

One might wonder if this vital force in nature can be thought of as a conscious activity. Bergson is cautious in answering this question, but he does speak at one point of "the consciousness, or rather supra-consciousness, that is at the origin of life." He even suggests the possibility of applying the term "God" to this creative force that is the source of all things. However, he never elaborates on these remarks, and not until his last publication on morality and religion did he work out their full meaning.

The Two Sources of Morality and Religion

Having exposed the opposition between the static and the dynamic in his epistemology and metaphysics, Bergson uses this contrast to illuminate morality and religion, the theme of his last important work, *The Two Sources of Morality and Religion.* When we look at the way in which morality has developed in history, Bergson says, we find two sets of phenomena: static morality and dynamic morality. One type of morality manifests itself as enduring moral traditions. This sort of morality provides the continuity essential for maintaining a stable community. This is static or closed morality. We find static morality in obligations and those structures that make society stable. A large portion of the self is a social self, so that even when society's direct pressures are absent, we internalize its values, which impinge on us.

The type of morality that is open and dynamic results from the moral genius and insights of creative people. Such individuals rise above the standard of their society to present a vision of a new, higher moral ideal. In so doing, they bring their society to a new level of moral awareness. Although dynamic morality originates in the great moral idealists and prophets, ultimately it flows from the creative source of life itself. "It is the mystic souls who draw and will continue to draw civilized societies in their wake" (TSMR 84). Whereas the morality of obligation makes its claims on us through social pressure, open morality solicits our convictions through appeal and aspiration. Open morality is the creative movement of life; closed morality is the fixed residue left behind. Static morality is propelled by the inertia of tradition and is largely something below the activity of reason, while dynamic morality transcends reason. Reason, therefore, mediates between the two.

Morality includes both "a system of *orders* dictated by *impersonal* social requirements and a series of *appeals* made to the conscience of each of us by *persons* who represent the best there is in humanity" (TSMR 84). They are constantly pulling in opposite directions, but intermingle in most societies, for society needs the strengths of each of them. Open morality infuses fresh life into the closed morality, while the latter makes the insights of the former a part of society's structures. In religion the same dynamics are at work. Religion presents itself as a historical and sociological phenomenon in which doctrines, traditions, and institutions prevail. Yet there is also the deeper, more personal level of extraordinary religious consciousness. The great mystics, prophets, and religious leaders represent this dynamic form of religion. The ultimate end of religious experience is

a contact, consequently of a partial coincidence, with the creative effort which life itself manifests. This effort is of God, if it is not God himself. The great mystic is to be conceived as an individual being, capable of transcending the limitations imposed on the species by its material nature, thus continuing and extending the divine action. (TSMR 220– 221)

A complete mysticism is a twofold movement that goes from a participation in the divine life to bringing this vision down to earth within the human community.

Bergson's Influence

Bergson's impact spread beyond the narrow domain of professional philosophy, and writers, social activists, and theologians all felt the impact of his ideas. However, though Bergson left behind a small number of disciples who carried on his philosophy, a well-defined Bergsonian movement never developed. For the most part, his influence was reflected in the writings of other philosophers who admired Bergson while eclipsing him, such as the pragmatists. Bergson anticipated themes that would find their way into different philosophies in the twentieth century. These include the priority of processes over things, a concern for the limits of reason and language, the role of evolution in explaining human nature, and the central importance of immediate experience.[3] Although the enormous fame Bergson enjoyed dwindled after his death, William James's congratulatory letter on the release of *Creative Evolution* indicates the admiration Bergson received from many of his contemporaries.

> *O my Bergson, you are a magician, and your book is a marvel, a real wonder in the history of philosophy.*[4]

ALFRED NORTH WHITEHEAD

Although Bergson tried to integrate his philosophy with current scientific thinking, many philosophers still dismissed his ideas as hopelessly vague and poetic. However, process metaphysics surged forward with new vigor when Alfred North Whitehead (1861–1947) took up its defense. He had already established his fame in the field of mathematical logic, and when he turned to speculative metaphysics his colleagues were shocked to discover that this hardheaded logician had the soul of a romantic poet.

Whitehead's Life: From Mathematics to Metaphysics

Alfred North Whitehead was born on February 15, 1861, in Kent, England.[5] He received his university education at Trinity College, Cambridge, where, by his own admission, he never attended lectures on any topic other than mathematics. However, Whitehead says this was balanced out by the equally important education he received from after-dinner discussions with students and faculty on literature, history, religion, and philosophy. Later on, he said that it was his wife's "vivid life," her appreciation of beauty and capacity for love, that taught him to appreciate the moral and aesthetic values that lie beyond the domains of logic and science. After completing his studies, he stayed on at Trinity College to teach, and there he first became acquainted with Bertrand Russell, who was first his most distinguished pupil and later his colleague and friend.

Whitehead's intellectual career falls into three main periods. During the first period he worked on the foundations of mathematics. He and Russell found that they shared some of the same ideas, and this led to their coauthorship of *Principia Mathematica* (1910–1913). In this work they provided an elaborate demonstration that mathematics can be deduced from the principles of formal logic. It has been called "one of the great intellectual monuments of all time." In the second phase of his life, Whitehead moved to London in 1910 where he worked at the University of London and then became a professor of applied mathematics at the Imperial College of Science and Technology. Most of his work on the philosophy of science came out of this period. The third phase of Whitehead's life began in 1924. Although he was sixty-three, an age when most professors would be wrapping up their career, Whitehead started a new one and became a professor of philosophy at Harvard. In the early years of his career, his writings on mathematics, nature, and science were very technical in nature. However, his ideas gradually developed to the point where they could not be separated from philosophical concerns. During this remaining period of his life, he marched boldly into the center of philosophy, expanding his earlier ideas into a full-scale metaphysical vision of reality.

Whitehead's Task: Finding the Ultimate Categories

At a time when many of his contemporaries were growing skeptical of the possibility of attaining a grand vision of reality as a whole, Whitehead was a dauntless metaphysician. He sought to discover the ultimate categories that apply to all reality. His vision of philosophy was breathtaking in scope:

> Speculative Philosophy is the endeavour to frame a coherent, logical, necessary system of general ideas in terms of which every element of our experience can be interpreted. By this notion of "interpretation" I mean that everything of which we are conscious, as enjoyed, perceived, willed, or thought, shall have the character of a particular instance of the general scheme. . . .
>
> It will also be noticed that this ideal of speculative philosophy has its rational side and its empirical side. The rational side is expressed by the terms "coherent" and "logical." The empirical side is expressed by the terms "applicable" and "adequate." (PR 4–5)

Whitehead was not satisfied with any view that assumes the mind imposes patterns on the world that cannot be found within the world's own structure. Hence, he rejected both Nietzschian

subjectivism and Kantian constructivism. Since science has been successful in finding general truths about nature, Whitehead argued, why not carry this process of generalization to its metaphysical completion?

The Method and Possibility of Metaphysics

METAPHYSICS AND THE IMAGINATION

The way to do metaphysics, Whitehead said, is to first start with a system of concepts that seem illuminating for some region of experience and then, using this "free imagination" and logical criteria, see if these concepts can be generalized and used to coherently interpret the other regions of experience:

> The true method of discovery is like the flight of an aeroplane. It starts from the ground of particular observation; it makes a flight in the thin air of imaginative generalization; and it again lands for renewed observation rendered acute by rational interpretation. (PR 7)

Whitehead started from several regions of experience from which he made his metaphysical generalizations. First, he was impressed with the developments in twentieth-century physics that made events and not particles the fundamental unit. Second, he took the dynamic, vital processes of biological organisms as a clue to the nature of reality. For this reason, he referred to his system as the "Philosophy of Organism" (PR v). Finally, his most common point of reference was our own, immediate experience. With Bergson, he believed that if we could have an accurate picture of what goes on in the flow of experience, we would have a window to the larger world of which it is a part.

To those, such as the positivists who doubted whether metaphysical speculation was useful or even possible, Whitehead countered that metaphysics is unavoidable. The only alternatives we have are either a metaphysics that is self-critical or one that is naively assumed:

All constructive thought, on the various topics of scientific interest, is dominated by some such [metaphysical] scheme, unacknowledged, but no less influential in guiding the imagination. The importance of philosophy lies in its sustained effort to make such schemes explicit and thereby capable of criticism and improvement. (PR x)

Whitehead believed that a metaphysical system had to adhere to the logical principles of coherence and consistency, but he also believed that intuition, not argument, is the final court of appeal. In effect, he enjoined his reader to "try on" his scheme, to view the world through the lens of his metaphysics, and see if it made sense of things.

METAPHYSICS AND LANGUAGE

One problem facing the metaphysician is the limits of language. This problem has burdened all creative thinkers, for, as Whitehead said, the history of ideas has been the constant "struggle of novel thought with the obtuseness of language" (AI 120). For this reason, many readers find that their first attempt to understand Whitehead's terminology is strenuous, if not frustrating. The problem is that Whitehead thought the concepts and their associated terms we have used for thousands of years to think and speak about reality have given us a misleading picture of its structure. This is because our conceptual equipment is infected with questionable philosophical assumptions and contains the sediment of philosophical ideas that have made their mark on culture. To use an analogy, it is as though Whitehead sees reality as circular in nature, but our current conceptual categories and terms are made to hold only triangular shapes. To overcome this problem, Whitehead had to create his own technical terms, using such peculiar words as "prehension," "nexus," and "superject." He also stretched ordinary terms far beyond their customary usages. For example, he said electrons have "feelings" and things such as chairs are "societies." However, these sorts of linguistic oddities are inevitable if philosophy is the "attempt to express the infinity of the universe in terms of the limitations of language."[6]

The Fallacies of Scientific Materialism

One factor that motivated Whitehead to shift his emphasis from science to metaphysics was that he believed classical physics was built on a questionable metaphysical outlook he called "scientific materialism." According to Whitehead, this view consists of the following fallacious doctrines. (1) *The irrelevance of time to the essence of things*: the physical universe consists of particles of matter whose essential identity and characteristics remain the same throughout their temporal duration. (2) *The thesis of external relations*: the characteristics of each particle are self-contained such that its essential nature is independent of its relationship to any other particles. (3) *The thesis of simple location*: at any given moment each particle has a definite location within space and time. (4) *Determinism*: the state of a given particle at a particular time is completely determined by its antecedent causes.

Whitehead was aware that developments in twentieth-century physics cast doubts on every one of these principles.* However, he was concerned not only to develop a metaphysics that would fit with contemporary science, but one that would also heal our sense of alienation from nature that began with the rise of the modern outlook in the sixteenth century. Hence, he attacked what he called "the bifurcation of nature." This results from the distinction that Galileo and Locke (among others) made between (1) the world of immediate experience, a world consisting of sounds, scents, colors, tastes, celebrated by the poets, and (2) the world of science in which "nature is a dull affair, soundless, scentless, colourless; merely the hurrying of material, endlessly, meaninglessly" (SMW 54). This dichotomy results, according to Whitehead, from the "Fallacy of Misplaced Concreteness"

---

*For example, a discovery known as "Heisenberg's indeterminacy principle" suggested that there is spontaneity in nature. This caused problems for classical determinism and forced physicists to formulate their discoveries in terms of probability laws instead of deterministic laws. Furthermore, the theory of relativity showed the interrelatedness of space and time, making time as much an essential feature of things as their spatial dimensions.

(SMW 51). This is the fallacy of taking the abstract entities of science (such as material particles) and mistaking them for what is most concrete and real. After quoting the romantic poets he says,

> We forget how strained and paradoxical is the view of nature which modern science imposes on our thoughts. . . . Is it not possible that the standardised concepts of science are only valid within narrow limitations, perhaps too narrow for science itself? (SMW 84)

Consequently, an adequate philosophy overcomes the dichotomies of mind-matter, subjective-objective, and human experience-science by recognizing that "the red glow of the sunset should be as much part of nature as are the molecules and electric waves by which men of science would explain the phenomenon" (CN 29).

Metaphysics: The Philosophy of Organic Process

EVENTS AS THE PRIMARY REALITIES

In contrast to the emphasis on substance in the history of philosophy, Whitehead starts with the conviction that *process* is the fundamental feature of all reality. To be actual, he says, is to be in process. Things that appear permanent and unmoving are really abstractions from the basic reality. To use an analogy, suppose you see what appears to be a log lazily floating on a pond. On closer inspection you discover it is actually a dense school of fish rapidly swimming together in one location. In your initial judgment you committed the "Fallacy of Misplaced Concreteness," for what you thought was a single, large, motionless mass was actually a very superficial appearance of the primary reality that was a collection of rapidly moving, individual fish circling around one point in the lake.

Even though reality is a temporal process, it is not one, indivisible flow. Whitehead's philosophy is atomistic, in that he thinks basic, irreducible, discrete units make up reality. However, these units are not the bits of matter of scientific materialism, but are *events* or momentary happenings. White-

head calls them "actual entities" or "actual occasions." Even God is to be understood in terms of this basic category. "God is an actual entity, and so is the most trivial puff of existence in far-off empty space" (PR 28).* A particular event or actual occasion could be, for example, a single vibration of an electron that is one among the many momentary vibrations that make up the series of events we collectively call "the electron." Again, another type of actual occasion could be a single, momentary event in your stream of consciousness (a twinge of pain or the perception of a flash of light).

According to scientific materialism, the spatial extension of an entity is crucial to its identity, but its temporal extension is not. However, Whitehead disagrees. To take an example from our common experience, the ultimate entities that make up reality are more like a sneeze, in that their temporal extension is just as important a feature of their identity as is their spatial extension.† If we consider half the time period it takes a sneeze to occur, we do not have a sneeze lasting half as long. Instead, we have only half a sneeze. The sneeze is not a complete entity lasting through several moments of time. Instead, its existence is possible only if it has a certain temporal duration. The fundamental units of reality, actual entities, have this same feature. "*How* an actual entity *becomes* constitutes *what* that actual entity is. . . . Its 'being' is constituted by its 'becoming' " (PR 34-35).

FEELINGS: HOW EVENTS ARE RELATED TO ONE ANOTHER

Descartes divided the world into two kinds of realities, minds and bodies. However, the problem with his dualism was that the two realities were so different it was not clear how they were related. The materialists argued that this showed

---

*The sense in which God (and other persons) are changing aspects of the world's process, and yet endure through time, is discussed in a later section.
†This illuminating example was suggested by William Alston in *Readings in Twentieth-Century Philosophy*, ed. William P. Alston and George Nakhnikian (New York: The Free Press of Glencoe, Macmillan, 1963), 117.

we need a unified theory of reality in which there are no breaks in nature. Hence, they reduced all reality to a collection of physical particles in motion and tried to explain mental events as particular kinds of material motions.

Whitehead agrees we need a unified picture of nature, but says the materialist has started with the wrong model. If you start with inert hunks of matter, having no interior life, you will never be able to explain the phenomenon of subjective feelings. However, maybe our metaphysics will be more successful if we start with our own experience of being subjective centers of feeling and then view entities such as electrons or crystals as rather low-level examples. Whitehead draws the extraordinary conclusion that *no entity in reality is devoid of subjective experience.* Accordingly, he describes actual entities as brief but unified, "drops of experience."

Returning back to our own experience, any particular human feeling can fall on a continuum ranging from those feelings we are fully conscious of (a headache) to those we are only dimly aware of and that are recessed in the background of our conscious experience (our feelings of our general bodily state), all the way down to unconscious feelings (the bodily experiences we have when asleep). Other sorts of organisms (such as a worm or an amoeba) have very low levels of feeling. Still, at a very low level, they are active, feeling, and valuing subjects. Even though they have no conscious awareness, they respond to their environment and seek out conditions conducive to their survival. Do feelings fade out entirely at any point in nature? Whitehead thinks not, for even electrons feel their environment and respond to it. Electrons are not passive entities mechanically imposed on by external forces. Instead, they are active centers of energy whose characteristics are substantially affected by the way in which they incorporate their environment and respond to it by becoming "excited," "agitated," "attracted," and "repelled." Thus the difference between the entities the psychologist studies and those the physicist studies is only a difference of degree. "The energetic activity considered in physics is the emotional intensity entertained in life" (MT 168).

This view is sometimes called **panpsychism**, the claim that everything in reality has some degree of mental life. There are obvious similarities between Whitehead and Leibniz on this point.*

The technical term Whitehead uses for an entity's perception of its environment is "prehension." This notion is similar to apprehension, except that prehending is a lower-level way of relating to the world that does not involve conscious awareness. Prehensions include all the modes by which one actual entity is affected by another, from human ways of experiencing down to the electromagnetic energy transmitted from one electron to another. A positive prehension is identical with a feeling, for it is the activity by which an actual entity includes a datum within itself. A negative prehension is that activity within an entity's self-creation in which it excludes data. To use an analogy, a block of marble is creatively transformed into a statue by chipping away some of the pieces (corresponding to negative prehensions) so as to reveal a new form within the marble that is preserved (corresponding to positive prehensions).

Contrary to the mechanistic picture of the world in which things are what they are, independent of how they are related to other things, Whitehead says that the unique character of each entity in the universe is a function of its relationship to everything else. Physicists tell us that each electron is affected by the energy transmitted by every other particle in the universe, although the intensity of a particle's effect, of course, is diminished the further away we get from it. Hence, the causal relationship between events is not an external one, but it is a relationship in which one event enters into the experience of another event:

> *In a certain sense, everything is everywhere at all times. For every location involves an aspect of itself*

---

*In fact, Whitehead was impressed with Leibniz's writings and continually came back to Bertrand Russell's book on this seventeenth-century logician and metaphysician. The main difference between their positions is that, contrary to Leibniz's view, Whitehead's actual occasions are not "windowless." They are open to the world and enter into one another's experience.

in every other location. Thus every spatio-temporal standpoint mirrors the world. (SMW 91)

For this reason, Whitehead rejects "the thesis of simple location" and claims that reality is a web of interconnected events.

CREATIVITY: THE ULTIMATE CATEGORY

Any metaphysical theory must account for the phenomena of causality and freedom, continuity and spontaneity, and multiplicity and unity. For Whitehead, the ultimate metaphysical category that characterizes everything that exists is the category of *creativity*. Creativity characterizes not only the activity of the artist, but also describes the activity of an amoeba, a plant, and an electron as well. Each new entity comes into existence by emerging out of a background of previous events, and forms itself by unifying its causes in a novel way, bringing a new synthesis into the world.

In Whitehead's metaphysics, *concrescence* is the temporal process that constitutes the existence of an actual occasion. "Concrescence" is derived from Latin words that mean "growing together" and "becoming concrete." This process of becoming a concrete actuality consists of the following phases:

1. As a new actual occasion emerges, it *prehends its immediate past.** Hence, every occasion is partly the result of causes acting on it in which it is influenced (but not determined) by previous events. The events that have just become past are the objective "data" to which the emerging event must conform.

2. As an entity emerges out of the immediate past, there is a process of *self-creation*. Even though the past moment shapes its successor, there are alternative ways in which the emerging present event can incorporate its inheritance. The objective content of a prehension is *what* is felt, while the "subjective form" is *how* it is felt. There

---

*To give a rough indication of what he means by "immediate past," Whitehead says "it is that portion of our past lying between a tenth of a second and a half second ago" (AI 181).

are many species of subjective forms, "such as emotions, valuations, purposes, adversions, aversions, consciousness, etc." (PR 35). As an actual entity takes into account the data of its past, it unifies them in a novel, unique way. In this way it produces a new synthesis that is not simply the blind, logical outcome of the initial ingredients.

3. When this state of "satisfaction" has been achieved, the activity of self-creation has reached its culmination and the actual entity simply is what it is. It has realized its unique identity as a distinct moment in the universe related to yet different from everything else. However, nothing is static in the universe, and as soon as the present moment is achieved it immediately gives itself over to its offspring. Hence, there is a creative urge within everything to thrust itself into the future as a cause of further events.

4. Finally, while presenting itself as an objective datum for the next occasion, the event fades into the past and perishes. However, the past is never completely dead and gone, for it has made a difference to the universe and in this way everything that happens achieves what Whitehead calls "objective immortality." These successive phases characterize the life span of every temporal event, including the most trivial physical event as well as the moments within our own stream of consciousness.

THE REALM OF POSSIBILITIES: ETERNAL OBJECTS

Thus far, we have a picture of the world as a continuous process, a rhythm in which actual occasions come to be for a brief duration and then perish as the next event emerges from them. But something is missing. For change to occur, possibilities must be actualized. Furthermore, we need a principle of definiteness, for we can say about any actuality that it is *this* but not *that*. We can speak about the world because things that are actual always manifest intelligible and repeatable forms and characteristics. To fill in this gap, Whitehead says there must be "eternal objects" or "forms of definiteness." These are somewhat like Platonic forms in that they are universals such as colors, shapes, and numbers that may be conceptually intuited. The process of becoming actual involves the selection and exclusion of forms from among this domain of possibilities. Hence, some forms become part of an event and others not. Whitehead says that eternal objects "ingress" into actual entities (a concept similar to Plato's notion of "participation"). Since an actual entity may be simultaneously definite in many ways, it must be able to manifest more than one eternal object.

ENDURING OBJECTS: SOCIETIES OF ACTUAL ENTITIES

The important question that now arises is, How do we get from the spatially and temporally minute actual entities making up reality to the everyday objects that we see around us? The answer is that the larger entities that make up our commonsense world (rocks, chairs, trees, dogs, human beings) are not irreducible individual entities, but are groups or "societies" of actual entities. Contrary to common sense, they are not "things" but are continuing, repeated patterns within the temporal process. At any given point in time, a physical object (a rock) is the collection of subatomic events that are occurring within it, whereas a biological organism (a tree or human) is an organized collection of many individual cells, each with their own individual experiences and activities. From the temporal perspective, an object that endures through a span of time is really a series of actual occasions who come into being and perish while maintaining a stream of continuity by passing on their characteristics to the next emerging occasion.

The difference between organic and inorganic objects is the way they are organized. A rock is simply an aggregate. There is only a loose connection between its parts. In contrast, a plant, such as a tree, is like a democracy (AI 206). Its parts are mutually interdependent and what happens to one part will affect the whole society. A high-level organism, such as a human being, is more like a monarchy, for it is an intimately related society of cells organized and directed by a dominant actual entity (the mind) that imparts its subjective aims throughout the smaller entities composing the organism.

THE MIND–BODY PROBLEM

Whitehead offers a distinctive solution to the classic mind–body problem. Previously, the main options were dualism, materialism, and idealism: the mind and body were viewed as two completely different substances (Descartes), or the mind was reduced to bodily motions (Hobbes), or physical bodies were reduced to mental ideas (Berkeley). In Whitehead's view, however, there are neither pure mental substances nor pure physical substances. These are abstractions from the more fundamental reality, which is the series of actual occasions, each of which is a continuum having a mental pole and a physical pole.

> No actual entity is devoid of either pole; though their relative importance differs in different actual entities. . . .
>
> Thus, an actual entity is essentially dipolar, with its physical and mental poles; and even the physical world cannot be properly understood without reference to its other side, which is the complex of mental operations. (PR 366)

In other words, in each part of reality there is that aspect (the physical pole) that tends to conform to the patterns of its immediate past, is passive, and causally determined. There is also that aspect (the mental pole) that is creative, active, and self-determining.

In nonliving beings, the mental pole is negligible, for it is "canalized into slavish conformity. It is merely the appetition towards, or from, whatever in fact already is" (FR 33). For example, the primary mental activity of a crystal consists of resisting the intrusion of novelty by continuing the patterns of the past (the crystal simply persists) or allowing them to fade away (the crystal disintegrates), but it does not introduce anything new. The apparent stability of physical objects results from the fact that they are collections of events whose diversity is averaged out at the level of the totality.

In complex organisms such as humans, the mental pole predominates. This allows us to creatively and subjectively respond to our causal influences, giving us the capacity to respond to a wider range of possibilities, and thereby producing greater amounts of diversity. If the mental and the physical are two poles of the same continuum, then nature is not divided into separate compartments (mind matter, organic inorganic), but is a unified reality.

> In a sense, the difference between a living organism and the inorganic environment is only a question of degree; but it is a difference of degree which makes all the difference—in effect, it is a difference of quality. (PR 271)

Whitehead's Natural Theology

GOD AND THE HARMONY OF THE WORLD

Although many of the aspects of nature can be explained by the categories introduced thus far, Whitehead believes something is still missing. There must be a principle of order. If all actualities exercise some degree of freedom, their unbridled creativity would produce a tumult of random occurrences without any direction or coherence. For this reason, Whitehead introduces a version of the teleological argument (the argument from design). The harmony in the world is explained by the activity of God. "The immanence of God gives reason for the belief that pure chaos is intrinsically impossible" (PR 169). To achieve a definite form, each emerging actual occasion must draw on the realm of possibilities (the eternal objects). But possibilities are abstract and provide no agency for introducing themselves into the actual world. God is the agency that mediates between the sphere of possibilities and the process of the world.

A GOD IN PROCESS

Whitehead's God is very different from the God of classical theism we find in philosopher-theologians such as Augustine, Aquinas, and Leibniz. Historically, the development of Christian theology drew not only on the biblical tradition, but also on Greek conceptions. The Greeks (Plato is a prime example) tended to depreciate becoming. What was immutable and free of influence from others was considered superior to what was changing and affected by others. In assimilating this Greek prejudice, traditional Christian theism held that God was a radically different sort of being from the world, for he was thought to be completely independent, fully actualized, and, therefore, unchanging. Whitehead, however, says that God has the same metaphysical character as any other entity. "God is not to be treated as an exception to all metaphysical principles, invoked to save their collapse. He is their chief exemplification" (PR 521).

God's nature is dipolar, consisting of two aspects. First, there is his *primordial nature*. This aspect of God is eternal, fully complete, unchanging, and the ground of all the possibilities in the world. This sphere of possibilities, the realm of eternal objects, exists in the sense that it is comprehended by God as part of his nature. Hence, God "does not create eternal objects; for his nature requires them in the same degree that they require him" (PR 392). But Whitehead says that if this was the whole of God's nature, then he would be static, wholly apart from the world, and unable to value, to love, or to interact creatively with a changing world. Traditional Christian theists would agree that the world is in process and that God relates to it, but at the same time they try to hold onto God's immutability and independence. According to Whitehead, however, this is a contradiction, for to relate to something is to be affected by it. Hence, in knowing the world and loving it, God is affected by it and changes as it changes.

The God of process philosophy is immanent within the world's process and intimate with it. This temporal, relative, dependent, and changing aspect of God is what Whitehead calls God's *consequent nature*. To say that God has an unchanging primordial nature and a changing, consequent nature is not to say that God is divided into parts. Imagine a circle on a computer screen that maintains its shape while changing color from red to blue to green as you press the keys on the keyboard. One aspect of the figure, its circularity, is unchanging and unaffected by your input. But this abstract, unchanging aspect is actualized and manifested through the successive changes of color in response to your activities. The fact that the world and God are interactive means that "it is as true to say that God creates the World, as that the World creates God" (PR 528).

Whitehead says the consequent nature of God is enriched by his prehensions of the temporal world. He is the repository of all value achieved in this world. No event is ever totally lost even though it perishes into the past, for every event achieves "objective immortality" by contributing to God's being. "The consequent nature of God is his judgment on the world. He saves the world as it passes into the immediacy of his own life" (PR 525).

Strictly speaking, Whitehead's view is not theism, for he denies that God is transcendent to the world. "[God] is not *before* all creation, but *with* all creation" (PR 521). Nor is his view pantheism—the claim that God and the world are identical. In contrast to pantheism, Whitehead's God is an independent entity that interacts with the world. Instead, Whitehead's position is commonly called **panentheism**. This is the view that God includes the world in his being (since he is affected by every event within it) at the same time that he is more than the events in the world (God has his own unique aims and actions). Thus, we can consider the world "God's body." Looked at in this way, God's experience is analogous to yours, for your experience includes the experiences of all the cells in your body. At the same time, Whitehead would say that your thoughts, values, decisions are something more than the physical processes in your body.

GOD'S INFLUENCE ON THE WORLD

Whitehead provides a unique account of how God causally influences the world. A key feature of Whitehead's position is the conviction that God cannot violate the integrity or the freedom of his creatures. He cannot use his sheer power to impose his will on the world, for then every creature's actions (including human actions) would no longer belong to that creature but would simply be God's actions. Whitehead proposes that instead of controlling events through brute force, God allows the world to feel his influence through persuasion. "He is the poet of the world, with tender patience leading it by his vision of truth, beauty, and goodness" (PR 526).

God is an immanent presence in the emergence of every actual entity. "Thus each temporal occasion embodies God, and is embodied in God" (PR 529). In every moment within the history of an electron or a human being, we are continually prehending God, even though we are not fully aware of this (except, perhaps, in moments of mystical insight). As an actual entity is being formed, God presents to it those possibilities or eternal objects that are relevant to its situation and that will maximize the realization of its potential. Thus, when a snowflake forms it can represent an unlimited number of geometrical forms, but a snowflake will never take the shape of a kangaroo. In this way, there is both order and spontaneity in the changing world as the result of God selecting and presenting possibilities for each entity to realize. In doing so, each emerging actual occasion "receives that initial aim from which its self-causation starts" (PR 374):

> [God] is the lure for feeling, the eternal urge of desire. His particular relevance to each creative act, as it arises from its own conditioned standpoint in the world, constitutes him the initial "object of desire" establishing the initial phase of each subjective aim. (PR 522)

Thus, although Whitehead's God does not transcend the world, he does transcend every other actual entity within the world.

THE PROBLEM OF EVIL

Every metaphysical system that postulates God's existence must come to terms with the problem of evil. Whitehead does not try to explain the problem away by saying that evil is only "apparent" or that it is always a stepping-stone on the way to a greater good. For him, evil is an irreducibly real presence in the world. God is continually enticing the world to fulfill his purposes, which always involves producing the greatest intensity of enjoyment and value. However, as discussed, finite actualities are not compelled to conform to his will. Thus, each entity, from a human being to a biological cell, has the freedom to resist God's persuasion and can fail to conform to his aims. "So far as the conformity is incomplete, there is evil in the world" (RM 60). The problem is, a greater capacity for good is always correlated with a greater capacity for evil. If there were no conscious beings, there would be no suffering in the world. However, such a world would be of minimal value compared to ours. When God seeks to maximize the good by supporting his creatures' capacity for freedom and creativity, he risks that they will use their powers to resist his desire for harmony. Nevertheless, God is not the passive spectator of the world, he is a God in process. "God is the great companion—the fellow-sufferer who understands" (PR 532). He is actively involved in his creation and is working with us to increase both his and our fullest satisfaction. However, "there is no totality which is the harmony of all perfections" (AI 276). There is always more for God and us to do, and there will always be values that have not yet been realized.

The Impact of Process Philosophy

Many philosophers (as well as writers, scientists, artists, historians, sociologists, and others) were inspired by the majestic vision, if not the details of Bergson's and Whitehead's philosophies. The process philosophers had much in common with the pragmatists in viewing philosophy as the search for a unifying perspective that would incorporate the full range of human experience. Both groups of philosophers tried to give us a sense of the whole and our relationship to it, which can serve as a basis for integrating our aesthetic, moral, and spiritual values into the nature of the universe. Particularly Whitehead sought to do this in a way consistent with contemporary physics.

Bergson and Whitehead boldly kept alive the project of speculative metaphysics in a time when it had fallen into disrepute. However, while appreciating this point, more traditional metaphysicians argued that the process view that reality is a flow of momentary events did not provide the stability necessary to make the world intelligible. On an even more practical level, critics claimed that process philosophy does not provide the category

of "person" with enough continuity through time to account for the notion of moral responsibility. Traditional philosophical theologians accused Whitehead's God of being a mere "godling," a relatively weak, finite deity, buffeted about by causal influences while bobbing in the flow of time, and lacking the sovereignty, power, and transcendence of the God of traditional theism.

A group of philosophers who composed the movement known as *analytic philosophy* did not quibble over the details of process philosophy, for they thought the quest to know the ultimate nature of reality was doomed from the start. They claimed that philosophy simply cannot answer all our questions and that we must lower our expectations, seeking only to establish humble bits of truth that can be decisively verified through the methods of logic and science. The analysts thought Bergson's method of intuition and Whitehead's "play of a free imagination" did not give us the ultimate categories for understanding our world. Instead, these metaphysicians provided inspiring but cognitively barren, emotional poetry. Even Bertrand Russell, who had collaborated with Whitehead on the logical foundations of mathematics, said about his friend's later work, "I must confess that the metaphysical speculations of Whitehead are somewhat strange to me."[7] In the next chapter, on analytic philosophy, therefore, we must shift gears and look at a radically different conception of the goals of philosophy.

Questions for Understanding

1. What is the main difference between substance metaphysics and process metaphysics?

2. What are the two ways of knowing the world, according to Bergson? How are they different?

3. According to Bergson, what is the one reality that we know directly or "seize from within"? What does this window to reality reveal to us?

4. What distinction does Bergson make between "scientific time" and "duration"?

5. What are the two aspects of the self in Bergson's philosophy? How is this distinction similar to and different from the one Kant

makes? What is Bergson's view of psychological determinism?

6. In what way is Bergson's metaphysics similar to yet different from Charles Darwin's evolutionary view?

7. What is the *élan vital*? What sorts of phenomena does it explain?

8. What is the difference between static morality and dynamic morality in Bergson's ethics? Why are both important?

9. In your own words, describe what Whitehead took to be the task of speculative philosophy.

10. According to Whitehead, what is the role of the imagination in metaphysics?

11. What are the four fallacies of scientific materialism according to Whitehead?

12. What does Whitehead mean by the "Fallacy of Misplaced Concreteness"?

13. What are actual occasions and why does Whitehead think they are the primary units of reality?

14. How does Whitehead attempt to avoid Descartes's dualism without lapsing into scientific materialism?

15. What is panpsychism? Why is this an apt name for Whitehead's metaphysics? What is his surprising thesis concerning feelings?

16. What does Whitehead mean by "prehension"?

17. What does "concrescence" mean? What are the four phases of becoming a concrete actuality?

18. What are eternal objects? What role do they play in the world?

19. What are some examples of "societies" of actual objects?

20. What is Whitehead's unique solution to the mind-body problem?

21. What is Whitehead's argument for God?

22. What does Whitehead mean by his distinction between God's primordial nature and his consequent nature?

23. How is Whitehead's panentheism different from both theism and pantheism?

24. What is Whitehead's view of how God causally influences the world?

25. How does Whitehead address the problem of evil?

Questions for Reflection

1. Using Bergson's categories, which do you trust more, intuition or intellect? Why?

2. Do you agree or disagree with Bergson that the self as studied by science is an abstraction or distortion of the self that is lived through in subjective experience?

3. In what way is it true to say "Both Bergson and Whitehead view the world on the model of biology than on the model of a machine"?

4. In what ways is Whitehead's philosophy an attempt to reconcile the scientific and romantic views of the world?

5. Do you think Whitehead's view that our subjective experience and relation to the world differs only in degree from that of an electron is plausible?

6. What does Whitehead mean when he says "it is as true to say that God creates the World as that the World creates God"?

7. Do you think that Bergson's and Whitehead's project of trying to arrive at a comprehensive metaphysical vision of the universe is possible or worthwhile?

Notes

1. References to Henri Bergson's works are made using the following abbreviations:

CE   *Creative Evolution*, trans. A. Mitchell (New York: Holt, Rinehart & Winston, 1911).

CM   *The Creative Mind*, trans. Mabelle L. Andison (New York: Philosophical Library, 1946).

IM   *Introduction to Metaphysics*, trans. T. E. Hulme, rev. ed. (Indianapolis: Library of Liberal Arts, Bobbs-Merrill, 1955).

TFW   *Time and Free Will*, trans. F. L. Pogson (New York: Macmillan, 1913).

TSMR   *The Two Sources of Morality and Religion*, trans. R. Ashley Audra and Cloudesley Brereton (Notre Dame: University of Notre Dame Press, 1977).

2. Quotations from the works by Whitehead are referenced within the text using the following abbreviations. The numbers in the reference refer to page numbers.

AI   *Adventures of Ideas* (New York: The Free Press, 1961).

CN   *The Concept of Nature* (Cambridge, England: Cambridge University Press, 1964).

FR   *The Function of Reason* (Boston: Beacon Press, 1958).

MT   *Modes of Thought* (New York: The Free Press, 1966).

PR   *Process and Reality*, corrected ed., ed. David Ray Griffin and Donald W. Sherburne (New York: The Free Press, 1978). The page numbers of this work are given using the pagination of the original 1957 Macmillan edition, which are also provided in brackets in the 1978 corrected version.

RM   *Religion in the Making* (Cleveland: Meridian Books, World Publishing, 1954).

SMW   *Science and the Modern World* (New York: The Free Press, 1953).

3. These points have been made by William Alston in *Readings in Twentieth-Century Philosophy*, ed. William P. Alston and George Nakhnikian (New York: The Free Press, Macmillan, 1963), 56.

4. *The Letters of William James*, ed. by Henry James (Boston: Atlantic Monthly Press, 1920), 2:290.

5. A personal account of Whitehead's life can be found in his brief autobiographical sketch in the first chapter of *Essays in Science and Philosophy* (New York: Greenwood Press, 1968).

6. *Essays in Science and Philosophy*, 14.

7. Bertrand Russell, *Wisdom of the West* (London: Crescent Books, 1959), 297.

32

Analytic Philosophy and the Linguistic Turn

The Turn to Language and Analysis

In the early part of the twentieth century and continuing on today, a group of philosophers united around the conviction that clarifying language is the most pressing, if not the sole, task of philosophy. This movement is known as **analytic philosophy** or **linguistic philosophy**. These labels signify the fact that, in spite of their diversity, the philosophers within this movement believe that analysis is the correct approach to philosophy and that language is its primary subject matter. There are at least two reasons for this "linguistic turn" in philosophy. First, these philosophers felt science had taken over much of the territory formerly occupied by philosophy. The questions of metaphysics had been inherited by physics, they said, those of epistemology and philosophy of mind were now being answered by physiology and psychology, and the concerns of social and political philosophy were better left to sociology and political science. If the mission of acquiring knowledge about our world has been taken over by science, then the only task that remained for philosophy was to clarify linguis-

tic meaning. As Moritz Schlick, an early member of the analytic movement, put it, "Science should be defined as the '*pursuit of truth*' and Philosophy as the '*pursuit of meaning*.'"[1] Second, new and more powerful methods of logic had been developed in the twentieth century that promised to shed new light on some of the old, philosophical stalemates. With these logical techniques, expressions that appeared to be meaningful propositions, but that were actually vague, equivocal, misleading, or nonsensical, could be exposed and eliminated by careful analysis.

Although the analytic philosophers proposed many different theories of language and methods of attacking philosophical problems, they all embraced three fundamental doctrines: (1) philosophical puzzles, problems, and contradictions are not found in the world, but in the things we say about the world; (2) philosophical problems can first be clarified and then solved or dissolved by either analyzing or reforming the way that language works; and (3) if any problems remain that cannot be resolved in this way, they are pseudo-problems and are not worth worrying about.

Analytic philosophy can be divided up into five stages or movements.[2] The first stage was *early realism and analysis*, introduced by G. E. Moore and Bertrand Russell in his early period. They reacted against the grandiose metaphysics of the Hegelians and brought British philosophy back to the search for clarity by means of a piecemeal analysis of particular propositions.

Second, the philosophy of *logical atomism* was developed in the work of Russell from 1914–1919 and in Ludwig Wittgenstein's early work, represented by his *Tractatus Logico-Philosophicus* (1921). During this period, Russell and Wittgenstein saw the task of philosophy as constructing a logically perfect language whose syntax would mirror the metaphysical structure of the world. By applying new techniques in logic, they hoped to find the fundamental, "atomistic" units of language that relate to the corresponding units that compose the world of facts.

Third, *logical positivism* arose in the 1920s and early 1930s. This widespread movement included a number of significant thinkers. Like the logical atomists, these philosophers tried to construct a logically perfect language. However, while the first two movements made metaphysics one of their concerns, the logical positivists claimed that metaphysical statements were meaningless. Hence, their ideal language would be able to articulate clearly all scientific and logical truths, while making it impossible to express any metaphysical claims.

The fourth stage in the analytic movement could be called *ordinary language philosophy: the Wittgensteinian model*. This movement resulted from the radical shift in direction taken by Wittgenstein in his later period. Repudiating the assumptions of stages 2 and 3, including his own work, he now thought there was no such thing as a logically perfect language. Ordinary language was now said to be perfectly adequate as it is. Philosophical problems arise, however, when philosophers become confused about how language functions, and therefore they get caught in a tangle of pseudo-problems. The unique feature of this stage of analysis was that Wittgenstein thought that the linguistic analyst, like a therapist, merely "cures" philosophers of their distortions. Philosophical problems are not solved but are dissolved by taking a more careful look at how language works. Once this is done, there is no more need of philosophy.

The fifth stage, which we will call *ordinary language philosophy: conceptual analysis*, was initiated by such thinkers as Gilbert Ryle and John Austin. They and many other heirs of the analytic movement turned Wittgenstein's linguistic "therapies" into a positive method for doing philosophy. Unlike Wittgenstein, they did not see language analysis as simply a way to cure philosophers of their philosophical pathology. Instead, they engaged in systematic explorations of traditional philosophical topics, using ordinary language as a guide for mapping the regions of our conceptual landscape.

BERTRAND RUSSELL

Russell's Life: Mathematician, Philosopher, Reformer

Bertrand Russell (1872–1970) was born into an aristocratic British family. (He inherited the title of Earl Russell in 1931.) He was the godson of John Stuart Mill, "so far as is possible in a non-religious sense," as Russell put it. His parents died

when he was three and even though they were freethinkers, he ended up being raised by his fervently religious grandmother. When he was a teenager, he wrestled intensely with the intellectual credibility of theism and abandoned it by the time he was eighteen. The rest of his life he was an outspoken critic of all forms of religious belief. He studied mathematics and philosophy at

Cambridge and went on to become a lecturer in philosophy at Trinity College. Russell was never reticent about speaking his mind, and throughout his life his iconoclastic and liberal opinions caused a stir wherever he went. He was fired from two academic positions because of his controversial views on politics and sexual morality. His confrontational political protests also landed him in jail several times. Even at the age of eighty-nine, he was still going strong and was jailed for leading a protest against nuclear arms in London.

In spite of these troubles, Russell was a respected international figure because of his groundbreaking work in logic and philosophy. Although he held several academic positions in England and America for short periods of time, he supported himself on his writings and public lectures for most of his life. Throughout his long career, Russell received many distinguished honors, including the Nobel Prize for literature in 1950. In addition to numerous articles, he wrote over ninety books, both technical and popular, on a wide range of topics. Russell died in 1970, two years short of living a century.

Background: The Revolt Against Hegelianism

BRITISH IDEALISM

During Bertrand Russell's student days, a form of Hegelianism known as British Idealism was the prevailing orthodoxy. The two most famous spokesmen of this outlook were F. H. Bradley and J. M. E. McTaggart. Russell enthusiastically read Bradley's books and sat in on McTaggart's lectures at Cambridge. The captivating vision of their philosophies caused the young Russell to become a Hegelian himself. The Idealists taught a form of monism in which reality was viewed as a single, eternal, all-comprehensive, experiencing being (sort of an atemporal version of Hegel's Absolute Spirit). Consequently, no particular could be understood on its own, for everything is merely an aspect of the whole. Eventually, Russell came to realize this contradicted the principles of mathe-

matics, where we first study isolated, fundamental units and then learn about their relations to other units. Consequently, he rebelled against Hegelian philosophy and asserted that reality is a plurality of fundamentally independent particular things.

G. E. MOORE

Russell was supported in his rebellion against Idealism by his fellow student G. E. Moore (1873–1958). Moore was upset by the way in which the British Idealists violated common sense. They claimed that particular physical objects are not real but are merely appearances, that nothing exists that is not related to a mind, and that time is unreal. In reaction to the Idealists, Moore and Russell affirmed a form of **realism** that asserted that the components of reality exist on their own, independent of their relationship to minds, that time is real, and that things can be known apart from their relationship to anything else. In their early period, their realism was somewhat Platonic, for they believed in the full reality not only of particular things such as minds and material objects, but also of universals such as redness, numbers, and equality.

In responding to the Idealists, Moore developed a new method for analyzing the meanings of philosophical questions and answers. Guiding his method was the conviction that our fundamental concepts and the linguistic meanings that express those concepts arise out of common sense and ordinary language. Most philosophical perplexities, he believed, result from philosophers using concepts and terms in peculiar ways.

In one of his most famous analyses, which has become an important position in ethical theory, Moore examined the concept of goodness. He argued that good is an indefinable notion (in the same sense that "yellow" cannot be given a purely verbal definition). Good is a property that cannot be reduced to any nonethical natural quality such as pleasure or desirability, but can only be known through an intellectual intuition. He argued that the attempt to reduce ethical claims to factual, empirical claims commits a logical error that he called the **naturalistic fallacy**.

Moore's persistent search for clarity and his detailed dissection and analysis of the meanings of philosophical propositions provided a model for the analytic philosophers after him. In particular, Moore's appeal to ordinary language had an impact on the later stages of analytic philosophy's development. While Moore and Russell both started out as Hegelians and then converted to anti-Hegelian realism, their philosophical interests gradually grew further apart. Moore continued to engage in piecemeal analyses of the meanings of perplexing philosophical statements, while Russell attempted a large-scale reconstruction of our ways of speaking and thinking about reality.

Russell's Task: Developing a Logically Perfect Language

Russell tells us that the "constant preoccupation" of his life was "to discover how much we can be said to know and with what degree of certainty or doubtfulness."[3] "I wanted certainty in the kind of way in which people want religious faith."[4] Accordingly, Russell did not value achieving finality in his thinking as much as he valued being correct. Thus he was his own, harshest critic, and throughout his career he continually revised or abandoned positions he had earlier defended vigorously.

Russell was one of the twentieth century's greatest minds in logic and mathematics and the whole of his philosophy reflects the work he did in these disciplines. Particularly important to Russell was the groundbreaking work he did with Alfred North Whitehead on the foundations of mathematics and logic. Together they wrote the three-volume classic of modern logic, *Principia Mathematica*, published in the years 1910–1913. This work demonstrated that the whole of mathematics could be reduced to a set of fundamental statements in logic in which numbers did not appear. This remarkable discovery served as the key to the whole of Russell's philosophical program, for he continually tried to show that what is complex can be reduced to a collection of elementary units.

Russell's central assumption through most of his life was that there was a necessary link between the nature of language and the truths of metaphysics. Since language is capable of describing the world and expressing true propositions about it, then there must be, he argued, some correspondence between the logical structure of language and the necessary structure of reality. Although the later analysts would be decidedly antimetaphysical, Russell enthusiastically believed that the new, powerful tools of modern logic he had developed would let us put metaphysics on a sound foundation at last.

Russell's Logical Atomism

Russell called his philosophical perspective **logical atomism**. This label expresses his conviction that the logical analysis of language would show it consisted of a relatively small number of irreducible, "atomistic" linguistic units that would, of necessity, correspond to the basic entities within the world. As with all the analytic philosophers, he begins with the conviction that many of the muddles in philosophy result from confusions about our ordinary language.

Russell's concern can be made clear with an example. Consider the following argument:

(1a) There is a fire in my kitchen.

(2a) My kitchen is in my house.

(3a) Therefore, there is a fire in my house.

Now compare that argument with this one:

(1b) There is a pain in my foot.

(2b) My foot is in my shoe.

(3b) Therefore, there is a pain in my shoe.[5]

In the first example, there seems to be no problem. But something has gone wrong in the second argument. Although the second argument is valid and its premises are relatively unproblematic, the conclusion (3b) is absurd when interpreted literally. Since the corresponding statements in the two arguments seem grammatically identical, what is the source of the problem? The problem, Russell would say, is that the syntax of ordinary language does not represent the true logical form of statements. Although statements (1a) and (1b) are *grammatically* similar, they are *logically* quite different. The sense in which a fire is "in" my kitchen is a straightforward spatial notion, leading to the conclusion in (3a). However, the sense in which a pain is "in" my foot does not let us transfer this property to the larger spatial context of my shoe.

The task, therefore, according to Russell, is to reformulate ordinary language statements in terms of an ideal language whose syntax would be logically precise. This ideal language would serve two purposes:

> *First, to prevent inferences from the nature of language to the nature of the world, which are fallacious because they depend upon the logical defects of language; secondly, to suggest, by inquiring what logic requires of a language which is to avoid contradiction, what sort of structure we may reasonably suppose the world to have.*[6]

In this way, a logically ideal language would both prevent and solve problems in metaphysics.

To begin with Russell's theory of language, he assumes the primary function of language is to represent facts. Thus, a proposition will be true if it corresponds to a fact and false if it doesn't. What is needed is an improved language where this correspondence can be set out clearly.

> *In a logically perfect language the words in a proposition would correspond one by one with components of the corresponding fact, with the exception of such words as 'or', 'not', 'if', 'then', which have a different function.*[7]

This correspondence is revealed by the parallel activities of analyzing complex propositions down to their simplest components (called "atomic propositions") and likewise analyzing facts down to their simplest components (which he called "atomic facts").*

*In referring to "atomic facts," Russell is not talking about anything that has to do with nuclear physics. Instead, he is talking about whatever is logically and metaphysically fundamental. As we will see, Russell's position implies that even our concepts of the elementary particles postulated by physics (electrons, neutrinos, and so on) are actually constructions from elements in our experience that are logically, epistemologically, and metaphysically more primary.

An atomic proposition ascribes a simple property to an individual or asserts a relation among two or more individuals. Examples of each of these cases are "This is red" and "This is taller than that." Atomic propositions can be combined to form complex propositions called *molecular propositions*. These compounds are created by using logical operators such as "and," "or," "not," "if . . . then." An example of a molecular proposition is "This is red, and that is blue." However, Russell believed there were no complex or molecular facts, so the conditions that would make this statement true are *two* atomic facts, namely the first thing being red and the second being blue. Russell thinks this analysis provides us with the logical skeleton of any meaningful language. English, German, and all other ordinary languages are imperfect and confused versions of this logically precise language.

All this seems very straightforward. However, Russell's theory of language is packed with a number of metaphysical implications. Since the truth or falsity of atomic propositions are independent of one another, the world they describe must be made up of wholly independent, discrete entities. Hence, from one fact we cannot logically infer another fact. Furthermore, since there is no logical necessity to the contents of the world, whether or not a particular statement corresponds to a fact in the world is wholly an empirical matter to be decided by scientific observation. So, while the logical structure of language provides us with the logical form of the world, a metaphysics of this sort cannot tell us what particular things exist. This can be accomplished only by an appeal to experience. As we will see, the more Russell tried to get clear on the sort of facts we can actually know, his position became increasingly radical.

How Language Connects with the World

So far, we have a general overview of how Russell thinks language and the world are structured. However, we need to say more about how to determine the meaning of a proposition. Russell's theory of meaning follows from two fundamental principles. First, Russell believes every word has a meaning: the entity to which it refers. This is often called the "referential" or "naming theory of meaning."* Second, this definition of meaning implies that "if we can understand what a sentence means, it must be composed entirely of words denoting things with which we are acquainted or definable in terms of such words."[8] A word that directly refers to a particular entity with which we are acquainted is a "logically proper name." Since we cannot analyze an atomic proposition any further, it must describe a particular fact in the world, and therefore the subject of an atomic proposition must be a logically proper name. You might suppose that the name of your best friend is a proper name, since you *are* acquainted with this person. However, Russell makes the startling claim that, in the logically precise sense, you *do not* have direct acquaintance with your best friend nor with familiar physical objects such as your favorite chair. Rather than being proper names or denoting terms, the terms you use to refer to your friend or your chair are actually descriptions of complicated systems of sense data. To make this puzzling notion clear, let's look at Russell's account of logical constructions.

Russell's Theory of Logical Constructions

Russell embraced the methodological principle known as Ockham's razor (after the fourteenth-century logician). This principle advises us that "explanatory entities are not to be multiplied without necessity." In other words, "Keep your explanations as simple as possible." As Russell says,

> I always wish to get on in philosophy with the smallest possible apparatus, partly because . . . you run less risk of error the fewer entities you assume.[9]

*Although this theory of meaning appeals to common sense, it is controversial. The ordinary language philosophers, whom we encounter later in this chapter, contend this account of meaning is inadequate.

Russell's philosophical development was a continuous quest for those elements of the world that were absolutely simple and fundamental and that could be known with absolute certainty based on our direct acquaintance with them. These particulars with which we are directly acquainted are what Russell called "hard data." The problem is that a good number of our beliefs concern "soft data," which are inferred entities. Russell's task is to show that a great deal of the soft data can be reinterpreted as constructions from the indubitable hard data. To achieve this goal, he formulated another methodological principle: "Whenever possible, logical constructions are to be substituted for inferred entities."[10]

Consider your experience of a chair. A chair appears within your visual field as a series of color patches whose size and shape vary, depending on the angle and the distance from which you view it. Each distinct, particular sense datum you experience at a given moment is a piece of hard data, for you cannot doubt that what is directly appearing to you is a series of rectangular patches of a certain color. However, by psychological habit and for practical purposes, you group these particular patches of color data together and treat them as parts of a class you refer to as "the chair." This is not something you *consciously* do, but if Russell's atomistic empiricism is correct then this is what you *actually* do.

In this way, Russell thinks, science and ordinary experience can be set on a rock-solid foundation. Instead of making the word *chair* refer to an inferred entity outside of experience as the seventeenth-century empiricist John Locke would have, Russell reduces the word *chair* to a class term referring to a collection of "hard," sensory data that we directly experience. Russell does not deny that there could be a "chair substance" beneath all the appearances, he just concludes we cannot know it and don't need to postulate it to speak meaningfully about the chair. If the notion of a "chair" is a logical construction from our immediate sense data, it is even more obvious that scientific objects such as electrons and protons are logical constructions. Of course, the same sort of analysis applies to your experience of your friend. The friend's name is actually a class term for the collection of sense data you associate with him or her.

When he first started working on these ideas, Russell thought we directly experience three sorts of things: particular sense data, universals, and our self. However, he came to doubt we have direct knowledge of the self, and claimed it, too, was a logical construction from the particular data of experience. In his later work, the only logically proper name Russell would allow was the word *this*. Thus, propositions such as "This is red," said when referring to a certain sense datum, are the only sort of solid claims we can make about the world. To prevent someone from thinking that "this" refers to some sort of metaphysical substance, he preferred to state "This is red," as "Redness is here."

This account of experience—as a flow of sense data grouped together under class names such as "chair"—does not seem a sufficient basis for ordinary life or science. If we don't have a basis for asserting the existence of enduring physical objects nor for believing in causal relations, how can we make inferences and predictions from the sense data? Since logical atomism rejects the claim that there are logically necessary relationships between facts, we will not be able to make deductive inferences about anything in the world. However, Russell says that we can make cautious nondeductive inferences from our experiences. Therefore, he tentatively proposes a set of five postulates that provide minimum foundation for science and practical living. The nature of his postulates may be illustrated by quoting one of them, "the postulate of quasi-permanence." He says we can use this postulate "to replace the common-sense notion of 'thing' and 'person' in a manner not involving the concept of 'substance.' " This postulate states that

> Given any event A, it happens very frequently that, at any neighboring time, there is at some neighboring place an event very similar to A.[11]

Thus, if I have chairlike or personlike appearances in one moment, I am reasonable to expect experiences "very similar" in the next moment without appealing to a metaphysical substance.

Still, we may ask, What is the justification for these postulates? The only answer Russell comes up with is that they are acquired habits or "animal inferences" rooted in our biological nature.[12]

This shows that, despite his complicated conceptual apparatus, when we get down to the basis of Russell's position he has made very little progress beyond David Hume's skepticism. Even worse, in the final analysis, he speaks as though everything rested on a subjective choice.

> If we are to hold that we know anything of the external world, we must accept the canons of scientific knowledge. Whether . . . an individual decides to accept or reject these canons, is a purely personal affair, not susceptible to argument.[13]

There is tremendous irony here. Russell began with a Cartesian search for absolute certainty, but in the end it seems all we can know about the world are such barren truths as "Redness is here." To get beyond this level, we have to place our trust in the canons of scientific knowledge, but this requires a Kierkegaardian leap of faith in which "an individual decides to accept or reject these canons."

Russell says that at the beginning of his career, he had hoped to find in philosophy an intellectually and emotionally satisfying substitute for religion. However, at age seventy-one he concluded that "my intellectual journeys have been, in some respects, disappointing."[14] Even though Russell's philosophical labors did not accomplish all he hoped they would, his contributions were enormous. Particularly in the area of logic, Russell expanded and sharpened one of our most important philosophical tools.

The difficulties in the logical atomists' attempt to base a metaphysical theory on an analysis of language led later analytic philosophers to lower their sights, giving up all expectations that philosophy tells us anything about ultimate reality or that it provides the meaning of human life. Instead, they put philosophy to work on a much more humble task, that of clarifying the expressions we use to speak about the world. Logical positivism, the third phase of analytic philosophy, represents this chastened, antimetaphysical turn in philosophy.

LOGICAL POSITIVISM

In the 1920s and early 1930s a group of philosophers took it as their mission to search for a body of positive knowledge based on science, much as Auguste Comte did a century earlier. They called their position **logical positivism** (or *logical empiricism*, as it was also known) to distinguish their specific program from earlier positivisms, as well as to indicate that logical analysis was the core of their method. This movement originated with a group called the Vienna Circle. The most influential members of the Circle were Rudolf Carnap, Otto Neurath, Herbert Feigl, Friedrich Waismann, and Kurt Gödel. A. J. Ayer attended a number of the sessions and introduced logical positivism to England in his classic book *Language, Truth and Logic.* Hans Reichenbach led a similar group in Berlin. Their goal of rebuilding philosophy on a sound logical and scientific foundation was very appealing. Because they vigorously promoted their philosophy at international congresses and through their publications, logical positivism became an international movement that spread throughout most of Europe and became very powerful in the English-speaking countries.

The logical positivists were strongly influenced by the logical atomism of Bertrand Russell and Ludwig Wittgenstein. Although they disagreed with some of the details of logical atomism, the positivists carried forward the vision of a logically ideal language and the attempt to anchor the meaning of terms in irreducible sense data. They were also influenced by David Hume's empiricism and sought to provide an updated version of it. Although they joined with many of their contemporaries in the attack on metaphysical systems such as Hegel's, they thought philosophy needed stronger logical artillery to vanquish metaphysics once and for all.

The logical positivists had three main goals: (1) to develop a logically adequate theory of language that would provide a criterion of linguistic

meaning, (2) to use this criterion as a sieve to separate meaningful scientific statements from meaningless metaphysical statements, and (3) to use this theory of language to set out the epistemological and logical foundations of science.

The spirit of logical positivism is captured by Hume's famous statement:

> When we run over libraries, persuaded of these principles, what havoc must we make? If we take in our hand any volume; of divinity or school metaphysics, for instance; let us ask, Does it contain any abstract reasoning concerning quantity or number? No. Does it contain any experimental reasoning concerning matter of fact and existence? No. Commit it then to the flames: for it can contain nothing but sophistry and illusion.[15]

Like Hume, the logical positivists believed that all genuine knowledge falls within the two realms of science: (1) the formal sciences of logic and mathematics and (2) the empirical sciences. The first sort of knowledge is expressed in what are called analytic propositions. The truth or falsity of these sorts of statements is based on the logical form of language or on the definitions of words. Thus "All lemons are lemons," "2 + 2 = 4," and "All bachelors are unmarried" are examples of true analytic statements. Wittgenstein called such statements **tautologies**.* A false analytic statement, such as "John is an unmarried bachelor," is identified by the fact that it contains a contradiction. Since tautologies are always true and contradictions are always false, no matter what is the case, analytic statements do not give us any factual knowledge about the way the world is.

---

*Such statements express what Hume called "relations of ideas" and what Kant called "analytic *a priori* judgments." Kant, however, treated mathematical statements differently, claiming they fell into the class of "synthetic *a priori* judgments." Neither Hume nor the logical positivists acknowledged the existence of such a category.

The second category of statements consists of empirical statements.* Statements such as "Lemons are yellow" or "The sun rises in the east" are true, empirical statements. In contrast, "The moon is made out of green cheese" is a meaningful empirical statement, even though it is false. Unlike analytic statements, both true and false empirical statements do, of course, make claims about the way the world is. Since analytic and empirical statements are the only sorts of meaningful statements there are, any proposition that does not fall into either category is not simply false, nor is it merely unknowable, it is *meaningless*. Plato's metaphysical claim that "beyond individual human beings there exists the nonphysical Form of Humanity" makes no more sense than the following pieces of nonsense: "Is the number 7 holy?" or "Which numbers are more athletic, the even or the odd ones?"

The Verifiability Principle

The rules of logic and language give us clear-cut methods for determining the meaning of analytic statements. However, to carry out their program the logical positivists also needed a definitive method for separating meaningful empirical statements from meaningless pseudo-statements. They therefore developed the **verifiability principle**, and this criterion of meaning became the centerpiece of their program. Note that they were not trying to decide whether a given statement about the world was true or not, for this is the task of science. The role of philosophy is to decide what it means to say that a statement has *cognitive* meaning. A cognitively meaningful statement is one that provides information about the world. (As we will see, they acknowledged there may be noncognitive meaning as well.)

The verifiability principle can be stated thus: *a factual statement is meaningful if it can be verified in experience*. The corollary of this principle is *the*

meaning of a factual statement is the method of its verification. Suppose, for example, someone claims that "it is raining outside." This claim (whether true or false) is meaningful because I can specify concrete experiences that would verify it. The entire meaning of the claim can be translated into a series of sentences referring directly to possible sense experiences. These were sometimes called "protocol statements." In our example, the meaning of the claim could be captured by sentences such as "If I look out the window, I will see water falling" or "If I stand outside, I will feel water droplets."

The logical positivists found themselves continually modifying the verifiability principle in the attempt to remedy problems that kept arising. First, they said we may not be able to actually verify a statement, but it must be verifiable *in principle* to be meaningful. In other words, we must be able to state what sorts of experiences would count for or against the claim, even if we cannot subject it to the test. This allows historical statements to be meaningful even if we cannot verify or falsify them. An example would be "Julius Caesar had breakfast the day he died." Also, verification in principle allowed statements to be meaningful that cannot be actually verified because we lack the technology to do so. Statements about an unexplored planet would be such a case.

Second, the positivists originally dictated that for a statement to be factually meaningful, it must be capable of being *conclusively* verified by experience. This was later called "strong verification." However, a great many important statements in science would fail this test. Statements expressing large-scale scientific theories are only indirectly and incompletely supported by particular observations. For example, a collection of observation statements such as "this rock is falling to the earth" will not verify Newton's theory of gravitation. Also, universal statements such as "all oxygen is combustible" cannot be conclusively verified, because there is always the possibility that the next experiment will produce a counterexample. Therefore, the logical positivists decided that it is enough if a statement can be "weakly verified." Roughly, the principle of weak verification declares that a

---

*Hume said these statements express "matters of fact," and Kant said they express "synthetic *a posteriori* judgments."

statement is cognitively meaningful if experience can render it probable. The logical positivists thought this revised version would draw the boundaries of cognitive meaning so as to include scientific statements, while excluding the philosophical statements they wished to reject.

THE DEMISE OF METAPHYSICS AND THEOLOGY

What made the logical positivists unique in the history of philosophy was that, unlike previous critics of metaphysics, they did not simply say metaphysical statements are false or unfounded. Instead, they insisted all metaphysical statements, in principle, are totally nonsensical. Consider the statement "Blue ideas sleep furiously." It doesn't violate any rules of English grammar, but is obviously a piece of nonsense. It is not so obvious that metaphysical statements are nonsense. Yet under the logical positivists' analysis these statements are a form of disguised nonsense and are just as empty of cognitive content as the statement about blue ideas. To make this point, A. J. Ayer quotes a statement from the Neo-Hegelian F. H. Bradley: "The Absolute enters into, but is itself incapable of, evolution and progress." Applying the verifiability principle, Ayer remarks, "One cannot conceive of an observation which would enable one to determine whether the Absolute did, or did not, enter into evolution and progress."[16] Similarly, statements such as "all reality is material" go beyond the bounds of experience and therefore are neither true not false, but are pseudo-propositions.*

Since theological statements make claims about ultimate reality, the logical positivist would say they also are unverifiable and meaningless. For example, the statement "there is a loving God" cannot be translated into any observation statements. Religious people still maintain there is a loving God even when their lives are filled with

suffering and arbitrary, cruel misfortunes. This demonstrates that claims about God do not have anything to do with what we will or will not experience. Of course, it follows that the denial of any metaphysical claim will have no empirical content either. So the atheist's assertion that "there is no God" is also an example of an unverifiable and meaningless claim. At best, metaphysical and theological statements express our feelings about the world. As Rudolf Carnap expressed it, metaphysical propositions "are, like laughing, lyrics, and music, expressive."[17]

The Status of Ethics

Traditionally, ethics was an important branch of philosophy. Ethical statements make claims about how people ought to act and what sorts of things have intrinsic value. However, logical positivism cast them in a new light. The positivists made several different kinds of responses to ethics. Moritz Schlick said that ethical statements are factual claims about how people use the word *good* and why a person approves of this or that action. Hence, ethics can be understood as a division within psychology. Of course, if ethics is merely a type of behavioral science, it cannot make normative pronouncements about what the word "good" *should* mean nor can it provide an absolute justification of ethical norms.

Rudolf Carnap and A. J. Ayer represented the majority opinion on ethics within the positivist's camp. Their ethical theory came to be known as *emotivism*. In their analysis, ethical statements do not make factual claims capable of being verified and, therefore, they have no cognitive meaning. However, ethical statements do have *emotive* meaning. They are best understood as verbal ways of expressing certain attitudes of approval or disapproval. Thus, when someone says, "You acted wrongly in stealing that money," this does not make a factual claim about stealing, because no sense data corresponds to the quality of "moral wrongness." Instead, when a person morally condemns an act of stealing, what they are actually doing is (1) stating a fact plus (2) expressing an

---

*Insofar as Russell's logical atomism made claims about the structure of reality, these claims would be rejected by the logical positivists' criterion as meaningless intellectual baggage.

emotion or attitude toward it such as "You stole the money!—Ugh, Boo, Hiss!" Carnap and Ayer also believed that moral claims may be used to influence the attitudes and behavior of others. In this case, the statement "It is your moral duty to tell the truth" means nothing more than "I recommend you tell the truth."[18]

The final verdict rendered by the logical positivists is that philosophy cannot be a source of truth. Knowledge comes to us only through the formal propositions of mathematics and logic or through the empirically verified observations of science. As Carnap said, "We give no answer to philosophical questions and instead reject all *philosophical questions*, whether of metaphysics, ethics or epistemology. For our concern is with *logical analysis*."[19] Nevertheless, because philosophy is the activity of clarifying language, the logical positivists believed philosophers, as the caretakers of language, could still make three contributions. First, philosophers could be put in charge of the "environmental quality" of the intellectual realm. They could use the verifiability test to clear our intellectual discourse of the verbal pollution of meaningless statements. Second, the philosopher could be an "efficiency expert" who clarifies complex and murky scientific statements by analyzing them into the clean and crisp statements of direct observation. Third, the philosopher could be an "organizational administrator" who tries to realize the dream of the unity of the science. Here, philosophers could use their logical techniques to show how all the sciences may be reduced to physics, the most fully developed and well-grounded of the sciences.

Problems with Logical Positivism

As with a leaky ship at sea, problems with logical positivism were continually being discovered, and its advocates spent much time patching its leaks instead of carrying out their positive program. First, as mentioned, the verifiability principle went through a number of modifications. If the principle was made very narrow (strong verifiability), it eliminated a good deal of science. Scientific state-

ments expressing general laws or referring to unobservable entities such as electrons cannot be conclusively and directly verified. According to the strong verifiability principle, such statements would have to be classified as meaningless. In other words, the logical positivists found, as Russell had, that conclusively verifiable observation statements such as "Redness here now" provide too thin a foundation on which to build knowledge. To remedy this problem, the logical positivists made the principle more liberal (weak verifiability). Under this version, statements about unobservable subatomic entities are meaningful because observations are relevant to assessing their truth. The problem was that by preserving the more theoretical regions of science, weak verifiability allowed some metaphysical statements to creep back in. For example, many arguments in natural theology use observations about the world as evidence that the existence of God is probable. Hence, by the standards of the weaker principle, statements about God, Plato's Forms, and Hegel's Absolute were cognitively meaningful.

Second, critics were quick to drag the logical positivist's principle of verification before its own tribunal of judgment. Let's consider this statement of the verifiability principle: "A meaningful statement will either be analytic or empirically verifiable." We may ask, Is this itself a meaningful statement? It doesn't seem to be an analytic statement based on a rule of logic or a definition. However, it doesn't seem to be an empirical statement, either. What sort of sense data could possibly verify it? Pressed up against the wall, many logical positivists had to admit the principle is simply a recommendation they were making about how to use the terms "meaningful" and "meaningless." But this response reduces their theory of language to simply a matter of subjective, personal preference.

Somewhere between 1930 and 1940 logical positivism lost its momentum. As a movement it is now dead, although some philosophers still retain some of the spirit of this philosophy. Their interest in the philosophy of science brought this area of philosophy into prominence. Ironically, the model of scientific language they set forth was an ideal refuted by a closer look at the empirical facts of how scientific theories actually develop.* Eventually, analytic philosophers found that the major shortcoming of logical positivism was that it assumed all meaningful language had to conform to the model of scientific language. In 1959 A. J. Ayer, one of the most famous of the logical positivists, repented of his earlier one-sided perspective. Speaking of what the logical positivists had accomplished, he said,

> The most that has been proved is that metaphysical statements do not fall into the same category as the laws of logic, or as scientific hypotheses, or as historical narratives, or judgments of perception, or any other common sense descriptions of the "natural" world. Surely it does not follow that they are neither true nor false, still less that they are nonsensical.[20]

Similarly, Ludwig Wittgenstein, a guiding light of logical atomism and logical positivism, discovered that his original position was misguided and that a new way of looking at language was needed. Wittgenstein took analytic philosophy to the next stage of its development. However, before we can look at how he changed the course of analytic philosophy, we must follow the path of his earlier ideas to see why they led to a dead end.

LUDWIG WITTGENSTEIN

Wittgenstein's Life: From Engineer to Philosopher

Ludwig Wittgenstein (1889–1951) was born in Vienna into a family that was not only financially wealthy, but rich in intellectual and artistic talents as well. The composer Johannes Brahms was a close friend of the Wittgenstein family and a frequent visitor to their home. Wittgenstein's father was a Jewish convert to Protestantism, but Wittgenstein himself was raised in his mother's faith, Roman Catholicism.

Wittgenstein began his university education at the University of Manchester, where he studied engineering and researched aeronautical design. His work toward a career in engineering ended when he became interested in pure mathematics and then in the philosophical foundations of mathematics. Pursuing this, he discovered the work of Bertrand Russell and enrolled in Trinity College at Cambridge in 1912 to study with Russell. Very quickly, Russell realized his student's great genius and told Wittgenstein's sister he believed the next great advance in philosophy would be made by her brother. Russell became one of Wittgenstein's closest friends and had an important influence on his career, even though they came to differ on a number of issues. Like many great geniuses, Wittgenstein was an extraordinarily intense person, and this intensity, combined with his thirst for personal and intellectual honesty, tormented him his whole life. His sister says that when he was pursuing a career as an engineer,

> he was suddenly seized so strongly and so completely against his will by philosophy, i.e., by reflections about philosophical problems, that he suffered severely. . . . One of several transformations which he was to undergo in his life had come over him and shaken his whole being.[21]

From this intensity came the fulfillment of Russell's prediction, for in the 1920s Wittgenstein's ideas reverberated throughout the halls of philosophy departments. However, Russell underestimated the genius of his student, for Wittgenstein initiated not one, but two revolutions in philoso-

---

*See Thomas Kuhn, *The Structure of Scientific Revolutions*, 2d ed., enlarged (Chicago: University of Chicago Press, 1970), for the classic work on the history of science that undermined the logical positivists' view of science when it first appeared in 1962.

phy. Approximately ten years after he had made his first impact, Wittgenstein's driving demand for intellectual honesty forced him to repudiate the ideas that had made him famous and led him to chart a new course in philosophy.

The two periods in Wittgenstein's intellectual life center on his two major works. His early philosophy is represented by the *Tractatus Logico-Philosophicus*, published in 1921. His later philosophy was stated in the *Philosophical Investigations*, published in 1953. The two books differ radically in style as well as in their conceptions of philosophy and language. In his later period, when he attacks his earlier theories, Wittgenstein refers to the mistakes of "the author of the *Tractatus*" as though he were speaking about a completely different person. Although Wittgenstein's general approach to language in his early period has been covered in our discussion of logical atomism, we must sketch out some of the features of the *Tractatus* to understand the radical shift he made.

The Early Wittgenstein: From Logic to Mysticism

THE TASK OF THE *TRACTATUS*

The *Tractatus* was written before Wittgenstein was thirty years old. Running fewer than eighty pages in length, it consists of a series of short, numbered statements. The composition of the book and its range of topics is very unusual. Although most of the book is a collection of very precise statements on the nature of logic, the last four pages take a very strange shift in direction and consist of poetical and mystical utterances. The philosophy of language Wittgenstein developed during this period linked Russell's logical atomism and logical positivism. Despite their differences, all these philosophies united around three common projects: (1) the repudiation of traditional metaphysics, (2) the attempt to reduce language to a series of elementary propositions that would correspond with observable facts, and (3) the attempt to develop a theory of language that would establish the boundaries of meaning. In Wittgenstein's

case, his project takes the form of a "linguistic Kantianism." Kant tried to set out the limits of reason by distinguishing what, in principle, is knowable from what is unknowable. Since Wittgenstein believes whatever can be thought can be spoken, it follows that the limits of thought can be set out by determining the limits of language. This will give us the limits of what can be intelligible.

THE PICTURE THEORY OF LANGUAGE

Russell believed the world was a collection of atomic facts. Using the term "states of affairs" for "atomic facts," Wittgenstein gives us a similar account of the world.

(1) The world is all that is the case.

(1.1) The world is the totality of facts, not of things.

- •
- •
- •

(2) What is the case—a fact—is the existence of states of affairs.

(2.01) A state of affairs (a state of things) is a combination of objects (things).[22]

Similar to Russell's logical atomism, Wittgenstein took for granted that the function of language is to represent states of affairs in the world. This was known as his "picture theory of language":

(4.01) A proposition is a picture of reality.
A proposition is a model of reality as we imagine it.

Obviously, a proposition does not give us a spatial representation of a situation. Instead, the logical relationships among the elements of a proposition represent the logical relationships among objects in the world. A proposition has a sense if it describes a specific, possible situation within the world; otherwise, it is meaningless. The logical positivists considered this a statement of their principle of verification. Consequently, they wrongly

Penn Station, New York City, 1934. The skeletal structures produced by modern arthitects provide a visual image of Ludwig Wittgenstein's early philosophy of language. Wittgenstein attempted to get below the surface of our language to reveal the logical structure of any possible language. However, just as the unbounded sky can be seen through the confining framework of the building, Wittgenstein stressed that there is much that is beyond the boundaries of language: "There are, indeed, things that cannot be put into words. They make themselves manifest. They are what is mystical."

assumed Wittgenstein was one of them. However, Wittgenstein did agree with them on at least three points. First, he claims that the only meaningful language is the fact-stating language of the natural sciences. "The totality of true propositions is the whole of natural science" (T 4.11). Second, Wittgenstein also agrees a correct understanding of the logic of language would eliminate most traditional philosophy:

(4.003)   Most of the propositions and questions to be found in philosophical works are not false but nonsensical. Consequently we cannot give any answer to questions of this kind, but can only establish that they are nonsensical. Most of the propositions and questions of philosophers arise from our failure to understand the logic of our language.

Third, like the logical positivists, Wittgenstein believes philosophy does not give us any information about reality. Its job is simply to straighten up our thought and language by removing misunderstandings. "Philosophy is not a body of doctrine but an activity. . . . Philosophy does not result in 'philosophical propositions', but rather in the clarification of propositions" (T 4.112).

WITTGENSTEIN'S MYSTICISM

Thus far, the doctrines of the *Tractatus* simply seem to repeat the main ideas of logical atomism and logical positivism, adding a few, unique flourishes. However, what makes this work so fascinating is the startling set of implications Wittgenstein draws from his position and the ways he deviated radically from his contemporaries. Following the example of Kant once again, Wittgenstein said that if we can draw a boundary, then something must be on both sides of the boundary. Within the boundary of meaningful language is nothing but the propositions of science. But what lies beyond the limits of language? It would, of course, be something inexpressible. The positivists thought what is inexpressible could never be anything more than sheer nonsense. However, Wittgenstein believed something transcends the limits of language, which he called "the mystical." "There are, indeed, things that cannot be put into words. They *make themselves manifest.* They are what is mystical" (T 6.522).

Paradoxically, among the inexpressible things are the propositions of the *Tractatus* itself. Wittgenstein came to this conclusion by reasoning as follows. The doctrine he and Russell embraced was "A proposition is meaningful only if it can be analyzed down into one or more elementary propositions each of which refer to an atomic fact." According to this theory, the relationship between a proposition and the world is one of "referring to" or "picturing" and can be illustrated with the following diagram:

Proposition ———→ Atomic fact

But given this picture, what is the status of Russell and Wittgenstein's proposition? Clearly, it does not make a claim about some particular fact in the world. Instead, this proposition and the others Wittgenstein expresses describe the relationship between propositions and facts or, to put it more generally, they are making claims about the relationship between language and the world. This may be diagrammed in this way:

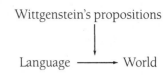

Wittgenstein's propositions

Language ———→ World

The problem is that according to his own theory of language, Wittgenstein's propositions stand outside the domain of meaningful language. Wittgenstein "bit the bullet" and accepted this conclusion. For this reason, he acknowledges,

(6.54)   My propositions serve as elucidations in the following way: anyone who understands me finally recognizes them as nonsensical, when he has used them—as steps—to climb up beyond them. (He must, so to speak, throw away the ladder, after he has climbed up it.)

In other words, Wittgenstein's propositions are attempting to say the unsayable (and this applies to those of Russell and the logical positivists as well). Nevertheless, these propositions are "elucidations" for they can help trigger an insight into the nature of the world, even though this insight cannot be expressed.

Another aspect of the mystical is the realm of ethical and spiritual values. Wittgenstein says we will not find values among the facts of the world, for everything just is what it is (T 6.41). Therefore, the sense of the world, what constitutes its value, must lie outside the world. It cannot be one more mundane fact among the scientifically observable facts in the world. Consequently, "ethics cannot be put into words. Ethics is transcendental" (T 6.421). A little bit later he says,

(6.432)   *How* things are in the world is a matter of complete indifference for what is higher. God does not reveal himself *in* the world.

Wittgenstein closes his discussion of the mystical and ends the *Tractatus* with proposition 7, his final, oracular statement:

(7) What we cannot speak about we must pass over in silence.

At first glance, this seems a truism and the logical positivists took it as such. But Wittgenstein is actually making the significant point that there is *something* to be silent about. He once wrote to a friend concerning the *Tractatus*, "My work consists of two parts: the one presented here plus all that I have *not* written. And it is precisely this second part that is the important one."[23] Eventually, through meetings with Wittgenstein, the logical positivists realized with horror that the man who had inspired their antimetaphysical polemics really wasn't one of them. Wittgenstein agreed with them that it is hopeless to "thrust against the limits of language," at the same time he insisted, "the tendency, the thrust, *points to something*."[24]

The Later Wittgenstein: The Turn to Ordinary Language

In the preface to the *Tractatus*, Wittgenstein claimed his conclusions seemed "unassailable and definitive" and he had found "the final solution of the problems" (T 5). After showing that scientific statements constitute the whole of what we can think and say—and that the rest, what can only be shown but not spoken, is left to mysticism—Wittgenstein concluded that the task of philosophy was finished. Ending his work with the summons to philosophical silence, he followed his own advice and stopped doing philosophy. First he became an elementary school teacher in an Austrian village from 1920 to 1926; then he served as a gardener's assistant in a monastery for several months. After that, he spent two years using his architectural skills to design a house for one of his sisters. Gradually Wittgenstein began to think about philosophy again. He had a gnawing suspicion that, somehow, he had not gotten it right in his early work and he needed to rethink his whole approach.

Wittgenstein returned to Cambridge in 1929 to do research in philosophy and eventually was made a Fellow of Trinity College. In 1930 he began giving informal lectures to a carefully, screened group of advanced students. Actually, they could hardly be called *lectures*, for Wittgenstein was really thinking out loud about various philosophical problems in front of his students, without the benefit of notes. In the midst of this extemporaneous philosophizing, he frequently engaged in intense, question-and-answer dialogues with his students, much like Socrates. During two of the years he taught, Wittgenstein dictated his thoughts to his inner circle of students, who then circulated transcripts of these meetings around Cambridge. After Wittgenstein's death, these notes were published as *The Blue and Brown Books* (referring to the original covers of the typewritten copies). Finally, Wittgenstein retired from teaching in 1947 in order to devote his time and energies to his research. After a period of ill health, he died on April 29, 1951. Two years after Wittgenstein's death, the *Philosophical Investigations*, the most significant work of his later period, was published. Through the impact of Wittgenstein's lectures and his later writings, analytic philosophy took off in a completely new direction.

There are a number of striking differences between the *Tractatus* and the *Investigations*. First, the *Tractatus* used an *a priori*, logical method. The early Wittgenstein thought the results of his analysis showed that language necessarily *must* conform to the logician's ideals. In contrast, the *Investigations* uses an empirical, descriptive method. He now cautions, "One cannot guess how a word functions. One has to *look at* its use and learn from that" (PI §340).[25] The *Tractatus* had a linear, logical format, each proposition fitting neatly into its appointed place. The later book, however, has neither a beginning nor end. When you start reading it, you are thrust into the middle of a rambling album of sketches, remarks, questions, descriptions, dialogues, jokes, stories, and confessions that unfold in almost a stream-of-consciousness style.

It is easy to find contrasts between Wittgenstein's earlier and later work. However, there is also a sense in which he was wrestling with the same questions in both periods, albeit with different methods and assumptions.* In the *Tractatus* he said that philosophical problems arise because "the logic of our language is misunderstood" (T, preface). In the *Investigations* he says we have these problems because "we do not *command a clear view* of the use of our words" (PI §122). In both works he was concerned to find the limits of legitimate language and to confront the problems that arise when these boundaries are violated. However, there is a considerable change from his earlier writings in how Wittgenstein conceives the method of clarifying language and his notion of the limits and boundaries of language.

LANGUAGE-GAMES

One of the most important analogies Wittgenstein draws in his later work is that between language and games. He captures this comparison with his notion of "language-games." He makes numerous uses of the metaphor of language-games; three will be discussed here. First, the term "language-games" is used to emphasize the plurality of our ways of speaking. To get the analogy off the ground, consider the many kinds of games and the ways they differ in purposes, rules, and the kinds of action response interactions that characterize them. Wittgenstein asks the following question concerning games:

> *What is common to them all?—Don't say: "There must be something common, or they would not be called 'games' "—but look and see whether there is anything common to all.—For if you look at them you will not see something that is common to all, but similarities, relationships, and a whole series of them at that. (PI §66)*

Similar to the diversity of literal games, our multiple ways of speaking (language-games) do not

conform to a single model. Wittgenstein's repeated insistence on this was meant to refute "the author of the *Tractatus*" (as Wittgenstein sometimes referred to his earlier phase). The earlier theory had supposed the sole function of a word was to name an object. In response to this theory, Wittgenstein says we do use words in this way in some language-games, but this does not describe the whole of language:

> *It is as if someone were to say: "A game consists in moving objects about on a surface according to certain rules . . ."—and we replied: You seem to be thinking of board games, but there are others. You can make your definition correct by expressly restricting it to those games. (PI §3)*

In contrast to the one-dimensional "naming" theory of language of the *Tractatus*, Wittgenstein gives a random list of language-games to illustrate their diversity. He includes giving orders and obeying them; describing the appearance of an object; speculating about an event; making a joke; translating from one language into another; asking, thanking, cursing, greeting, praying (PI §23). To illustrate the relationship of language-games to one another, Wittgenstein uses yet another analogy. He says the different uses of language are like "family resemblances" (PI §67). The people at a family reunion will share many similar features, such as eye color, temperament, hair, facial structure, and build. However, there will be no one particular feature that they all share in common. A daughter may have her father's eyes, her mother's hair, and her aunt's smile. With this analogy, Wittgenstein is attacking the theory of essentialism, which is the Platonic thesis that for things to be classed together they must share some essence. Wittgenstein's point, however, is that while our modes of discourse are all examples of *language*, the fact that they belong to the same category does not imply there is a single essence they all possess. Instead, the different language-games "are *related* to one another in many different ways" (PI §65).

A second reason why Wittgenstein compares the use of language to the playing of different games is to emphasize that the speaking of language is

---

*Wittgenstein is reported to have said that "the *Tractatus* was not *all* wrong: it was not like a bag of junk professing to be a clock, but like a clock that did not tell you the right time." Reported by G. E. M. Anscombe in *An Introduction to Wittgenstein's Tractatus*, 2d ed., rev. (New York: Harper & Row, Harper Torchbooks, 1959), 78.

an *activity*. As he says, "the whole, consisting of language and the actions into which it is woven, [is] the 'language-game' " (PI §7). For example, the problem with the "naming theory" of language is not only that there are other uses of language besides naming objects, but also that the act of naming objects plays no role unless it is an activity within the context of a particular language-game (PI §49). Suppose I point to a piece of furniture and say "chair." So far, I have done nothing other than uttering a sound. However, in the right sort of circumstances it could be a move in a language-game. For example, if I am teaching you English, you would point to the object and repeat "chair." If I am drilling you on your German, you would try to respond with the correct German equivalent. If I am rearranging the living room, you might respond to the word by bringing the chair to me. Apart from the linguistic responses and activities that make up such language-games, my saying "chair" would make no sense. We don't simply speak—we do things by means of speaking.

Third, Wittgenstein used the notion of language-games to illustrate that we run into confusion when we aren't aware that the way in which words function will vary from one language-game to another. In literal games, for example, catching the ball in one's hands is important in basketball, but in soccer if someone other than the goalie uses hands to catch the ball that is an illegitimate move. With respect to language, the logical positivists treated scientific discourse as the only language-game and judged all other ways of speaking (religious and ethical discourse) to be meaningless. But this is like supposing that ducks are the only kind of fowl there are and, therefore, like judging swans to be deficient and malformed ducks. According to Wittgenstein, language-games (like ducks and swans) must be judged on their own terms, by their own standards.

Not paying attention to the different ways in which language functions is the cause of many traditional philosophical problems. Wittgenstein thinks the proper role of the philosopher is not to propose new and exotic theories but to remove "misunderstandings concerning the use of words, caused, among other things, by certain analogies between the forms of expression in different regions of language" (PI §90). To illustrate Wittgenstein's point, consider whether or not the questions "Where was it lost?" and "Can I help you find it?" would be appropriate responses to each of the following statements: (1) I lost my contact lens. (2) He lost consciousness. (3) I lost my train of thought. (4) I lost my job. (5) I lost my faith. The preceding questions clearly apply in some of these cases and not in others; and in some of the cases, whether the questions make sense or not might depend on the context. Even in situations where one or the other question does apply, the questions have a different sense from one context to another. Clearly, losing a lens differs from losing consciousness. Although we could try to find the lens, it would be senseless to try to find the consciousness. The reason for this difference, of course, is not because consciousness is so much harder to detect than a lens. The point of the examples is that the language-games in which we speak of physical objects follow different rules (have a different grammar, Wittgenstein would say) from the language-games in which we talk of mental states, abilities, relationships, religious commitments, and so on. To use one of Wittgenstein's own examples, if you *know* the height of Mont Blanc you know a certain proposition that can be stated. But you can *know* how a clarinet sounds without being able to say it (PI §78). Again, this is because the word *know* functions in different ways.

It would be misleading to leave the impression that Wittgenstein is saying that the boundaries of language-games are clear-cut, hard-and-fast lines. Boundaries are drawn for special purposes, and they may vary depending on our purposes (PI §499). The general purpose of the language-games metaphor was not to catalogue linguistic usages but to remove confusions. Wittgenstein says that the language-games serve as

objects of comparison *which are meant to throw light on the facts of our language by way not only of similarities, but also of dissimilarities. (PI §130)*

The mistake of the *Tractatus* was to impose on language the standards of "the crystalline purity of logic" as though human language were some sort of calculus (PI §107). However, to suppose that the inexactness of our language is a defect would be like supposing that the light from a reading lamp is not a real light because it has no sharp boundary (BB 27).

MEANING AND USE

In his earlier work, Wittgenstein explained meaning in terms of the logical relations between a name and its object or between a proposition and a fact. Gradually, however, he came to understand that words and sentences do not have meanings all by themselves, for they have the meanings we give to them. They are intimately tied to human purposes and activities, and in this context they have their life. Some have speculated that Wittgenstein received a new appreciation of how language functions from his experience as an elementary school teacher. Little children do not acquire new words by learning formal, exact definitions, but by learning how a word performs a job within an particular kind of context. To make us aware of the close relationship between meaning and use, Wittgenstein offers the following, tentative definition: "For a *large* class of cases—though not for all—in which we employ the word 'meaning' it can be defined thus: the meaning of a word is its use in the language" (PI §43). To emphasize the point that "use" can mean many sorts of things, Wittgenstein compares words to tools, each having a distinctive function (PI §11).

FORMS OF LIFE

The *Tractatus* account views language as an autonomous system of symbols in which the human speaker is mysteriously absent. In striking contrast, Wittgenstein now emphasizes that speaking is one sort of activity that takes place within the broader, concrete circumstances of human life. Wittgenstein uses the notion of "form of life" to capture this insight:

> To imagine a language means to imagine a form of life. (PI §19)

> Here the term "language-game" is meant to bring into prominence the fact that the speaking of language is part of an activity, or of a form of life. (PI §23)

Linguists have been able to decode long-dead ancient languages because there is something universal within human life.

> The common behaviour of mankind is the system of reference by means of which we interpret an unknown language. (PI §206)

In contrast to his earlier views, Wittgenstein does not think there is anything logically necessary about the ways in which our language is structured. At the same time, our ways of speaking are not completely arbitrary, either. They are intimately tied into the common human practices, needs, interests, goals, and understandings we seem to have. That language only has meaning within this broader context implies that simply uttering meaningful English sounds (such as a parrot does) is not yet to speak *our* language. In one of his typically striking epigrams, Wittgenstein says, "If a lion could talk we would not understand him" (PI II, p. 223). If the lion said, "I'm going to see a lawyer," while still behaving like a typical lion, basking in the sun, his words would not be serving a purpose within the activities or contexts where they have meaning for us.

Philosophers such as Descartes supposed a philosophical justification had to be given for every belief we have. However, Wittgenstein thinks this is a hopeless and useless task. There is simply a point where justifications come to an end:

> If I have exhausted the justifications I have reached bedrock, and my spade is turned. Then I am inclined to say: "This is simply what I do." (PI §217)

> What has to be accepted, the given is—so one could say—forms of life. (PI II, p. 226)

What makes possible our agreements in the forms of our language and practice? There seems to be no basis apart from human practice to ensure we will so agree. As Stanley Cavell puts it,

> That on the whole we do [agree] is a matter of our sharing routes of interest and feeling, modes of response, senses of humor and of significance and of fulfillment, of what is outrageous, of what is similar to what else, what a rebuke, what forgiveness, of when an utterance is an assertion, when an appeal,

when an explanation—all the whirl of organism Wittgenstein calls "forms of life." Human speech and activity, sanity and community, rest upon nothing more, but nothing less, than this.[26]

There can be no justification for our most basic concepts and ways of viewing the world because "what people accept as a justification—is shewn by how they think and live" (PI §325).

ORDINARY LANGUAGE VERSUS PHILOSOPHICAL LANGUAGE

One of the most important features of Wittgenstein's later philosophy is the distinction he makes between ordinary uses of language and philosophical uses. Previous philosophers had thought our understanding of terms such as "knowledge," "goodness," "mind," "time," and "reality" was confused. Hence, they tried to develop new definitions and theories to replace our ordinary conceptions. However, is it conceivable people never knew what they meant by these words? By what other standard than our ordinary practices could we critique our use of these terms? To say generations of people did not know what they meant when they said, "I know *X*," is like saying the rules of baseball we have used since the beginning of the game are wrong. The philosopher may come up with a new conception of knowledge, but would it improve our pre-philosophical understanding of knowledge? We seem to communicate and understand one another when we use the term "know" in ordinary discourse. Speaking about our ordinary ways of speaking, Wittgenstein says,

> *Is this language somehow too coarse and material for what we want to say? Then how is another one to be constructed?* (PI §120)

Philosophers such as Russell created an ideal language against which our ordinary language was to be judged. According to Wittgenstein, the judge and the defendant should be reversed. The technical ways in which philosophers analyze and use ordinary terms create pseudo-problems because language has been taken out of the practical contexts where it is functioning just fine:

> *For philosophical problems arise when language goes on holiday.* (PI §38)

> *The confusions which occupy us arise when language is like an engine idling, not when it is doing its work.* (PI §132)

> *It is wrong to say that in philosophy we consider an ideal language as opposed to our ordinary one. For this makes it appear as though we thought we could improve on ordinary language. But ordinary language is all right.* (BB 28)

PHILOSOPHY AS THERAPY

If traditional philosophical problems result from the misuse of ordinary language, then the role of the Wittgensteinian philosopher is to show the source of the puzzlement:

> *When philosophers use a word—"knowledge", "being", "object", "I", "proposition", "name"—and try to grasp the* essence *of the thing, one must always ask oneself: is the word ever actually used in this way in the language-game which is its original home?—.* (PI §116)

If the answer to this question is no, then the remedy is to "bring words back from their metaphysical to their everyday use" (PI §116). Wittgenstein speaks of traditional philosophy as though it were a pathology. For example, he describes the philosopher's search for essences as "our craving for generality" (BB 17). To heal this deep discomfort, therefore, what is needed is a sort of "linguistic therapy" that will cure us of our search for Platonic perfection and that will make us feel at home in the ambiguous world of ordinary life and discourse. It was the purpose of Wittgenstein's work to accomplish this healing. "There is not *a* philosophical method, though there are indeed methods, like different therapies" (PI §133).

Just as the *Tractatus* ended in philosophical silence and Wittgenstein went on to pursue other things, so in his later period he hoped that once we saw things clearly, there would be no more need for philosophical theories and explanations and we could return to the peace of philosophical silence again:

Philosophy simply puts everything before us, and neither explains nor deduces anything.—Since everything lies open to view there is nothing to explain. (PI §126)

The real discovery is the one that makes me capable of stopping doing philosophy when I want to.—The one that gives philosophy peace, so that it is no longer tormented by questions which bring itself in question. (PI §133)

That Wittgenstein never accomplished this goal in his personal life nor in his culture, and that others used his methods to carry on the task of philosophy, leaves the haunting feeling that maybe philosophical questioning is just inextricably a part of our human form of life. Perhaps Wittgenstein, in spite of himself, realized this when he said that philosophical problems are "deep disquietudes; their roots are as deep in us as the forms of our language and their significance is as great as the importance of our language" (PI §111).

THE IMPACT OF WITTGENSTEIN'S LATER PHILOSOPHY

Wittgenstein once wrote, "Our language continually ties new knots in our thinking. And philosophy is never done with disentangling them."[27] This quote illustrates Wittgenstein's conviction that philosophy has only a negative, therapeutic mission. It also illustrates the fact that he did not think there was any way to systematically do philosophy. When trying to untangle the knots in a fishing line, one can start just about anywhere, attacking the problem first at this point and then at that one. For this reason, Wittgenstein's later writings are a loose collection of rambling remarks, dealing with a multitude of philosophical tangles. However, a number of philosophers who were inspired by Wittgenstein's example believed his techniques could be used to produce sustained and systematic analyses of traditional philosophical topics. Hence, many of the later ordinary language philosophers did not agree with him that philosophy simply attacks confusions. They saw his method of linguistic analysis as a positive method for doing philosophy of mind, epistemology, philosophy of religion, ethics, and so on.

This new method of doing philosophy benefited from the fresh, new way of looking at language that Wittgenstein provided. Previously, the logical positivists had banished religious, ethical, and aesthetic language from the realm of meaningful discourse. However, Wittgenstein showed that there are other kinds of discourse besides scientific reports and descriptions of sense data. The philosopher cannot improve on our ways of speaking, much less condemn language-games that have a function. The cardinal rule is "Philosophy may in no way interfere with the actual use of language; it can in the end only describe it" (PI §124). Although Wittgenstein did motivate a return to some of the traditional topics in philosophy, those who used his method still refrained from producing elaborate theories, and they remained skeptical of speculative metaphysics. Instead, analytic philosophy in the Wittgensteinian tradition engaged in the much more humble task of "mapping" the geography of our linguistic concepts. This new approach to language and philosophy is best described by looking at some representatives of post-Wittgensteinian analytic philosophy who labored at the task of conceptual analysis.

CONCEPTUAL ANALYSIS

Gilbert Ryle

Gilbert Ryle (1900–1976) was educated at Oxford and taught there until his retirement. He was a powerful influence on philosophy in the English-speaking world. In 1949, four years before the publication of Wittgenstein's *Philosophical Investigations*, Ryle published *The Concept of Mind*. Many of his contemporaries called it one of the major events of philosophy in the postwar years. It was the first sustained investigation of a classical philosophical problem (the mind–body problem) that used the new techniques of ordinary language analysis. Ryle shared Wittgenstein's conviction that philosophical problems are not to be solved as much as they are to be dissolved. In other words, a proper analysis of the terminology of a problem area in philosophy will show that what initially appeared to be a problem was only a pseudo-problem. Thus, Ryle claimed he was not putting forth any philosophical theories, but was trying to make us attentive to the features of our linguistic terrain we have misconstrued:

> The philosophical arguments which constitute this book are intended not to increase what we know about minds, but to rectify the logical geography of the knowledge which we already possess. (CM 7)[28]

CATEGORY MISTAKES

The organizing principle Ryle uses for mapping our conceptual terrain is that of "categories." He says that "the logical type or category to which a concept belongs is the set of ways in which it is logically legitimate to operate with it" (CM 8). According to Ryle, a typical source of philosophical perplexity is that philosophers tend to confuse the differences between categories in their thought and language. Ryle gives the following example of a category mistake (CM 16). Suppose a visitor to the Oxford University campus is shown the libraries, playing fields, museums, laboratories, residences, the administration building, and so on. After com-

pleting the tour he or she now says, "I have seen all the classroom buildings, research centers, and dormitories, but when are you going to show me the university?" This person has committed what Ryle calls a category mistake. He or she has placed the university in the wrong category, assuming that the university is another particular thing, along with the buildings on the campus. The university, however, is not one more part within the whole, but the way in which all the parts are organized to form a whole. This sort of mistake occurs frequently in philosophy, Ryle claims, when we suppose that what we refer to with words such as "mind" and "body" belong to the same conceptual category, when they are actually serving different logical functions.

DESCARTES'S MYTH

Ryle believes Descartes made a similar sort of category mistake when he analyzed the mind–body problem. Descartes said the mechanical theories of Galileo apply to physical bodies but do not apply to minds. Therefore, since minds are not physical things governed by mechanical laws, he concluded that minds must be nonphysical, nonspatial sorts of things whose activities are mysterious, nonmechanical processes. It follows from Descartes's view that every person is a divided being. Some of a person's activities are bodily events that are in space and are publicly observable. Running parallel to these are mental events that are internal and private. Ryle describes Descartes's view of the mind as that of "the dogma of the Ghost in the Machine." This image trapped Descartes into asking questions about how and where a nonphysical mind can interact with a physical body. This picture has been so influential that Ryle says it is "the official doctrine" on the nature of the mind.

Ryle's solution is to argue that mental conduct words and physical thing words belong to different categories such that trying to figure out the relationship between mental events and bodily events is as absurd as asking if Oxford University is east or west of the chemistry building. The problem is, when we encounter a noun (such as "mind"), we tend to suppose it refers to some sort of distinct *thing*, even if a ghostly thing. To use an example (this one is not Ryle's), if you say, "He gives me the creeps," it would be a mistake for me to ask, "How many creeps does he give you?" We know what was meant by the first statement, and it didn't mean to imply that some sort of transferable entity exists called a "creep."

The thesis of Ryle's book is that *"the mind"* is a misleading term that can best be translated into the manifold mental conduct terms we use to describe certain aspects of one another's public activities. Thus, he tries to make clear what we are doing when we talk about thinking, understanding, and willing or when we say something was done intelligently, carelessly, purposefully, and so on. It is important to note that, as an ordinary language philosopher, Ryle does not intend to rob us of any of the ways we normally speak:

> I am not, . . . denying that there occur mental processes. Doing long division is a mental process and so is making a joke. But I am saying that the phrase "there occur mental processes" does not mean the same sort of thing as "there occur physical processes", and, therefore that it makes no sense to conjoin or disjoin the two. (CM 22)

In other words, he wants to describe how language functions and not reform it. His problem is not with how we use mental terms but with philosophers' *theories* about mental activities.

RYLE'S ANALYSIS OF MENTAL TERMS

Typical of Ryle's method is his analysis of the notion of intelligence. The official doctrine says that acting intelligently consists of two activities: (1) doing something and (2) thinking what one is doing while doing it. It is true we often deliberate before we do something, as in playing chess, but deliberation is not a necessary feature of intelligent performances. When we drive a car, make a humorous response in a conversation, or address a letter, we usually do not mentally rehearse our

intended action. Furthermore, if intelligence is defined in terms of a hidden, private process that occurs behind the scenes, then we could never know if someone was intelligent, for we would not have access to the private theater of the mind. Similarly, we could not know a host of other things we do know about people, such as that they are vain, creative, conscientious, or observant. The correct analysis, Ryle believes, is to view an attribute such as intelligence as a kind of competence or skill similar to knowing how to tie a knot or play a musical instrument. Hence, "overt intelligent performances are not clues to the workings of minds; they are those workings" (CM 58). Ryle points out that dispositional properties are a different sort of property from properties such as color or shape. For example, being brittle is a dispositional property. When we say a glass is brittle, we are saying that under certain circumstances the glass will break. Similarly, when we say Smith is intelligent (or devious, or cautious, and so on), we mean that in certain sorts of circumstances he will tend to respond in certain sorts of ways.

One problem with the view that bodily activities are directed by mental acts is that it leads to an infinite regress. If acting intelligently requires the bodily action to be preceded by some sort of intellectual operation, then for these mental activities themselves to be intelligent, their execution must be preceded by another prior act of theorizing, and so on. Similarly, if we say a bodily action is voluntary if it originated in an act of the will, then if that mental action of willing is to be voluntary, it must have itself been preceded by yet another volition, and so on endlessly. Ryle argues that "voluntary" does not refer to a mental act that precedes or accompanies an action, but indicates the manner in which it was done.

One argument that Descartes and other dualists use to defend their position is based on the phenomenon of self-knowledge. We have privileged access to the private theater of our minds, they claim, in ways other people do not. In critiquing this thesis, Ryle points out that we do not have a totally unique, privileged access to our own mental life because (1) we are often wrong in interpreting our own motives and emotional states and (2) people sometimes understand us better than we do ourselves. For the most part, however, "the sorts of things that I can find out about myself are the same as the sorts of things that I can find out about other people" (CM 155). To illustrate this, he asks us to consider the answer to the following sorts of questions:

> How do I discover that I am more unselfish than you; that I can do long division well, but differential equations only badly; that you suffer from certain phobias and tend to shirk facing certain sorts of facts; that I am more easily irritated than most people but less subject to panic, vertigo, or morbid conscientiousness? (CM 169)

To answer such questions, I do not "peep into a windowless chamber, illuminated by a very peculiar sort of light" (CM 168–169). In knowing how to answer such questions about myself as well as others, I observe the activities of the person in question, his or her tendencies, dispositions, and patterns of behavior in certain circumstances. Finally, if the mind is not a private arena of mental states, the dualist asks, how can the hypocrite be outwardly contrite while he remains inwardly unrepentant? Ryle says we judge that someone is contrite from his or her gestures, accents, words, and deeds. If we were not usually correct in making inferences from such behavior, the hypocrite could not deceive us by simulating this behavior. To conclude, Ryle would, perhaps, say that whether or not you consider his own philosophical intellect to be brilliant or mediocre, you did not find this out by peering into the hidden recesses of his mind. Any judgments you make about a philosopher's intellectual powers are necessarily made on the basis of the publicly available data of his or her scholarly achievements.

John Austin

John Austin (1911–1960) was a professor of moral philosophy at Oxford University from 1952 until his death in 1960. He once said that early in his career he had to choose between publishing as much as possible or devoting the major portion of his time to teaching. He chose to concentrate on

training students in the philosophical method he had developed and so did not publish as much as some of his contemporaries. Nevertheless, the few journal articles he published during his lifetime created a stir because of the new techniques he had developed for analyzing concepts. Happily, several books published after his death enabled the philosophical community to benefit from the labors of this great mind. The essays he wrote were collected under the title *Philosophical Papers* (1961). A reconstruction of Austin's lectures and notes on the theory of perception were published, as *Sense and Sensibilia* (1964). Finally, a series of lectures he gave at Harvard University in 1955 were published, as *How to Do Things with Words* (1962). All three books have since become classics within analytic philosophy.

AUSTIN'S PHILOSOPHICAL METHOD

Unlike Wittgenstein, Austin believes philosophy can make a positive contribution to the understanding of our language and concepts rather than simply serving as a therapy to our linguistic pathology. In response to the question "How many kinds of sentence are there?" Wittgenstein gave the inexact reply "There are *countless* kinds" (PI §23). However, Austin thinks we can classify various forms of expression much as a botanist classifies species of flowers, producing an orderly array. He thinks that analyzing and cataloguing the rich and diverse varieties of linguistic phenomena is worthwhile in itself, independently of the practical results of eliminating conceptual confusions. Austin does not claim the analysis of ordinary language is the only method that should be used in philosophy, but he insists it is a useful one. As he says, "Ordinary language is *not* the last word: in principle it can everywhere be supplemented and improved upon and superseded. Only remember, it is the *first* word" (PE 386).[29]

Austin lists several reasons why the analysis of ordinary language is important to philosophy. First, "words are our tools, and, as a minimum, we should use clean tools: we should know what we mean and what we do not, and we must forearm ourselves against the traps that language sets us." Second, since our ways of speaking (like biological species) have evolved over a long period of time, those that have endured are likely to be the most effective ones. As Austin expresses it,

> Our common stock of words embodies all the distinctions men have found worth drawing, and the connexions they have found worth marking, in the lifetimes of many generations: these surely are likely to be more numerous, more sound, since they have stood up to the long test of the survival of the fittest, and more subtle, at least in all ordinary and reasonably practical matters, than any that you or I are likely to think up in our arm-chairs of an afternoon—the most favoured alternative method. (PE 383–384)

Finally, linguistic analysis is not simply words about words, even though words and things must not be confused. Careful attention to words can give us insight into the world of experience:

> When we examine what we should say when, what words we should use in what situations, we are looking again not merely at words (or "meanings," whatever they may be) but also at the realities we use the words to talk about: we are using a sharpened awareness of words to sharpen our perception of, though not as the final arbiter of, the phenomena. (PE 384)

AUSTIN'S ANALYSIS OF EXCUSES

Austin's seminal essay "A Plea for Excuses" gives us a paradigm example of the method of conceptual analysis. Instead of offering us a full-scale ethical theory, Austin uses his conceptual microscope to focus in on one, manageable area of ethical discourse, namely, those situations where we offer excuses for our actions. Nevertheless, he is convinced this sort of microanalysis will be useful for ethics because it will help clarify the nature of action, the differences between permissible and prohibited acts, as well as the notions of responsibility, blame, and freedom. When we want to offer an excuse for an action we performed that was unacceptable in some way, we use such words as "involuntarily," "inadvertently," "accidentally," "unwillingly," "unintentionally," and so on. He notices that some words come paired in positive and negative forms, such as "voluntarily" and "involuntarily," but some

words do not have these dual forms. For example, I can knock over the teacup *inadvertently* when I pass the butter. But if I did not upset the cream jug, I did not avoid it *advertently*. Furthermore, he argues that contrary to appearances, "voluntarily" and "involuntarily" are not true opposites. When we did not do something voluntarily, we did not do it involuntarily either, but we did it under constraint, under duress, or in some other way were compelled by factors that impinged on us. However, the opposite of an involuntarily action is one done deliberately, on purpose, or the like. Furthermore, these terms do not exhaust the possibilities, for when I do something routine such as eating breakfast, we do not say I did it either voluntarily or involuntarily unless some extraordinary circumstances require one of these descriptions. In this way, Austin shows the connections, the differences, and the subtle nuances among these important words in our moral vocabulary.

HOW TO DO THINGS WITH WORDS

Wittgenstein employed the notion of "language-games" to indicate that speaking is not simply making sounds but is a type of activity. Similarly, in his important work *How to Do Things with Words*, Austin introduces the notion of "speech acts." Whenever someone says something, a number of distinguishable acts are performed. First, the *locutionary act* is simply the act *of* uttering (or writing) a set of words with a certain meaning. Second, the *illocutionary act* is what a person intentionally does *in* performing the locutionary act (such as reporting, warning, confessing, suggesting, ordering). Third, the *perlocutionary act* consists of the actual response on the part of the listener the speaker hopes to bring about *by* performing the illocutionary act (for example, persuade, deceive, frighten, inspire, and so on).

To illustrate Austin's analysis, I can say, "It is raining outside" (locutionary act). In saying this, there are several possibilities as to what action I am actually performing (illocutionary act): reporting a fact, expressing dismay at the weather, suggesting that you stay, telling a lie, and so on. Let us suppose I am simply reporting a fact. Then, by means of this act, there is some effect on the listener I am intending to bring about (perlocutionary act). For example, I could be trying to get the listener to *believe* correctly it is raining, *distract* the listener from her self-pity, *cause* the listener to realize that the driving will be dangerous, and so on. As a result of Austin's investigations, speech act theory has blossomed into a very complex but fruitful approach to understanding language. From this brief account it is clear the theory of language has come a long way from Russell's view that the function of language is simply to refer to a fact in the world.

The Significance of Analytic Philosophy

The analytic movement has provided philosophy with new methods, new tools, and new territories for philosophical exploration. It has made philosophers aware of the importance of language both as a philosophical resource and as an impediment to clear understanding. Its importance is signified by such slogans as "the linguistic turn in philosophy" and "the revolution in philosophy" that have been used to describe its impact. Analytic philosophy, in all its different varieties, has become dominant in the English-speaking world and has produced many brilliant practitioners of the method as well as a wealth of illuminating, twentieth-century philosophical classics. No one can be a serious student of philosophy today without giving careful attention to the accomplishments of this movement.

Despite the influence of analytic philosophy, however, it has had its detractors. For the most part, Marxist philosophers have never been fond of it. Herbert Marcuse, a contemporary Marxist theorist, describes it as "one-dimensional philosophy."[30] He claims that ordinary language contains the sedimented ideology of the prevailing power structures. Hence Wittgenstein's assurance that philosophy "leaves everything as it is" prevents any sort of radical critique and change of the status quo. Those within the Continental (European) movements of phenomenology and existentialism

charge that an analysis of language is irrelevant because our current ways of speaking may obscure rather than reveal the rich dimensions of our lived experience, which they think is the proper subject of philosophical exploration. The last few decades of the twentieth century, however, have seen signs of increased understanding between the proponents of these diverse philosophical movements. Some have made attempts to build bridges from both sides of the gulf between analytic and Continental philosophy in order to learn from the insights of the opposing camp.

Questions for Understanding

1. What are three fundamental points of agreement among analytic philosophers?
2. What are the five stages of analytic philosophy?
3. Why did Russell call his philosophy "logical atomism"?
4. Why did Russell believe there was a need to construct an ideal language?
5. In Russell's ideal language, what are atomic propositions and molecular propositions and how are these related to atomic facts?
6. What sorts of things are logical constructions, according to Russell?
7. According to Russell, what is the nature of a logically proper name? In his later work, what was the only expression he would have recognized as a logically proper name?
8. What were the three main goals of the logical positivists?
9. What are the two kinds of genuine knowledge according to the logical positivists?
10. What are tautologies?
11. What is the verifiability principle? Why was it modified several times and in what ways?
12. Why did the logical positivists say the statements of metaphysics and theology are not simply false but meaningless?
13. What were the two different ways logical positivists explained ethical statements?
14. What was the task of Wittgenstein's *Tractatus*?

15. What was the earlier Wittgenstein's picture theory of language?

16. What were the implications of Wittgenstein's *Tractatus* for traditional philosophy?

17. Why did Wittgenstein call his own propositions in the *Tractatus* "nonsensical"?

18. In the *Tractatus*, why does Wittgenstein refer to "the mystical"?

19. In what ways was Wittgenstein's philosophy different in his later period?

20. In spite of all the differences, what were the common concerns in both Wittgenstein's earlier and later work?

21. What features of language is Wittgenstein drawing our attention to in using the expression "language-games"?

22. What is Wittgenstein's point concerning "family resemblances"?

23. What does Wittgenstein suggest is a good way to view the meaning of a word?

24. What does Wittgenstein mean by "forms of life"? What does he say about their justification?

25. Why does the later Wittgenstein think there is no need for a special philosophical language or an ideal language?

26. Why does Wittgenstein speak of philosophy as a kind of therapy in his later period?

27. What does Gilbert Ryle mean by "category mistakes"? What are some examples?

28. According to Ryle, what is Descartes's "myth"? What is Ryle's remedy to Descartes's way of talking about the mind?

29. What account does Ryle give of each of the following: acting intelligently, acting voluntarily, self-knowledge? In what way do his explanations attempt to undermine Descartes's notion that the mind is a separate entity in which special mental activities take place?

30. What is J. L. Austin's philosophical method?

31. What is the distinction Austin makes between locutionary, illocutionary, and perlocutionary acts? How does his account of language differ from the view that the purpose of language is simply to refer to a fact in the world?

Questions for Reflection

1. Take a philosophical problem that you have encountered previously. How might an analytic philosopher translate that problem into one concerning the meaning and use of our terms?

2. Browse through the previous chapters and find philosophical claims that would be rejected as meaningless by the logical positivists. Do you agree with their verdict on these claims?

3. What are the strengths and weaknesses of the verifiability principle?

4. Taking the standpoint of the later Wittgenstein, Ryle, or Austin, argue against the thesis that the purpose of language is simply to name objects in the world.

5. Think of examples that illustrate Wittgenstein's and Ryle's claim that philosophical pseudo-problems can result from misunderstanding the use of a word.

Notes

1. Moritz Schlick, "The Future of Philosophy," in *The Linguistic Turn: Recent Essays in Philosophical Method*, ed. Richard Rorty (Chicago: University of Chicago Press, 1967), 48.

2. This method of organizing the positions is taken from Barry R. Gross, *Analytic Philosophy: An Historical Introduction* (New York: Pegasus, 1970), 13–14.

3. Bertrand Russell, *My Philosophical Development* (New York: Simon & Schuster, 1959), 11.

4. Bertrand Russell, *Portraits from Memory and Other Essays* (London: Allen & Unwin, 1956), 53.

5. This example was taken from Jerrold J. Katz, *The Underlying Reality of Language and Its Philosophical Import* (New York: Harper Torchbooks, Harper & Row, 1971), 6.

6. Bertrand Russell, "Logical Atomism," in *Contemporary British Philosophy*, vol. 1, ed. J. H. Muirhead (London: Allen & Unwin, 1924), 377.

7. Bertrand Russell, *The Philosophy of Logical Atomism*, ed. David Pears (La Salle, IL: Open Court, 1985), 58.

8. Russell, *My Philosophical Development*, 169.

9. Russell, *The Philosophy of Logical Atomism*, 86.

10. Bertrand Russell, "The Relation of Sense-Data to Physics," in his *Mysticism and Logic* (Garden City, NY: Doubleday Anchor Books, 1957), 150.

11. Bertrand Russell, *Human Knowledge, Its Scope and Limits* (New York: Simon & Schuster, 1948), 488.

12. Russell, *Human Knowledge*, 495.

13. Bertrand Russell, "Reply to Criticisms," in *The Philosophy of Bertrand Russell*, The Library of Living Philosophers, vol. 5, ed. Paul A. Schilpp (Evanston, IL: Northwestern University, 1944), 719.

14. Bertrand Russell, "My Mental Development," in *The Philosophy of Bertrand Russell*, 19.

15. David Hume, *An Enquiry Concerning Human Understanding*, sec. 12, pt. 3.

16. A. J. Ayer, *Language, Truth and Logic* (New York: Dover, n.d.), 36.

17. Rudolf Carnap, *Philosophy and Logical Syntax*, in *Readings in Twentieth-Century Philosophy*, ed. William P. Alston and George Nakhnikian (New York: The Free Press of Glencoe, Macmillan, 1963), 432.

18. A. J. Ayer, 107–108.

19. Rudolf Carnap, "The Physical Language as the Universal Language of Science," in *Readings in Twentieth-Century Philosophy*, 393–394.

20. A. J. Ayer, "Editor's Introduction," in *Logical Positivism*, ed. A. J. Ayer (New York: The Free Press, 1959), 15–16.

21. Hermine Wittgenstein, "My Brother Ludwig," trans. Bernhard Leitner in *Ludwig Wittgenstein: Personal Recollections*, ed. Rush Rhees (Totowa, NJ: Rowman & Littlefield, 1981), 2.

22. Ludwig Wittgenstein, *Tractatus Logico-Philosophicus*, trans. D. F. Pears and B. F. McGuinness (London: Routledge & Kegan Paul, 1961). Block quotations from this work place the paragraph numbers in the left margin as in the original. Short quotations within the text place the paragraph numbers at the end in parentheses, and the abbreviation "T" indicates the *Tractatus*.

23. Quoted in Paul Engelmann, *Letters from Ludwig Wittgenstein, with a Memoir*, ed. B. F. McGuinness, trans. L. Furtmüller (New York: Horizon Press, 1974), 144.

24. Ludwig Wittgenstein, "Wittgenstein's Lecture on Ethics," *The Philosophical Review*, 74, no. 1 (January 1965), 13.

25. The following abbreviations are used to refer to works from Wittgenstein's later period.

    BB   "The Blue Book" in *The Blue and Brown Books* (New York: Harper & Row, Harper Torchbooks, 1958). Numbers in the citation refer to page numbers.

    PI   *Philosophical Investigations*, trans. G. E. M. Anscombe (New York: Macmillan, 1953). Numbers in the citation refer to section numbers, except when the passage is from part II of the book, in which case the numbers are page numbers.

26. Stanley Cavell, "The Availability of Wittgenstein's Later Philosophy," *The Philosophical Review*, 71 (1962), reprinted in *Wittgenstein: The Philosophical Investigations*, ed. George Pitcher (New York: Anchor Books, Doubleday, 1966), 160–161.

27. Quoted in Garth Hallett, *A Companion to Wittgenstein's "Philosophical Investigations"* (Ithaca, NY: Cornell University Press, 1977), 195.

28. Gilbert Ryle, *The Concept of Mind* (New York: Barnes & Noble, 1949). References to this work are abbreviated "CM," and the numbers refer to page numbers.

29. John Austin, "A Plea for Excuses," *Proceedings of the Aristotelian Society*, n.s., 57 (1956–1957), reprinted in *Classics of Analytic Philosophy*, ed. Robert R. Ammerman (New York: McGraw-Hill, 1965). References to this work are abbreviated "PE."

30. Herbert Marcuse, *One-Dimensional Man* (Boston: Beacon Press, 1964), chap. 7.

CHAPTER

33

Phenomenology and Existentialism

WHEN WE TURN FROM THE ANALYTIC PHILOSO-
phy that flourished on British and American terrain, to the philosophies that developed on
European soil in the twentieth century, we find
ourselves in an entirely different world. The Continental movements of phenomenology and existentialism were concerned with questions such as
"What is consciousness?" and "What does it mean
to be a person?" However, the phenomenologists
and existentialists saw no use in analyzing how we
use the *words* "consciousness" or "person," for this
would only give us the unclarified assumptions
and residues of our historical traditions. Instead,
they believed we must look to the *experience* of
being a conscious person to answer these questions. However, it will be clear that the notion of
"experience" that underlies their investigations is
a far cry from the analytical, scientific model of
classical empiricism.

Although their roots go back to such
nineteenth-century figures as Søren Kierkegaard, Friedrich Nietzsche, and Fyodor Dostoevsky, most of the twentieth-century Continental

thinkers cannot be understood apart from the
work of Edmund Husserl, the founder of phenomenology. Many seminal figures in twentieth-
century Continental thought either studied with
Husserl or studied his writings. There is a great
deal of irony in Husserl's impact, however, for his
philosophical offspring were influenced as much
by the insights of his philosophy as they were by
those features they considered dead wrong. The
existentialists, for example, gave philosophy a new
agenda by focusing on the dark, shadowy side of
human existence with their analyses of such phenomena as anxiety, dread, guilt, and death. They
were equally at home expressing their philosophy
in terms of poetry, novels, and plays and writing
ponderously worded philosophical essays. In
striking contrast, Husserl, their intellectual men-
tor, received his training in mathematics and took
it as his goal to make philosophy into a "rigorous
science." It is an interesting case study of philosophical "genetics," therefore, to find the seed in
Husserl's philosophy and method that gave birth
to such unlikely offspring.

527

EDMUND HUSSERL

|||

The Life of a Perpetual Beginner

Edmund Husserl (1859–1938) was born the same year in which Bergson and Dewey were born. He studied physics, astronomy, and mathematics at the University of Leipzig, continued his education in Berlin, and finally earned his doctorate at the University of Vienna in 1883 with a dissertation on mathematical theory. The turning point in his life occurred when he attended the lectures of the German philosopher and psychologist Franz Brentano in Vienna from 1884 to 1886. Under Brentano's influence, Husserl discovered that his true calling was philosophy. After several teaching appointments, he settled in at the University of Freiburg in 1916 where he remained until his retirement in 1928.

Although Husserl was Jewish, he had converted to Protestant Christianity in his twenties. Nevertheless, when the Nazis rose to power, this did not exempt him from their anti-Semitism. After 1933 Husserl was forbidden to engage in academics. He published several major works and numerous, lengthy articles. In addition, he left behind a massive collection of 45,000 pages of handwritten manuscript, recorded in shorthand and preserved in the Husserl Archives in Louvain, Belgium. His working notes are so extensive because he described himself as a "perpetual beginner" who had to continually rethink everything he had done before. In 1938 Edmund Husserl died at the age of seventy-nine, sparing him from the worst of the Nazi terrors to come.

Husserl's Task: Developing Philosophy into a Rigorous Science

The driving force throughout Husserl's career was the quest for certainty. As he noted in his diary,

> I have been through enough torments from lack of clarity and doubt that wavers back and forth. . . . Only one need absorbs me: I must win clarity, else I cannot live; I cannot bear life unless I believe that I shall achieve it.[1]

Husserl believed that Western culture was in a state of crisis because we have lost our belief that we can attain rational certainty. Among other consequences, this led to irrationalism in the social and political realm, an irrationalism that would eventually produce the bitter fruit of Nazism. Furthermore, by neglecting the foundations of our knowledge, the theoretical sciences were drifting, having ignored their roots in the activities of consciousness that produced them. As his thought developed, Husserl realized that the crisis of rational certainty was also a crisis of meaning. The sciences had severed themselves from their origins in pretheoretical experience (called the "life-world") where all meaning is constituted.

As Husserl saw it, a major cause of the crisis of the modern world was an outlook known as naturalism. **Naturalism** claims that physical nature encompasses everything real and that all reality can be exhaustively explained by the natural sciences.* But this implies that consciousness itself is just another item of nature that can be explained by the laws of physics, chemistry, and biology. Husserl argued, however, that if consciousness and our beliefs are simply products of blind and irrational physical causes, then we cannot have rational, justified beliefs (including the belief in naturalism). Dismissing these theories that undermine the foundations of knowledge, Husserl began the search for rational certainty where Descartes before him had sought it, by looking within to consciousness. Accordingly, he titled one of his books

---

*In the early years of his career, Husserl himself had embraced a form of naturalism known as *psychologism*. His first book, *The Philosophy of Arithmetic*, was an attempt to base the foundations of arithmetic on certain generalizations about human psychology. However, through the criticisms of the mathematician and logician Gottlob Frege, Husserl came to see that logic and mathematics contain *a priori*, necessary truths that cannot be reduced to the empirical truths of psychology.

Cartesian Meditations and closed it with a line from Augustine: "Do not wish to go out; go back into yourself. Truth dwells in the inner man." But if consciousness is to provide us with the foundations of knowledge, Husserl thought it must be approached in a special way. Hence, he spent his life charting a new course for philosophy.

Phenomenology as a Science of Experience

Husserl proposes a *method*, the method of phenomenology, which not only guides us in discovering new truths but also enables us to test the rational adequacy of any truth claim. Husserl's understanding of phenomenology has affinities with Hegel's massive work *The Phenomenology of Spirit*. For Hegel and Husserl alike, phenomenology is a systematic study of the phenomena, or of what appears within experience. By denying that any meaningful content exists in the notion of a reality that is, in principle, inaccessible to reason, both wish to avoid the trap Kant fell into when he postulated the unknowable "things in themselves." They both argue that once we suppose there is such a gap between the phenomena and reality, then skepticism is unavoidable.

Husserl's goal is to find an approach to philosophical truth that will be "presuppositionless." Minimally, Husserl meant by this claim that philosophers should not use any assumptions in their investigations that have not been thoroughly examined, clarified, and justified. The fundamental philosophical rule is to accept only what is directly evident. As Husserl puts it, there can be no higher justification for the truth of a claim than "I see that it is so" (I 76).[2]

The uniqueness of phenomenology is indicated by the fact that it can be characterized as both a type of rationalism and a radical empiricism. It is a rationalism because it searches for *a priori* principles and essences that are more than inductive generalizations and are known through rational intuition. Yet it is also a form of empiricism because it justifies its claims by reference to experience. It is a "radical" empiricism because

phenomenologists claim they are more empirical, more faithful to experience, than those who traditionally have called themselves *empiricists*. Phenomenology has a richer, broader, and deeper notion of experience than the British empiricists and most of the twentieth-century analysts. According to phenomenology, the content of experience includes more than the sensory impressions that come through the five senses. For example, Husserl claims we may also "experience" numbers, geometrical figures, ideal entities, universals, the meanings of propositions, values, moral duties, aesthetic qualities, and (perhaps) religious phenomena.* Furthermore, Husserl claims that perceptual experience is not the collection of discrete, unrelated sensations Hume talked about. According to Husserl, this picture is not what experience presents to us, but is the result of imposing onto experience the empiricists' *theory* of what they think experience *must* be like. Nobody experiences Hume's units of red-spherical-sweet sense data. Instead, we experience such things as apples, tomatoes, and cherries. At best, such sense data are abstractions artificially lifted out of certain moments within the complex unity of experience.

The Phenomenological Method

THE THESIS OF THE NATURAL STANDPOINT

According to Husserl, the phenomenological method involves taking a certain stance toward experience. All experiencing prior to our phenomenological investigations is characterized by what Husserl calls the "natural standpoint" or the "natural attitude." This is a particular way of viewing the world that is based on a number of unquestioned and implicit assumptions. The most basic assumption is that the external world is a

---

*Husserl himself never applied the phenomenological method to religious experience. However, besides the fact that he became a Protestant, his view of philosophy was such that he was as open to religious phenomena as he was to any genuine experience. Some thinkers who came after him did try to develop a phenomenology of religion.

spatiotemporal realm that exists independently of our consciousness and consists of objects that experience reveals to us (chairs, coffee cups, books, trees, and so on). Among the items in this world there are minds: my mind, your mind, and our neighbors' minds. In our everyday life we are immersed in our practical concerns and carry on our commerce with people and things in terms of this standpoint. To free us from this taken-for-granted standpoint, Husserl developed a number of techniques that would allow us to get back to pure experience, freeing it of the overlays and theories that philosophers have imported into experience.

BRACKETING THE WORLD

The point of departure for the phenomenological method is the "bracketing" of the world. This is done by initiating a shift of attention in which we take up a different stance from that of our everyday dealings with the world to clarify the sense and the structure of the world and our engagements with it. Husserl also called this procedure the phenomenological reduction or *epoche*.* This means that the world and its objects, as well as our beliefs about them, are put in mental brackets so that we can view this panorama of phenomena with a sense of objectivity and detachment. Besides initiating this shift of attention, bracketing also includes suspending judgment about the existence of the world as well as any theories about the causes of phenomena that appear within it.

Husserl's technique of withholding or disconnecting our beliefs about the world was inspired by Descartes's method of doubt. Unlike Descartes, however, Husserl is not asking us to doubt the existence of the world or our prephilosophical beliefs. Instead, the phenomenological reduction leaves everything within the natural standpoint as it was, except now we put our beliefs "out of action" and do not use them in describing experience. In other words, I do not cease believing in the world, but now I see it as "a-world-that-is-believed-in."

Epoche was the term used by the Greek skeptics when they recommended we withhold our commitment and suspend judgment about things that were uncertain.

Whereas previous philosophers theorized about experience, leading to a number of distortions, Husserl proposes a disciplined method of pure description. Phenomenological description explains the layers and strata within experience by making thematic what is operative and making explicit what is implicit, without adding to or subtracting from the phenomena:

> This cannot be emphasized often enough—phenomenal explication does nothing but explicate the sense this world has for us all prior to any philosophizing, and obviously gets solely from our experience—a sense which philosophy can uncover but never alter. (CM 151)

The basic thrust of Husserl's entire philosophy could be encapsulated in his famous slogan "To the things themselves!"

CONSCIOUSNESS AS INTENTIONALITY

One significant result of stepping back from the world and putting it in brackets is that consciousness is no longer submerged in the background of experience, but comes to the forefront of my reflective awareness. Ordinarily, when I am engaged with the world in the natural attitude, I have relatively little self-awareness, because I mainly attend to the objects of experience. However, when the world is put in brackets, when I am no longer straightforwardly engaged in it, I discover consciousness is at work in all my experiences. The next step in phenomenology is to uncover what we find when we bring consciousness to the center stage of our investigation.

Unlike Descartes, Husserl finds that when we examine consciousness, we do not discover some sort of metaphysical substance. Consciousness does not have the qualities of a thing—not even a ghostly thing. At the same time, Hume and the empiricists were wrong to suppose we find nothing but a flow of sensations. What we do find, Husserl insists, is a certain structure that we can describe independently of its particular contents. The turn to consciousness discloses not an entity but a series of acts of awareness that are always correlated

the intentional act (the experience): noetic correlate
the object of that act (what is experienced): noematic correlate

with some object. This, then, is the essential feature of consciousness. Consciousness is always a consciousness-*of* some object or another. This is known as Husserl's "doctrine of intentionality." Here "intentionality" does *not* mean the purpose of an action, as when we ask, "Did you intend to harm your opponent?" Instead, "intentionality" refers to that feature of consciousness characterized as tending toward, pointing to, or directedness toward an object. Since these two poles of experience are always correlated, the intentional act (the experiencing) is called the *noetic correlate*, and the object of that act (what is experienced) is the *noematic correlate*.

Two qualifications are necessary to understand Husserl's notion of intentionality. First, even though consciousness is essentially referential, its objects do not need to exist; for example, I can think of a unicorn or the perfect society. Second, the objects of consciousness are not always *physical* objects (real or imagined). For example, I can doubt a proposition, think about a prime number, worry about the emotional tone of a meeting, admire the values of another culture, desire moral goodness, or recognize the universal of redness as something different from red objects.

THE DISCOVERY OF ESSENCES

Husserl is not interested in simply an empirical, psychological description of various kinds of experiences. The search for certainty requires that we discover the essential features of the phenomena. Hence, the next step in Husserl's phenomenological method is what he calls the *eidetic reduction*. This is the process of reducing the phenomena to essences. The essence of something is its defining characteristics, what makes it the sort of thing it is. Essences are not discovered by means of empirical generalizations or abstractions from particulars, but through direct intuition. Suppose, for example, the phenomenon I am examining is perception and I begin by considering the specific case of my-seeing-an-apple. For the phenomenologist, the ultimate focus is not on the particular features of this concrete experience but on the essence of each of the three elements of the

experience. In other words, the phenomenologist uses this experience to examine what it means to be (1) a consciousness for whom there can be perceived objects, (2) an act of perceiving, and (3) a perceptual object. Through an exhaustive series of phenomenological investigations, Husserl hoped to uncover the sense that phenomena have for us, those acts through which the phenomena are revealed, and the ground of all meanings and human engagements in consciousness.

Transcendental Phenomenology

Husserl became increasingly radical in his later writings as he placed more emphasis on the role of consciousness in experience. Talk of consciousness as an activity became transformed into talk about a "transcendental ego" that is identical throughout its acts. Husserl had hoped to find a middle road between realism and idealism. However, there was always an ambiguity or a tension in Husserl's phenomenology that he could not resolve and that drove him, according to some interpreters, into the ranks of the idealists.

The tension in Husserl's position comes out in the following passage:

> *Objects exist for me, and are for me what they are, only as objects of actual and possible consciousness.* (CM 65)

The moderate interpretation of this would be that only through consciousness are things present to us as meaningful entities. The more radical interpretation is that things depend entirely on consciousness for their existence. The problem is, once we have bracketed the world to study what appears to consciousness, can we find some basis for asserting the world's objectivity and independence from the mind, apart from slipping back into the natural attitude?

This problem emerges as Husserl's understanding of the relation between consciousness and objects develops. In his earlier writings, he says the objects we experience are *given* in intuition (experience). Here, consciousness plays a partially passive role as the various aspects and structures of the phenomena reveal themselves to us. In his later writings, Husserl speaks of the phenomena as *constituted* by consciousness. For example, it is through the activities of a constituting consciousness that my experience of someone begins to take shape, from the initial perceptual data, to my observations of his or her behavior, then to the further level of the style and content of their speech, and so on. Layer by layer, "sedimentations" of meanings build up as consciousness constitutes the objects within experience. The process by which the many dimensions of a phenomenon take shape and are constituted in consciousness is studied by means of what Husserl called "genetic phenomenology." The question that remains throughout all this concerns the extent to which consciousness is active or passive in apprehending the phenomena and whether the objects constitute themselves or are constituted by consciousness.

Even some of Husserl's admirers worried that his later position had elevated the active role of the transcendental ego to the point that he had surrendered to idealism. There seemed to be a fine and fast-disappearing line between the notion of consciousness *constituting* the objects of experience and the transcendental ego *constructing* them. The following example illustrates how this issue arises. As I type this, I am perceiving a nearby coffee mug. However, it does not seem to depend on my mind, but seems to be an object existing across the room, sitting on the table by the window. Yet, for Husserl, we cannot escape the fact that when we call something "an objective and independently existing object" we are referring to an intentional object whose appearance has the aspect of *being-independent-of-me*, and this aspect is nothing more than the sense and meaning it has for consciousness. All our talk about realities apart from consciousness is always talk about one way in which objects can appear *to* consciousness. In the final analysis it seems that consciousness reigns supreme throughout the world.

The Shift to the Life-World

Toward the end of his life, Husserl moved from talking of the transcendental individual ego to focusing on the intersubjective community of individuals along with a social conception of cognition. Although we can only speculate on the causes of this shift, we can argue that it follows from his own view of consciousness. I do not simply experience the coffee mug, but I experience it as being on the table, which is by the window, which is located in my office, and so on. This process of the continually expanding horizons of any experience eventually leads to a sense of the totality or the horizon of all horizons. This all-inclusive region of ordinary experience, out of which all meanings must emerge, is what Husserl called the life-world (*Lebenswelt*). It is the total background of our pretheoretical experience. Yet Husserl discovered that even the world of everyday lived-experience has *a priori* structures for the phenomenologist to discover and explicate.

Since the Enlightenment, people had been increasingly convinced that it is science that truly reveals reality to us and that all other ways of comprehending our experience must be subservient to the scientific outlook. Husserl observes, however, that scientists are first and foremost human beings living in the world of everyday experience before they formulate their theories. Behind the objective, scientific account of the world is the scientist as a center of subjective consciousness, who is engaging in the mental activities of observing, counting, calculating, hypothesizing, theorizing, and explaining. But naturalism either ignores this fact or explains it away by supposing that these conscious acts of the scientist herself are just one more set of objective events in the world.

Notice that in scientific journals the subject is mysteriously missing in the report of an experiment. A laboratory report may say, "The test tube was heated, and a white precipitate formed." A more accurate account would say, instead, "*I* heated the test tube and waited with expectation until *I* observed a white precipitate forming, at which point *I* bubbled with excitement as *I* realized that *my* theory had been confirmed." For this reason, scientists are what Husserl called "self-forgetful theorizers." Everything a scientist does, whether reading her instruments, proposing hypotheses, or formulating theories, is an abstraction from what is first given in the concrete experiences within the life-world.

Many philosophers (Bertrand Russell, for example) believe the scientific outlook has replaced or invalidated the perspective of the life-world. In Husserl's account, however, the life-world is now revealed as the source of all meaning and concepts from which scientists begin their task:

> The investigator of nature, however, does not make it clear to himself that the constant foundation of his admittedly subjective thinking activity is the environing world of life. The latter is constantly presupposed as the basic working area, in which alone his questions and his methodology make sense. (PCEM 185)

According to Husserl, science gives us an "idealized and naively objectivized nature." He does not discount the fruitfulness of such an abstract, mathematical reformulation of the world, for he says science is "a triumph of the human spirit." Instead, Husserl simply insists we must remember that the world science presents us is an artificially structured world and that only by means of the conscious acts of the scientist as a subject has such a world been constituted.

Husserl's Significance

THE INFLUENCE OF PHENOMENOLOGY

The methods Husserl developed to understand the structures of experience have had a lasting influence on philosophy as well as the other disciplines. He helped spark a movement within the social sciences among those who believed the human subject cannot be understood on the same terms as the objects of the other sciences. Psychologists and sociologists who have been influenced by phenomenology claim that the human subject lives life from the inside out. Simply focusing on empirical facts, physical stimuli, and external causes will not explain human behavior, they say. Instead, the human sciences must understand how experience is structured by the subject and

must chart the structures of the life-world in terms of which the data are interpreted and made meaningful by the experiencing subject.

THE TRANSITION TO EXISTENTIAL PHENOMENOLOGY

The existentialists whom Husserl influenced, such as Martin Heidegger and Jean-Paul Sartre, modified the key features of his method. Two major points of disagreement arise between Husserl's conception of phenomenology and its existentialist versions. First, Husserl's focus on consciousness is too intellectualized, the existentialists claim. We are not simply cognitive spectators, holding the world at a distance as an object of contemplation. Hence Heidegger says we first engage with the world through concern and care, and only later do we intellectualize it. The existentialists focused on the experiences of anxiety, dread, guilt, aloneness, choosing, and the confrontation with the possibility of our own death as revelatory of the human situation. To translate these experiences into Husserlian terms of a conscious ego glaring at its intentional objects does not capture the reality of the human situation. Thus Husserl's notion of "intentionality" is broadened into a more general sort of precognitive engagement with the world.

Second, the existentialists who learned from Husserl dropped his method of bracketing the world. We are immersed in the world, they said, and cannot disconnect ourselves from it, as though it were nothing but a virtual reality displayed on the computer screen of the mind. As William Barrett expresses the problem that led Heidegger to reject Husserl's version of phenomenology,

> Husserl tells us we are to put within brackets absolutely everything that is given; but where does the given end, and suppose the reality of the world, as well as its appearance, is given? . . . The brackets bulge and break, the mass of the world is too great to be contained by them.[3]

MARTIN HEIDEGGER

|||

Heidegger's Life

Martin Heidegger (1889–1976) was born in a small town in southwest Germany in the region of the Black Forest. In the early part of his education he studied Catholic theology, preparing to enter the priesthood. While studying at the University of Freiburg, however, Heidegger became increasingly interested in philosophy and his change of focus became solidified under the influence of Edmund Husserl, then a professor at Freiburg. After receiving his doctorate, Heidegger worked for five years as Husserl's assistant. In 1923 he left to fill a chair in philosophy at the University of Marburg. In 1927 his extraordinarily influential work, *Being and Time*, appeared, dedicated to Husserl. On Husserl's recommendation, Heidegger was elected as his teacher's successor to the chair of philosophy in Freiburg in 1929.

When Hitler came to power in 1933, Heidegger joined the Nazi Party. Shortly after Hitler set up his new regime, Heidegger was appointed rector of the University of Freiburg, but resigned this post early in 1934. Although Heidegger made a number of statements supporting the Nazi movement, scholars continue to debate how long and to what degree he enthusiastically supported this ideology. Furthermore, scholars continue to differ on whether or not his philosophical ideas can be separated from his political views and whether the one naturally leads to the other.

After the war, Heidegger never completed the promised second volume of *Being in Time*. Instead his thought seemed to shift, and he published a number of shorter works, in which he turned to poetry as a way of revealing what our ordinary ways of speaking and approaching the world have concealed. Even though he was married and had three children, he was reclusive by nature. He spent his last years in seclusion in a mountain retreat in the Black Forest, emerging only occasionally to give a public lecture. Martin Heidegger died in 1976.

Heidegger's Task: Understanding the Meaning of Being

Acknowledging his debt to Husserl, Heidegger writes in the frontispiece of *Being and Time* that the book is dedicated to his teacher "in friendship and admiration." However, the contents of the book make a radical break with Husserl's philosophy. The difference is illustrated by the fact that Husserl thought "The wonder of all wonders is the pure ego and pure consciousness."[4] By way of contrast, Heidegger says, "Man alone of all existing things . . . experiences the wonder of all wonders: that there are things-in-being."[5] While Husserl bracketed the world to focus on consciousness, Heidegger responds that there is no "pure consciousness." Consequently, he turns to wonder at the world. Heidegger's deviation from his teacher and the sensation caused by his new approach mark the beginnings of existentialism as a distinctive philosophical movement.

Unlike Husserl, Heidegger engages in **ontology**, the science of Being. To understand this, we must recognize the distinction Heidegger makes between beings (or particular objects) and Being (what is manifested in anything that is). As an example of the first case, we can say a dog is a being. To illustrate the second case, when a suicidal Hamlet says, "To be or not to be—that is the question," he is trying to decide between Being or non-Being (Be-ing or not Be-ing).* We live in a world of plural beings: people, trees, cars, carrots, stars, kittens—the list is endless. Specific beings come into existence and pass out of it. What characterizes the Being of things? It is important to understand that Being is not an entity, for this would make it simply one being alongside other beings. For this reason, Heidegger denies that Being is to be identified

---

*Other languages, such as Greek, Latin, French, and German, make a distinction absent in English between "the thing that is" and "the Being of the thing that is."

with God. He believes that in traditional theology God is considered simply the highest among beings. Falling back on metaphors, he says Being is the light that illumines everything else.[6]

We can get a glimpse of Being in that experience of wonder that provokes us to ask, "Why is there anything at all, rather than nothing?" (IM 1).[7] The broad appeal of this question is indicated by the fact that it has been asked by professional philosophers such as Leibniz as well as by four-year-olds. To wonder at Being is to be open to the presence of Being. But we quickly lose this sense of wonder and return back to the crush of daily life, becoming wrapped up in the objects and tasks around us.

Heidegger thinks the early Greeks knew how to wonder at Being. But with the rise of Greek science and philosophy they quickly began to isolate things from their encompassing background in order to submit them to rational analysis. This yielded many wonderful and practical results, but Western thought forgot Being. The task for Heidegger, therefore, is to deconstruct the whole history of Western metaphysics to recover a kind of thinking that is responsive to Being.

Heidegger's Radical Conception of Phenomenology

Following his teacher Husserl, Heidegger uses the method of phenomenology to carry out his project. Accordingly, we will find very little in Heidegger's writings that resembles a philosophical argument. Instead, he tries to draw our attention to features of our experience, revealing what we have missed, covered up, or ignored. His only method of convincing us is to trigger a disclosure experience within us that will make his conclusions evident.*

With Husserl, Heidegger describes phenomenology as "the science of phenomena." However, Heidegger disagrees with Husserl's attempt to bracket the world and peel back the layers of experience until we are left with an intuition of pure consciousness. As we will see, Heidegger claims Being cannot be bracketed or doubted, but can only be forgotten, for it is the fundamental phenomenon in which all others (including our own existence) are grounded and from which they derive their meaning. Heidegger's modification of Husserl's method was so radical that it split the phenomenological movement in two. It is now necessary to distinguish Husserlian phenomenology and Heideggerian existential phenomenology, the latter giving birth to twentieth-century existentialism.

Our Existence as a Window to Being

The problem in studying Being is not with the scarcity of the data, but with their abundance. Everything we encounter is a manifestation of Being. So where do we start if we want to study Being? Heidegger's answer is to pick out a particular disclosure of Being that will best illuminate it. Accordingly, he proposes that we begin ontology with a study of our existence. To disassociate his philosophy from previous treatments of the topic, Heidegger uses the term *Dasein* as a technical term to stand for our being. The German word *Dasein* literally means "being there."[†] We are characterized as "being there" in the sense that we are always situated or related to the world in a certain way. Unlike other entities (and unlike previous discussions of human "nature"), Dasein cannot be defined in terms of a set of fixed properties. Instead, we each are characterized as a set of possibilities and we have the responsibility of choosing what we will be. For this reason, Heidegger says an object "is," but only humans *exist*.

---

*Heidegger's method can be compared to that of the later Wittgenstein, who said that "the work of the philosopher consists in assembling reminders" and that "philosophy simply puts everything before us, and neither explains nor deduces anything." Ludwig Wittgenstein, *Philosophical Investigations*, trans. G. E. M. Anscombe (New York: Macmillan, 1953), §§ 127, 126.

---

†To retain the unique content of Heidegger's concept, *Dasein* is not translated in most English versions of Heidegger's texts. This text follows this convention, and henceforth we will treat the word as a technical term in English.

What about our existence makes it a privileged standpoint for studying Being? We are unique in that we are the only kind of entity in the world able to raise questions about what it means to be. Accordingly, Heidegger says Dasein is not one object among others, but a clearing in the midst of the otherwise dense forest of Being. A clearing is an opening where the light can stream in. Thus, Dasein represents the region in Being where the latter is most fully revealed. Although Heidegger gives a very perceptive analysis of human existence, it is important to understand that this is not his ultimate goal. His hope is always that an analysis of what it means to be the sort of beings we are will open a window onto the larger issue. "The analytic of Dasein . . . is to prepare the way for the problematic of fundamental ontology—*the question of the meaning of Being in general*" (BT 227).

Heidegger refers to the basic *a priori* features of human existence as existential structures or *existentialia* (we will translate this as *existentials*). Since Heidegger is trying to draw our attention to what has been forgotten, our ordinary language is inadequate. Thus, he has to construct a unique vocabulary to speak about the extraordinary. There are, then, two levels about which he speaks. The *ontic* level refers to particular, ordinary facts within daily life. "In the last year, I have begun to care more about the environment" is an ontic fact. However, the *ontological* level refers to the fundamental structures of human existence that provide the framework within which mundane, ontic facts appear. Hence, when Heidegger refers to such things as care, anxiety, guilt, or death, he is not speaking about ordinary ontic events, but is speaking ontologically. For example, Heidegger does not speak of *care* as a particular attitude of a particular individual. Instead, it is the basic relationship we have to our existence.

Heidegger begins his analysis of Dasein at the most generic level of human existence, the realm of average, everyday experience. This is the world in which we all live prior to any philosophical speculation. Yet even at this level we implicitly understand Being. By unpacking this understanding through interpretation (hermeneutic phenomenology), we can move from our naive immersion in the world to a fully ontological appreciation of what is the ground and meaning of all things. In so doing, Heidegger introduces a complex set of interrelated *existentials* that characterize our mode of existence. For our purposes, the *existentials* we need to discuss are Being-in-the-world, concern, facticity, Being-ahead, and fallenness.

Being-in-the-World

Heidegger radically breaks with the philosophical tradition, which tended to separate the knowing subject and the object of knowledge and treat them as distinct entities. Descartes, for example, identified himself with his consciousness and then worried about how he could know that this consciousness was related to an external world. Husserl, likewise, bracketed the world in order to focus on the nature of pure consciousness. However, Heidegger considers this the first step to skepticism, for once we assume consciousness can be meaningfully considered in isolation from the world, they become difficult to reunite. In modern philosophy this is sometimes known as "the problem of the subject–object dichotomy."

Heidegger sweeps aside the whole problem with a single, fundamental concept. He refers to Dasein as *Being-in-the-world*. The hyphens in this phrase indicate that Dasein cannot be separated from the world, for our existence is a world-embedded existence.* Hence, Being-in-the-world is a fundamental structure of human existence. To clarify this phrase, we will discuss, in turn, the phenomena of "Being-in" and "the world," and then explain Heidegger's fundamental epistemological category of "concern."

*In reading the English translations of Heidegger, you may get the impression that if his typewriter didn't have hyphens he couldn't philosophize. There are two reasons for this excessive use of hyphens. First, the German language has the facility for connecting many words to create one big word. Translating such words into individual English words without hyphens would lose the sense that the German word is expressing one, unified concept. Second, because Heidegger is trying to get at phenomena that are ignored by our ordinary ways of thinking, he sometimes must manufacture words in this way to express original ideas for which there is no standard term.

BEING-IN

The notion of Being-in when applied to human existence differs from that of "being contained in." We are in the world in a different sense from the sense in which water is in a glass. Dasein is not a thinglike entity spatially juxtaposed with other objects. Instead, we *dwell* in the world, we are taken up with it, we are absorbed in it. Being-in-the-world is not a spatial notion, for it is closer to what we mean when we talk about "being in love" or "being in college." In these cases I am talking about a situation in which I am involved, which is tied to my interests, aspirations, and projects. Hence, the most important feature of the world is not the *what* (a collection of objects), but the *how* (the manner in which things present themselves to me).

THE WORLD

Next, we need to examine the notion of "world" phenomenologically. From the fact that he could doubt the existence of any particular object, Descartes mistakenly concluded he could doubt the world itself. However, it is only in terms of the total background of the world that we can resolve questions concerning the existence or nonexistence of a particular object. According to Heidegger, we are not Cartesian minds isolated within our private, inner rooms peering out at an alien, external reality (BT 89). Instead, we are "out there" dealing with a world that is familiar and meaningful.

When Heidegger says we "belong to a world," he is not referring to a collection of objects such as planets, trees, buildings, or chairs. Instead, he is using the term much as we speak of "the world of Shakespeare," "the nineteenth-century world," "the world of sports," "the world of the artist," or "the world of the corporate executive." We speak of people (such as an artist, or an executive) as being "worlds apart," or say, "They live in different worlds," even though they may live and work on the same street. Ultimately, of course, we sense that these regional worlds overlap with a larger, public world. When the world is understood in this way, then it can never be doubted, for it is a fundamental feature of our existence.

Although the world is not a collection of objects, we do relate to particular entities in the world. What does a phenomenological analysis reveal about the objects within our experience? First and foremost, it reveals that we do not encounter "things." A thing is a spatially extended object we can describe in terms of its geometrical properties. When an object is present as an explicit object of consciousness to be analyzed in a detached way, Heidegger says it is *present-at-hand*. However, this sort of relationship is an intellectualized mode of apprehension derived from our more fundamental encounters with the world. What we first and foremost encounter are not present-at-hand things but meaningful *ready-at-hand* items. Heidegger refers to things that are ready-at-hand with a term (*Zeug*) that means "equipment," "utensils," "tools," "gear," or "instruments." Something is equipment when its mode of presence is that of being used in my practical engagements.

To illustrate the way objects are present to us as ready-at-hand, Heidegger analyzes the experience of using a hammer to do a task, as opposed to treating it as an object for cognitive inspection. However, any of the thousands of moments in our daily life when we are engaged with a "tool" (such as a pen, a musical instrument, one's eyeglasses, a tennis racquet, or a car) can serve equally as well to make his point. For example, when you start your car, you don't have to explicitly think to yourself, "This is my car—this is the steering wheel—I will now turn the key and start the engine." Instead, the car is like an extension of your body. The familiar routine of starting the engine and pulling out of the driveway is carried out with the same unreflective ease that your hand reaches for a nearby cup of coffee. The car is "equipment" (in Heidegger's technical sense). It is not in the forefront of your attention. Instead, you are probably focusing on your intended destination.

Contrary to classical empiricism, we encounter things first and foremost not as collections of sensations nor as members of logical categories, but as instruments within our lived-space that are available for our projects and needs. Normally, objects in themselves are "transparent" to us, for they are experienced exclusively in relationship to their functions. In other words, we relate to an object as a "something-in-order-to" or a "for-the-sake-of-which."* Only when there is some interruption or breakdown in our normal precognitive Being-in-the-world (the car will not start) do we consciously focus on our equipment, turning them into objects that are present-at-hand to be inspected and considered in terms of their properties.

CONCERN

An implicit theme that has run through this discussion can now come to center stage. Heidegger complains that our philosophical tradition has given us a one-sided and artificial account of our primary relationship to the world. "The phenomenon of Being-in has for the most part been represented exclusively by a single exemplar—knowing the world" (BT 86). If knowing is not our primary way of relating to the world, then what is? The clue to Heidegger's alternative to traditional epistemology is found in our everyday dealings with things.

> The kind of dealing which is closest to us is . . . not a bare perceptual cognition, but rather that kind of concern which manipulates things and puts them to use; and this has its own kind of "knowledge." (BT 95)

Hence, *concern* is what characterizes our Being-in-the-world. *Knowing*, in contrast, is a second-level activity derived from our original encounter with the world. This original relationship to the world is found in practical relationships such as

> having to do with something, producing something, attending to something and looking after it, making use of something, giving something up and letting it go, undertaking, accomplishing, evincing, interrogating, considering, discussing, determining. (BT 83)

I can minimize this attitude of concern by relating to things by means of "leaving undone, ne-

glecting, renouncing." But even in these cases, I never reach a completely neutral cognitive state, free of concern, for I am still expressing an attitude toward the things I encounter.

Heidegger's notion of "concern" could be viewed as a replacement for Husserl's notion of "intentionality." Both terms seek to describe how we are related to the world. However, Husserl tended to focus on acts of cognition such as perceiving, believing, asserting, judging, recalling, or thinking. For Heidegger, however, these more intellectual operations arise out of the precognitive level of concern. Descartes had it all wrong when he said, "I think, therefore I am." If Heidegger is correct, then the slogan should be "I *am*, therefore I think." What this means is that our brute immersion in the world precedes all cognitive activities.

Modes of Dasein

FACTICITY AND THROWNNESS

Heidegger says our existence is characterized by "facticity." By this he means we always find ourselves in a situation where certain "givens" structure our existence. Some are the result of past choices (for example, choosing to be a student places you within a certain set of structures). Other givens are thrust on you by the features of your personal history that you did not choose, such as the century in which you live and your place of birth, race, gender, intelligence, and personality. Your facticity makes you the *you* that you are. Related to facticity is the concept of "thrownness." Because there is no reason or purpose for the fact *that* you exist and exist as *this* person in *this* situation, it is almost as though you have been thrown into the world.

Heidegger says this sense of alienation is a mood that discloses our facticity and thrownness. *Moods* are forms of disclosure, because we do not engage the world only with the cerebral cortex of the brain, but with our whole being. We do not first see the world and then assign a value to it. Instead, we encounter the world as something "attuned" to our mood. A person we are dating is

*This is the cause of the humorous situation in which people frantically search for their glasses but forget that the only reason they can see well enough to search for anything is that they are already looking through the glasses! Looking *for* the glasses is to treat them as present-at-hand, while seeing *with* the glasses is to use them as ready-at-hand.

fascinating, the movie is boring, the icy road is threatening, the chocolate dessert is enticing, the dreary weather is depressing. These moods are not experienced simply as subjective states within us but as aspects of our relationship to the world itself. "A mood assails us. It comes neither from 'outside' nor from 'inside', but arises out of Being-in-the-world, as a way of such Being" (BT 176). Hence, cognition and our affective states cannot be divorced, for our moods disclose the character of the world to us. As we will see later, Heidegger believes the most important mood is anxiety or dread.

BEING-AHEAD-OF-MYSELF

Human beings, unlike billiard balls, do not relate only to what exists in their present environment. We are always living-ahead in the sense that our here-and-now is oriented toward future possibilities. A future possibility presents itself as something-I-can-be, but realizing this possibility constitutes part of what I am now. Your present life may be oriented around completing a degree, and mine toward finishing this book. Heidegger calls this feature of Dasein's existence "Being-ahead-of-itself." This is why Heidegger and the existentialists influenced by him do not believe there is such a thing as human nature. We do not have a static essence, for we are always "on the way," creating ourselves by realizing this possibility and not that one. As Kierkegaard discovered, the question to ask is not "Who am I?" but "What shall I become?"

FALLENNESS

Another aspect of our Being-in-the-world is *fallenness*. Heidegger sometimes speaks of it as Being-along-with-the-entities-in-the-world.* Although this tends to lead to an inauthentic way of relating to existence, Heidegger seems to suggest it also can be simply a neutral aspect of our everydayness. In this sense, we are necessarily and continually

---

*I have used "Being-along-with" to express the sense of intimacy that is lost in the phrase "Being-alongside" used in the published English translation.

"falling in with" the things in the world that elicit our concern. Heidegger also says this immersion in the world involves coexistence with other people. "The world is always the one that I share with Others. The world of Dasein is a *with-world*. Being-in is a *Being-with* Others" (BT 155). Once again, Heidegger rejects the Cartesian notion that we are private, isolated minds for whom the existence of the world and others becomes a philosophical problem. On the contrary, we can become selves only in interaction with other selves.

Although *falling in with* and being involved with the things and people in my situation is an inescapable feature of my Being-in-the-world, I can lose myself in my situation and *fall away from* my authentic self. In this sort of fallenness we become preoccupied with the world of objects, but lose ourselves in the whirlpool of endless activity. Furthermore, instead of authentic relationships with other people, we identify ourselves with the anonymous, impersonal entity that Heidegger calls the "they" or the "one." The "they" becomes the authority, the standard of the way things are and is created by the voices of gossip and social pressure, as in the statements, "You know what *they* say about her . . ." or "*One* doesn't do that here." Within this inauthentic version of the public world, "Everyone is the other, and no one is himself" (BT 165). When we identify ourselves with the anonymous world of the "other," we interpret our experience in terms of the pregiven understandings that reside in our society:

> We take pleasure and enjoy ourselves as they take pleasure; we read, see, and judge about literature and art as they see and judge; likewise we shrink back from the "great mass" as they shrink back; we find "shocking" what they find shocking. (BT 164)

There is a "leveling off" or a "dimming down" of my possibilities "to what lies within the range of the familiar, the attainable, the respectable—that which is fitting and proper" (BT 239). For this reason, "the Self of everyday Dasein is the *they-self*." Heidegger says this is different from "the *authentic* Self—that is, from the Self which has been taken hold of in its own way" (BT 167).

The Fundamental Division: Authentic Versus Inauthentic Existence

Having analyzed our Being-in-the-world within the mode of everydayness, Heidegger now considers the possible ways in which we can relate to it. To summarize and reorganize his findings:

1. Dasein is *already-in-a-world*. We find ourselves "thrown" into a particular situation. This refers to our *facticity*, the unique deposit of given facts that makes up each person's *past*.

2. Dasein is *Being-along-with-the-world*. We engage with things that are ready-to-hand within the world as well as with other human beings. However, we tend to become absorbed into our situation, losing ourselves in the world of the impersonal, anonymous "they." We experience this *fallenness* within our *present* situation.

3. Dasein is *Being-ahead-of-itself*. Our past and present do not sum up what we are, for we are a field of possibilities that offer us choices in each moment of our existence. This existential structure of *possibility* includes the fact that our orientation toward the *future* provides part of the structure of who we are in the present.

This analysis indicates the importance of temporality to Dasein. My relationship to time is different from that of, say, a pencil, which simply is what it is within each isolated slice of time. However, I cannot understand my existence apart from what I have been, what I am, and what I will be. Heidegger says these three aspects of our existence are so interrelated that they form a single, unified phenomenon characterized as *care* (BT 237). This word is used both in the sense of (1) "I really *care* for her" and (2) "proceed with *care*." In other words, the phenomenon of care indicates both that (1) I am intimately involved with my Being and (2) how I respond to it is laden with consequences of great significance.

Previously, Heidegger said that "concern" is one of the *existentials*. But within the sphere of everydayness, this manifests concern for this or

that particular thing (my health, my career, my love life). By way of contrast, care is a "primordial structural totality" that lies before every specific attitude or situation.* It is not something I choose, for it is the *a priori* ground of all choices. Both our practical and our theoretical engagements arise out of care.

As human beings we make choices because we care about our existence. Unlike the busy ant following out the dictates of its biological programming, we are beings who are structured by our possibilities and whose existence necessarily involves making choices. The difficulty is, there are two ways of choosing:

> Dasein always understands itself in terms of its existence—in terms of a possibility of itself: to be itself or not itself. Dasein has either chosen these possibilities itself, or got itself into them, or grown up in them already. Only the particular Dasein decides its existence, whether it does so by taking hold or by neglecting. (BT 33)

If I consider my choices to be pregiven and just accept the situation I have drifted into or grown up with, as though I had no possibilities, I will live inauthentically. In this mode of existence, I am mired in my fallenness. In contrast, living authentically means that, in the face of my thrownness, I recognize I am the one who has to make choices and realize my possibilities. Authenticity is taking hold of my self in my own way (BT 167).

In a number of controversial passages, Heidegger repeatedly insists he is not interested in ethics. His discussions of the authentic or inauthentic modes of existence, he claims, merely provide ontological descriptions of Dasein and do not offer moral advice.† Yet aren't the terms "authentic" and "inauthentic" value laden? It would seem that authenticity is something to strive for and inauthenticity something to avoid. Heideg-

---

*It is worth noting that John Dewey was interested in Heidegger's thought, particularly in the notion of care (*Sorge*). Reported in Herbert Spiegelberg, *The Phenomenological Movement*, 2d ed. (The Hague, Netherlands: Nijhoff, 1965), 1:272.

†Jean-Paul Sartre adopted the terms "authentic" and "inauthentic" and, in contrast to Heidegger, used them for explicitly ethical purposes.

ger's reply is that fallenness and its accompanying inauthenticity are inevitable features of Dasein's condition. Hence, this level of existence is not condemned as morally deficient, for it is not something we can either choose or totally avoid.

If this is our natural condition, how, then, do we become open to the possibilities of our existence in an authentic way? The answer is that this new mode of existence comes on us "against all expectation and against our will" in a way that is "never planned, prepared, or willingly accomplished by ourselves" (BT 320). Heidegger says that the doorway to authentic existence is opened to us by the experience of dread or anxiety. Carrying forward the insights of Kierkegaard, Heidegger's discussion of anxiety has made it central to the twentieth-century existentialist's understanding of the human condition.

ANXIETY

According to Heidegger, anxiety differs from the experience of fear. Fear always has a specific object. I am fearful about an upcoming test, I fear going to the dentist, and so on. However, anxiety has ontological dimensions. Anxiety is not about this or that particular fact but is experienced with respect to what it means to be human. "That in the face of which one has anxiety is Being-in-the-world as such" (BT 230). Anxiety arises when we realize our whole system of meanings and our values have no ultimate ground other than that this is how our historical tradition has developed. This makes us realize that what we are is not what we could choose to be. We look around for some signposts to give us direction and discover we must invent the signposts. We have no absolute values to fall back on, no directions, no limits, no paths are laid out for us in advance to follow. We must make choices because we are finite and cannot realize all our possibilities. Hence, in the experience of anxiety we are forced to come face to face with our finitude. Our finitude is most concretely manifested in the fact that someday we will die. Our mortality, our Being-towards-death is one of the most important *existentials* that characterize Dasein.

BEING-TOWARDS-DEATH

Heidegger finds that facing the inevitability of death is a key to authenticity. For Kierkegaard, it was religious experience that individualizes me, that makes me aware of the "me-ness" of me. For Heidegger, however, realizing I am a "Being-towards-death" opens up this awareness. There is a big difference between entertaining the generalization "All people are mortal" and concretely realizing that "I will die."* In this sort of experience I become aware that one among my many possibilities is the termination of all possibilities. But in facing this possibility I become intimately acquainted with my own existence through realizing its boundaries and uniqueness.

In everything else in life (my job, my relationships) someone else can replace me. But no one can fill in the slot designated as "my death." That is the one role in life reserved for me alone. This perspective liberates me from my immersion in the mundane details of my life that ensnare me, and it snatches me out of the web of "comfortableness, shirking, and taking things lightly," so that I can begin to fully *exist* (BT 435). For this reason, Heidegger refers to it as "freedom towards death" (BT 311). A number of popular literary works have explored how a person's life would look to the person if he or she could look back on it after death. Others have depicted people who had a brush with death and returned to life with a new sense of who they were.†

CONSCIENCE

Since we can deny our own mortality and continually turn our minds away from it, even our attitude toward our own death can be inauthentic. What calls us to authenticity? Heidegger says it is

---

*In a footnote, Heidegger refers to Tolstoy's story, *The Death of Ivan Illyich*. In the character of Ivan, Tolstoy gives a powerful description of how an ordinary, average person moves from the abstract to the existential way of dealing with death.
†Thornton Wilder's play *Our Town* and Jean-Paul Sartre's play *No Exit* explore the first situation. Charles Dickens's classic *A Christmas Carol* and Frank Capra's sentimental film *It's a Wonderful Life* depict the second situation.

the voice of *conscience*. Obviously, conscience can be an ontic event, as when I feel a nagging guilt when I don't volunteer my time to someone who needs me. However, it should be clear by now that in Heidegger's analysis these passing ontic experiences are the surface of something deeper. Hence, the call of conscience Heidegger is pointing to is an ontological feature of human existence. As such, it is neither a product of our social conditioning, nor is it the voice of God, for the possibility of everyday experiences of guilt is grounded in the fundamental *existential* of conscience. What is the source of this call? "*In conscience Dasein calls itself*" (BT 320). Conscience is the self making itself aware of its own potential.

Conscience opens me to my own freedom by making me realize that neither my society nor my current identity (student, teacher, author) necessarily determines what I shall do or become. I have to take responsibility for my choices. Heidegger sums up authenticity as *resoluteness*. "When the call of conscience is understood, lostness in the 'they' is revealed. Resoluteness brings Dasein back to its ownmost potentiality-for-Being-its-Self" (BT 354). It is important to realize that authenticity is not achieved by retreating from life and becoming a mystical hermit living in the desert. Heidegger says "*authentic* existence is not something which floats above falling everydayness; existentially, it is only a modified way in which such everydayness is seized upon" (BT 224). Heidegger's philosophy may seem a burdensome, morbid obsession with anxiety, death, and guilt, but it has an optimistic strain. "Along with the sober anxiety which brings us face to face with our individualized potentiality-for-Being, there goes an unshakable joy in the possibility" (BT 358).

The Call of Being

To many readers, the heart of *Being and Time* is Heidegger's very perceptive phenomenological descriptions of human existence. His account of what it means to be an authentic human being has had an enormous influence on existentialists such as

Jean-Paul Sartre. However, Heidegger continually insisted that he was not an existentialist and that his earlier analysis of human existence was only a stepping-stone on the way to revealing the nature of Being itself. He never finished the promised second part of his project and, instead, he spent the last part of his life publishing essays and lectures on a number of topics. There is a definite change in style in his later period, for he becomes even more cryptic and mystical. The turning point in his thought seemed to occur in the early 1930s, when he began to view poetry as the field within human experience that Being reveals itself. In his later period, the focus on Dasein becomes secondary and Being comes to center stage.

There are considerable differences of opinion as to whether Heidegger began developing a completely new philosophy or whether the early and later Heidegger form a coherent whole. Some see the later work as a "turn," a change in direction, and others see it as a fulfillment of his original project. Heidegger himself claimed he never abandoned the project of *Being and Time*, but merely discovered that he had to approach the problem differently. Despite of his best efforts, he realized that his earlier work was too metaphysical, subjectivistic, and humanistic. It tried to clear a path to Being, but became entangled with our human understanding of Being. In his later work he no longer sees Being as something that must be approached, but as something to be listened to.

THE QUESTION OF TRUTH

An essential part of Heidegger's later work is his discussion of truth. We will first look at how he discussed it in his early work and then trace his understanding of truth as it emerges in his later discussions of language and poetry. In *Being and Time*, Heidegger starts by examining the traditional **correspondence theory of truth**. According to this theory, an assertion is true if it corresponds with its object. For example, the statement "The ball is red" is true if indeed the ball is red. However, it is not clear what we mean if we say that the string of words forming the preceding statement is related to some physical entity in the world, such as a ball.* To locate truth within the mind still raises the problem of how mental contents can "be like" an entirely different sort of entity.

To solve this problem, Heidegger changes the whole notion of truth as follows: "To say that an assertion 'is true' signifies that it uncovers the entity as it is in itself. Such an assertion asserts, points out, 'lets' the entity 'be seen' " (BT 261). Heidegger points out that the Greek word for truth is *aletheia*, which he translates literally as "unhiddenness" (BT 265).† This suggests that there can be truth only if something is disclosed, discovered, or revealed that was already present but hidden.‡

THE PROBLEM OF LANGUAGE

If truth is unhiddenness, what causes Being to be hidden in the first place? One answer is that in our fallenness we turn away from Being. A corollary is that language conspires with us to conceal Being. When functioning authentically, language discloses and makes things manifest. However, when we become lost within everydayness, our speaking becomes inauthentic and becomes simply a vehicle for our taken-for-granted perspectives:

> Words and language are not wrappings in which things are packed for the commerce of those who write and speak. It is in words and language that things first come into being and are. For this reason the misuse of language in idle talk, in slogans and phrases, destroys our authentic relation to things. (IM 11)

---

*We saw a very good example of the correspondence theory in Bertrand Russell's and Ludwig Wittgenstein's logical atomism discussed in Chapter 32. When Wittgenstein says in the *Tractatus* that thoughts or propositions "picture" facts, this metaphor makes the problem scream out at us rather than explaining anything.

†In Greek mythology, the river of forgetfulness was Lethe. Hence, the negative prefix in *aletheia* suggests that truth is an unforgetting of what was hidden.

‡Notice that in English we have the following words: (1) "discover," (2) "disclose," (3) "reveal." Taking these words in turn, their literal meanings are (roughly): (1) "to reverse the process of covering," (2) "to open" (undoing a closing), (3) "to draw back the veil."

Even when we try to speak philosophically, as Heidegger discovered in writing *Being and Time*, we must use a language overladen with conceptions deposited by twenty-five centuries of metaphysical thought. What we need is a kind of speaking that will open us up to Being rather than following the well-trodden paths of tradition. Heidegger discovers this in the language of the poets.

THE TASK OF THE POET

Heidegger rejects the notion that the poet simply says what everyone already knows, but says it in a colorful way. Instead, the poet brings into language and makes explicit what is so close to us that we do not notice it:

> Poetry is the inaugural naming of being and of the essence of all things—not just any speech, but that particular kind which for the first time brings into the open all that which we then discuss and deal with in everyday language. (HEP 283)

Thus, the poetic mode of speaking is the most fundamental form of language and the one that reunites us with the forgotten ground of our existence. It follows that literal language is derivative. It is a tool created by closing off the possibilities of language, making it uniform and necessarily dull. Instead of treating language like a tool we manipulate, Heidegger says we should see it is our dwelling place, as something toward which we have special responsibilities. "Language is the house of Being. In its home man dwells. Whoever thinks or creates in words is a guardian of this dwelling" (LH 193).§

---

§The comparisons that can be made between Wittgenstein and Heidegger are interesting. Wittgenstein ended his first book with the "mystical" and with the silence of what can be shown but cannot be said. In his later period, he thought we could recover our humanity by returning to everydayness and ordinary language. Heidegger, in contrast, finds that it is ordinary language that supports inauthenticity and in his later period says we must turn to the mystical, extraordinary language of the poet to rediscover our authenticity within what cannot be said but only shown.

LETTING-BE

Throughout the history of philosophy, the philosopher's task was frequently seen as a holy crusade, using the sharpened weapons of reason to assault the castle of truth to bring back its treasures. A particularly nice example is found in Hegel's inaugural lecture at the University of Berlin:

> The nature of the Universe, hidden and closed to start with, has no power to withstand the boldness of man's search for knowledge; it must open itself before him and disclose to his eyes its riches and its depths, offering them for his gratification.[8]

Heidegger himself, in *Being and Time*, had spoken of the appropriation of truth as a kind of "robbery" in which truth is "wrested" from entities (BT 265). However, Heidegger's study of Nietzsche in the late 1930s made him realize that Nietzsche's will-to-power was only the nihilistic version of an attitude toward truth that had driven metaphysics in the Western tradition from the time of Plato. However, he now understands this has been the problem all along. Finding an opening to Being is not something we do by our willing, but something we receive as a gift.

In his later period Heidegger now sees that dwelling in the presence of truth requires the *freedom to let-be* (ET 305-312). What he means by "freedom" here is something like being free of what would interfere with our ability to be open. Truth as an unconcealing results not from what we do, but from what we undo. It is a "letting-be of what-is." The poet cannot command inspiration to come to him, but must wait until it happens. In contrast, our Western approach to knowledge has been one of possessing, controlling, and manipulating in an attempt to wrestle the world into submission. In place of the Western tradition of epistemology, Heidegger proposes a way of thinking that revolves around the notions of being-available, listening, surrendering, and obeying. "Obedient to the voice of Being, thought seeks the Word through which the truth of Being may be expressed" (WM 360). Renouncing the humanism that began with the Greeks and was reborn in the Renaissance, Heidegger says, "Man is not the master of beings. Man

is the shepherd of Being" (LH 210). In the difference between mastering and shepherding, we have the difference between technology and poetry.

REDISCOVERING THE HOLY

In Heidegger's later work, Being is spoken of in very anthropomorphic terms as something that "calls" us, "conceals" itself from us, and "reveals" itself to us. At the same time, Heidegger rejects the attempt to identify Being with any sort of traditional notion of a divine person. The ambiguities in Heidegger's thought are indicated by the fact that both atheistic existentialists and Christian theologians have found resources for their thought in his writings.* Heidegger clearly is not a theist in the sense of believing in a transcendent, supernatural being. At the same time, if his outlook is a secular one, it is one surrounded with the aura of the sacred and inspired by an appreciation for the mysteries of Being that are both concealed and revealed in the visible world. For this reason, some have referred to Heidegger's philosophy as a "godless theology."

Our age is the culmination of 2,500 years of attempts to conceptualize the world metaphysically. However, according to Heidegger, after making technology possible, philosophy has run its course. Our age is now one in which we have been "given" the scientific and technological way of appropriating reality. We do not choose how things appear to us, any more than the medievals voluntarily decided to see everything as manifesting God. In our age, however, the sense of awe, mystery, sacredness, and reverence has been replaced by a fascination with atoms, quarks, black holes, and intelligent computers. For us, Heidegger believes, God is silent.

The supreme mistake would be to suppose that ours is the only way to view the world or that it will always remain our way of viewing the world. Our time is "the time of the gods that have fled *and*

---

*The difficulties we run up against in interpreting Heidegger are the same ones we encountered in Chapter 24 with Hegel's notion of Spirit. These two thinkers can be read in both secular and religious lights.

of the god that is coming" (HEP 289). Does Heidegger really believe a new revelation of the divine is possible? He says it is useless to ask that question unless we first rediscover the one dimension where this question can be asked, which is

> The dimension of the holy, which even as dimension, remains closed unless the openness of Being is cleared and in its clearing is close to man. Perhaps the distinction of this age consists in the fact that the dimension of grace has been closed. Perhaps this is its unique disgrace. (LH 216)

Although technology can conceal Being from us, Being is never far away. Heidegger believes that in our fascination with technology, we lose sight of what comes to presence in it. To remedy this, Heidegger calls us to step back from viewing the world technologically, to viewing ourselves as viewing-the-world-technologically. Once we understand technology as simply one way that the world is present to us today, it will have released its hold on us. "Thus the coming to presence of technology harbors in itself what we least suspect, the possible arising of the saving power" (QCT 32). Whether or not we will experience a new sense of the whole or the holy arising within the age of technology, and whether or not the voice of Being will call to us through Heidegger's writings, only the future will tell.

Heidegger's Significance

It is difficult to give a philosophical critique of Heidegger, for where no arguments have been provided, none can be refuted. A phenomenologist believes that the fundamental truths he sees cannot be revealed by analyzing language or deducing conclusions from premises that themselves need grounding. Hence, the only means of persuasion he has at his disposal is to be as illuminating in his descriptions of experience as possible, hoping that the phenomena will be disclosed to you as well. Naturally, many have looked in their experience where Heidegger tells us to look and have found that his insights have been illuminating. Others, particularly the analytic philosophers, deny he is doing philosophy at all. From the standpoint of his later thought, Heidegger would not deny the charge. "Future thought is no longer philosophy, because it thinks more originally than metaphysics" (LH 224). He thinks philosophy is so burdened with metaphysics it is unsalvageable. (He would add that the antimetaphysical analytic philosophers have not escaped metaphysics.) This assumes that Western philosophy has run its course and the only remedy is to break out of the structures that have alienated us from Being. Of course, this conclusion is more radical than many are willing to accept.

If a philosopher's significance can be measured in terms of the number of diverse disciplines he or she has influenced, then Heidegger certainly deserves his reputation as one of the most significant thinkers in the twentieth century. Existentialist phenomenologists such as Jean-Paul Sartre and Maurice Merleau-Ponty developed their thought in the light he had cast. Furthermore, Heidegger contributed to the development of existential theology. The foremost existentialist theologians Rudolf Bultmann and Paul Tillich were colleagues with Heidegger at Marburg. Their theological project was to make the Christian message relevant for our age by lifting it out of the ancient metaphysical categories in which it was first presented, in order to translate it into Heidegger's existential categories. Heidegger's thought also influenced the existentialist revolt against scientism and behaviorism within psychiatry and psychology. Psychiatrists Ludwig Binswanger and R. D. Laing were particularly influenced by Heidegger. Finally, Heidegger is alive and well among literary theorists. His writings on poetry, language, culture, and his notion that human experience is a text that needs to be interpreted, have all played a role in the literary theory known as *deconstructionism*.

JEAN-PAUL SARTRE

|||

A Life Lived Amidst Books

Jean-Paul Sartre (1905–1980) was born in Paris. His father died when Sartre was fifteen months old, and young Jean-Paul and his mother moved in with her parents. In his autobiography titled *The Words*, Sartre says he hated his childhood because of the suffocating atmosphere of his grandparents' household. Tutored at home, he was isolated and deprived of association with children his own age. Sartre's only friends were the books that filled his grandfather's study. "I began my life," Sartre says, "as I shall no doubt end it: amidst books." In his philosophy, Sartre describes the way we live out our lives by choosing projects in an attempt to define who we are. He says about himself, "I keep creating myself; I am the giver and the gift." As the title of his autobiography suggests, Sartre decided his life's project would revolve around words. As he puts it, "I was prepared at an early age to regard teaching as a priesthood and literature as a passion."

Pursuing his calling, Sartre received his university education at the prestigious École Normale Supérieure, after which he began his career teaching philosophy at a number of *lycées* (advanced high schools). During the academic year 1933–1934, he was a research student in Germany, where he studied the phenomenology of Husserl and Heidegger. In 1938 he published *Nausea*, his first novel. It became a surprising best-seller. Reading it in the light of his later work, it was an early statement of many of the existentialist themes that pervaded Sartre's literary and philosophical works for the remainder of his life. With the outbreak of World War II, Sartre was called into military service, but was captured and imprisoned by the Nazis for approximately a year. Pleading poor health, he was allowed to return to his life in Paris as a citizen. However, he became active in the underground movement of the French Resistance. Here he came to know Albert Camus, who went on to be a famous novelist and writer with affini-

ties to existentialism. Another member of Sartre's intellectual resistance group was Maurice Merleau-Ponty, who became a famous existential phenomenologist. Both of these friends eventually bitterly fell out with Sartre when they became disillusioned with the Communist Party and Sartre continued to sympathize with it.

Sartre's philosophical masterpiece, *Being and Nothingness: An Essay of Phenomenological Ontology*, came out in 1943. The work was clearly influenced by Heidegger's thought even though the latter was not pleased with the way Sartre used his ideas to articulate an existentialist humanism. As his fame spread, Sartre was able to live on his literary income alone. In his philosophical essays, novels, plays, and short stories, he put words to the experiences of both alienation and hope that characterized the twentieth century. His fictional works both stand on their own literary merit and brilliantly illustrate his philosophical and psychological insights into the human situation. Sartre was awarded the Nobel Prize for Literature in 1964, but he refused to accept the honor and the $53,000 prize money, because he did not want to become a tool of the establishment.

Consistent with the extreme individualism of his philosophy, Sartre lived a very unconventional life. He lived his adult life out of hotel rooms and had few personal possessions. When an interviewer asked to see a copy of Sartre's latest book, he confessed he didn't own one. While a university student, he met Simone de Beauvoir. They became lifelong companions, while avoiding the "bourgeois snares of matrimony." De Beauvoir became a world-famous author herself and contributed to French existentialism and political thought through her short stories, novels, and essays. Sartre and de Beauvoir did much of their writing in the Left Bank sidewalk cafés of Paris, particularly the Café de Flore and the Café des Deux Magots. The Paris café has traditionally been a gathering place for artists, intellectuals, and political radicals of all persuasions. Situated at his favorite table, Sartre was able to be a detached observer of the human situation while immersed in the hustle and bustle of daily life taking place on the sidewalks of Paris.

In the latter part of his life, Sartre's interests shifted toward social and political thought, and he tried to build a bridge between existentialism and Marxism. In very poor health throughout his life, he steadily declined in his later years. On April 15, 1980, Jean-Paul Sartre died of acute heart failure. As the hearse bearing his body drove to the cemetery, a crowd of about 50,000 people, most of them students, accompanied it through the streets of Paris.

Sartre's Task: A Human-Centered Ontology

Sartre's task, as evident from the subtitle of his major work, is to develop a phenomenological ontology. Phenomenology, as we have seen, is the study of the way the world is revealed through the structures of consciousness. Sartre believes this will also provide us with an ontology or an account of what the world must be like for experience to be the way it is. However, while ontology can describe the structures of being, it cannot answer metaphysical questions, such as why this particular world exists. Hence, Sartre tries to provide descriptive answers to "How?" and "What?" questions from within the scope of human consciousness, but with Kant he says it is meaningless to ask "why" questions that refer beyond the limits of reality as we experience it. All we can say is that "being is without reason, without cause, and without necessity" (BN 788).[9]

Sartre's philosophy owes more to Heidegger than to any other thinker. However, there were significant differences between the two.* For Sartre, the standpoint of the human subject is the beginning and the end of his philosophy. There is never any hint of Heidegger's Being that calls to us through the poets and in terms of which we

*Recall that Heidegger continually tried to disassociate himself from Sartre's existential humanism.

can find a "saving power." On the contrary, for Sartre human consciousness confronts a totality of being that is alien and meaningless. Sartre's writings return to the emphasis on human willing and action. Going along with this is the sort of subjectivism Heidegger tried so hard to avoid. According to Sartre, we must make our way in the world by subjectively creating meaning, rather than having it flood in on us by the "letting-be of what-is," as Heidegger proposed.

Two Kinds of Reality: Objects and Persons

Sartre says that when we analyze what appears to us, we discover two modes of being. First of all, one sort of being is manifested in objects. This is called the *in-itself* (*l'en-soi*). The term "in-itself" signifies that objects are self-contained or self-identical. Nothing in them transcends what they currently are. A table simply is what it is. The second sort of being is what characterizes human consciousness. Sartre calls this form of being the *for-itself* (*le pour-soi*). The term "for-itself" signifies that such beings are conscious and self-aware. Rather than being determined by external causes, we are bursting with spontaneous freedom and live our lives in terms of future possibilities. Unlike the table, we do not have static identities, for we are continually self-projecting beings. We are always incomplete, ongoing projects that are never finished, always being recreated anew by our own choices.

Descartes supposed a person's conscious acts are rooted in some sort of mental substance. But Sartre says consciousness is a nothingness. He is referring to the "no-thingness" of consciousness, the fact that it is not a thing. Instead, it is totally transparent, existing only as a consciousness of some object. We become aware of our own consciousness by being aware of the gap between ourselves and the world of causally determined objects. Like a bubble moving through a liquid, consciousness introduces nothingness into the world. Being-in-itself is simply there, without gaps, without possibilities, without any deficiencies, without the presence of any negations. When consciousness is present, however, "nothingness" is introduced into the world. Sartre speaks of coming to a café and finding that his friend Pierre is not there. In this awareness, consciousness introduces a negation, "the absence of Pierre," into the continuous, solid being of the café and its material objects. Similarly, consciousness looks at the world about it and sees not simply what is there, but also what it lacks, or possibilities that could be realized but that are not yet actual. Only the for-itself can become separate from the bare existence of things in the causal order in this way. As we shall see, the nothingness that is consciousness, its ability to separate from things and to live in the "what-is-not" (the realm of possibilities), makes us totally free. Since phenomenology only studies what appears to consciousness, Sartre never asks how the world divided into these two categories of being or how consciousness appeared in the midst of physical things. With Kant, Sartre believes that such metaphysical questions are unanswerable from within the human situation.

An Empty Universe

A fundamental feature of Sartre's philosophy is his outspoken atheism. As he describes his philosophy, "existentialism is nothing else but an attempt to draw the full conclusions from a consistently atheistic position" (EH 310). He provides at least two reasons why he rejects the theistic standpoint. The first reason takes the form of a syllogism:

(1) If a sovereign God existed, then persons would not be free agents.
(2) Persons are free agents.
(3) Therefore, a sovereign God does not exist.

Why does he assert the first premise? Apparently he agrees with Leibniz that a God who created the world would fill it with creatures having certain, given natures. If so, then everything a person does would simply be determined by the sort of nature that God had given people as part of his plan. As for the second claim that we are, indeed, free, Sartre believes that the anxiety we face when we

have to make a crucial choice shows that the decision is not already programmed into either our divinely created nature, our genes, or our social conditioning. Furthermore, Sartre says that even if God could create genuinely free creatures apart from himself, to have this sort of freedom would mean we would not depend on God nor be determined by him. Hence, what we chose to become would be the result of our own, sovereign choices, and for all practical purposes it would not make any difference, to the structures of human existence, how we came into the world (BN 26–27).

His second argument for atheism is based on the claim that the concept of God is contradictory, for it merges the two, incompatible types of beings. On the one hand, Sartre agrees with the medievals that a being such as God would have to be a fully realized, complete, unchanging, and absolute being. He could not have plans or desires, for these would imply he had unfulfilled potentialities. But this would mean he was a being-in-itself, the sort of being that characterizes objects. At the same time, the religious concept of God is the concept of a person. But, according to Sartre's analysis, a person is a being who has goals, values, projects. To be a person is to be incomplete because we are continually transcending our present by projecting ourselves into a still-unfinished future. Indeed, much of the religious language in the Bible describes God this way. Furthermore, to be a person is to be self-aware. But in self-awareness we step back from our being and become both a subject and an object for ourselves. Hence, unlike the table, if I have consciousness I never fully coincide with what I am. Therefore everything is either a fully complete being (in-itself) or a being continually transcending itself (for-itself)—but nothing (including God) can be both. Hence, the concept of a God that is an in-itself and for-itself is self-contradictory.

Existence Precedes Essence

In his most famous essay, "Existentialism is a Humanism" (1946), Sartre introduces the memorable statement, "Existence precedes essence." The essence of something is the set of its defining properties, what makes it the sort of thing it is. Sartre says an entity's essence precedes its existence only if it is a manufactured article. With respect to manufactured articles, we can ask, "What is it?" or "What is it for?" The initial idea of the statue in the artist's mind or the architect's blueprint are examples of how the essence of created things precede their actual existence. However, if we are not divinely created beings, then there was no plan and no blueprint for what we were intended to be. "Man first of all exists, encounters himself, surges up in the world—and defines himself afterwards" (EH 290). Sartre faults previous atheists for supposing they could remove the concept of God from their systems and still go on talking about human nature and objective values. Instead, "there is no human nature, because there is no God to have a conception of it. . . . Man is nothing else but that which he makes of himself" (EH 290–291).

One may wonder how Sartre can go on to philosophize about human existence if there is no common human nature. Sartre's answer is that nothing at the core of persons defines what they are. We cannot describe humans as naturally selfish, aggressive, good, social, rational, nor can we appeal to any other sort of defining essence. We are only social, say, if we choose to engage in social activities, but this does not define what we are. However, while there is no universal human nature, there is a common *human condition*. We face the same challenges, the same questions, and the same limitations. The existential structures of human existence are the same, but within these structures each person responds in his or her own, unique way.

CONDEMNED TO FREEDOM

Philosophers have debated for centuries about whether or not we have freedom. However, Sartre has the most radical and totalistic view of human freedom ever put forth in the history of thought. He says we do not *have* freedom, we *are* freedom. Freedom is not one property among many, but is intrinsic to the sort of beings we are, for at each moment of our existence we are creating ourselves anew. Most have assumed that having free will

would be a welcome condition, but in one of his most striking comments, Sartre says, "We are condemned to freedom" (EH 295). He wants to impress on us what an overwhelming burden it is that we cannot escape our freedom. He quotes Dostoevsky's pronouncement "If God does not exist, everything would be permitted" (EH 294). We want some direction in making decisions, we want to fall back on some objective realm of values that will assure us we are making the right choice. However, the fact is that

> we have neither behind us, nor before us in a luminous realm of values, any means of justification or excuse. We are left alone, without excuse. (EH 295)

Sartre tells about a Jesuit priest he met while they were both in a Nazi prison. Initially, this man's life was a total failure. He was orphaned, impoverished, had a disastrous love affair, and was denied a military career because he failed an exam. He took all these events as a sign that he was not destined for secular success but was being called to serve God. Sartre says this is the meaning that this individual *chose* to assign to these experiences. However, he could have just as easily decided that they meant he should become a revolutionary (EH 298). The crux of Sartre's position is that bare facts have no meaning until an individual assigns them a meaning.

FACTICITY

You might think that there are a number of obvious limits on freedom caused by past events over which we had no control. For example, I was born an American male and was raised in a middle-class home. These sorts of inescapable features of our existence Sartre calls our *facticity*. However, if facts do not have intrinsic meaning but are things to which we assign meaning, then to state the features of our facticity is, as such, to say very little. Our true freedom becomes clear in the ways in which we respond to our facticity. I was born an American. What does that mean to me today? Do I see it as a source of nationalistic pride? Or do I feel guilty over my country's affluence when compared to the rest of the world? Should I renounce my citizenship or even become a traitor, or should I be a flag-waving patriot? These are all choices I have to make. The same is true of my gender. In the latter part of the twentieth century, there has been a great deal of discussion and debate over what it means to be a female or a male. Should a man show his emotions? Should a woman be assertive? To be female or male as a biological fact tells us nothing about what it *means* to be this or that gender. Hence, scientific facts tell us very little about how to live our lives. As we face the bare givens of our facticity, we face an overwhelming amount of freedom in deciding what meaning these have for us.

THE PARADOX OF HUMAN EXISTENCE

In one of his typically enigmatic phrases, Sartre says that a feature of human existence is that *I-am-what-I-am-not* and *I-am-not-what-I-am* (BN 196, 798; EP 65). At first glance, this assertion seems contradictory if not completely impenetrable. However, a great deal of Sartre's philosophy can be unpacked from this brief formula. The first half of the statement ("I-am-what-I-am-not") refers to the quality of transcendence (which is the opposite of facticity). This means that we are always oriented toward the future.* Our possibilities, our freedom, the things we are striving for but have not yet realized are what shape our present life. My current life is oriented around the goal of finishing this book. Thus *I am* (someone trying to be) *what I am not* (a published author). To be a "being-for-itself" is always to be striving, always to be on the way. Our ongoing projects, those activities in which we seek to transcend what we are now, continually define us. "What we mean to say is that a man is no other than a series of undertakings, that he is the sum, the organization, the set of relations that constitute these undertakings" (EH 301).

The other half of the formula ("I-am-not-what-I-am") refers to the roles that we are playing out,

but that do not fully define us. Someone labeling me might say I am a husband, a father, a philosopher, and a professor. However, these identities are not woven into my being. In one sense, I am not fully and completely a teacher, but I am striving to be one (with various degrees of success). Furthermore, being a teacher (or any of the other labels) is not part of my essence, because it is something I am continually *choosing* to be or can choose not to be. A table is completely identified with being a table, because it has no choice about it. However, I choose to identify myself with one role or another. It might be thought that my being a father is a biological fact about my past I cannot change. Insofar as this is part of my facticity, that is true. But how I see this role makes an enormous difference to how I live my life and relate to my family. Furthermore, I can choose to identify myself with what it means to be a father or I can refuse to accept this role as part of who I am. Thus, *I am not* (essentially and unchangeably identified with) *what I am* (the roles and labels that I adopt for myself).

BAD FAITH VERSUS AUTHENTICITY

Sartre cautions us against falling into the trap of labeling ourselves, for this is simply an attempt to deny our freedom. I might say, "I am a loser" or "I can't change, because this is just the way I am." Labels become our identity only because we make them so. In his biography of the famous playwright Jean Genet, Sartre tells us that Genet stole something when he was a boy. When caught, he was told, "Jean, you *are* a thief!" He naively accepted this as his identity and ended up becoming a professional thief in his early adulthood. In many such ways we inauthentically identify ourselves with this or that role and think we are not free to be anything else. Consistent with his own philosophy, Sartre refused to identify his free, spontaneous self with the public's attempt to lock him into the identity of being a famous writer. In response to an interviewer's question, Sartre says,

> You know, the fame seems to go on in someone else's life, it has happened to someone else. There is me and then there is the other person. The other person

---

*Note how often we hear echoes of Heidegger in Sartre's descriptions of human existence.

has written books and is read. . . . He exists, I know, but he doesn't bother me; I use him . . . but I do not think of him as being me.[10]

Sartre uses the term *bad faith* to refer to the attempt to deny our freedom, to see ourselves as products of our circumstances, or the attempt to identify ourselves with our past choices while closing off our future possibilities. We feel a need to be an "in-itself," a being that is defined, that has an identity. But this is because, as Heidegger pointed out, facing our freedom brings with it the burden of responsibility and the experiences of anxiety, anguish, and despair. It is all up to us, for there is no meaning to the world or our lives but the meaning we create. When a young man came to Sartre seeking ethical advice, the only advice Sartre would give him was "You are free, therefore choose—that is to say, invent" (EH 297-298). Only when we take responsibility for the meaning of our past and present, and self-consciously choose our future, will we achieve *authenticity*, the one value Sartre seems to embrace in an otherwise valueless universe.

Alienation and Other People

What are the implications of Sartre's philosophy for our relationship to others? Try this thought experiment: look up, down, to the left, to the right, forward, and behind you. You have just demonstrated that you are the *center* of your lived-world. All the directions in the universe radiate out from you. If Sartre is correct in saying we cannot escape playing a godlike role in assigning meanings and values to our world, then each of us is sovereign in our own lived-world. The problem is, there are as many lived-worlds as individuals. However, there can only be one universe, with one God, and one center. Hence, there is an inevitable conflict among human beings.

I determine what meaning *you* have in *my* world. Are you interesting? dull? beautiful? plain? threatening? innocuous? *I* decide what value and meaning you have, for you are but one item in *my* world. Of course, others are doing the same for me. Hence, we are involved in a "war of the

Alberto Giacometti, The Forest, Seven Figures and a Head *(1950). The stark, elongated figures in Giacometti's sculpture reside forever in their individual spaces. Though in close proximity, they are forever alone. These figures provide an image of Sartre's philosophy and his emphasis on our experiences of alienation and anxiety as well as individual autonomy and personal dignity.*

worlds." Sartre talks about the feeling of discomfort we feel when someone stares at us. You are enjoying a moment of solitude in the park, thinking you are alone. You feel in control of your space. But then you become uncomfortably aware someone is staring at you. The presence of another consciousness means you have just become an item in someone else's world. Like water rushing to the drain of a bathtub when the plug has been pulled out, my whole world seems to drain toward that other center of consciousness. What is he thinking of me? What judgments is he making about me? The stare of another person is unsettling because it means you no longer fully control your psychological space. You continually struggle to be a fully subjective consciousness, giving meaning to the items in your world. But this means others can only be objects for *your* consciousness. Of course, the reverse is true as the other tries to absorb you within his or her conscious experience.

For such reasons, Sartre does not believe we can really share our experience with another, because individual autonomy is an inescapable feature of our way of experiencing the world. At best, a friendship can be like two separate ships moving in the same direction. As one of Sartre's characters says at the end of his play *No Exit*, "Hell is—other people."

Optimism in the Midst of Alienation

According to Sartre's analysis, there is something fundamentally absurd about human existence. Living in a universe without God, it is up to each one of us to answer questions about meaning and value. At the same time, we cannot fall back on any sort of rational order, for our lives are grounded in pure, subjective freedom. For this reason, Sartre says, "The existentialist . . . finds it extremely embarrassing that God does not exist, for there disappears with Him all possibility of finding values in an intelligible heaven" (EH 294). In practical terms, each of us must fill the slot occupied by God in previous philosophical systems. We also try to be like God in our efforts to find some sort of stable identity. Suffering from the anguish of always deciding, always being on the way, we thirst for completion and fulfillment. For this reason, Sartre says, "the best way to conceive of the fundamental project of human reality is to say that man is the being whose project is to become God" (EP 66). Yet Sartre has already argued that the idea of God is contradictory. Therefore, it follows that "man is a useless passion" (EP 199).

Despite all the negative features of Sartre's philosophy, he still thinks it is the most optimistic outlook possible. Unlike either theism or deterministic scientific philosophies, the future is not already decided, according to Sartrean existentialism. We face genuine possibilities, we are free, we can choose, we are in control. This philosophy gives us dignity and a hope that we can make ourselves what we decide to be. Neither nature, nor the gods, nor society have the last word, for each individual writes the next chapter of their own autobiography.

Sartre's Turn to Marxism

The ideas outlined thus far account for Sartre's enormous impact on existentialism, literature, and psychology. However, in the later part of his life he tried to weave his existentialism together with Marxism. Sartre felt lifelong regret over being a man of ideas instead of a man of action. Although never denying that freedom is inescapable, he began to focus on the way in which society limits people's ability to express their freedom. He hoped existentialism would make Marxism less dogmatic and deterministic.

Sartre's turn toward Marxism is expressed in his 1960 book *The Critique of Dialectical Reason*. In the beginning of the book he states, "Marxism is the inescapable philosophy of our time." Differing from orthodox Marxism, and the Hegelianism on which it is founded, Sartre does not believe Marxism is inescapable because history is determined. Instead, he is making the more modest claim that Marxism best expresses the human situation in our time. Sartre discusses two ways in which several individuals can relate together. One is the "serial collective," which would characterize a collection of isolated individuals waiting in line for a bus. They have no sense of unity, for each is engaged in his or her own projects and knows nothing of the other's concerns. The second type of plurality is a "group-in-fusion." In this case, people find that they face a common situation and that their individual projects can be merged, making them capable of concerted historical action, as in the French Revolution. Under capitalism, the individual workers are a serial collective in which they see themselves as powerless, oppressed, and alienated individuals. Realizing their shared alienation, and the fact that they are viewed by their bosses as just objects to be exploited, they begin to see themselves as an "Us-object." In turn, the oppressors become a "Them." With this new level of awareness, the workers can transform themselves from a collection of objects into a "We-subject." At this point, they define their aspirations toward individual freedom in terms of collective liberation and they can work together for a more humane society.

Sartre never was a true Marxist, for he always resisted the deterministic view of history that is intrinsic to Marxism. At the same time, many believe that by emphasizing the power of social structures and introducing the notion of collective identity, Sartre abandoned his existentialism. Sartre hoped, nevertheless, that existentialism would humanize Marxism, leading to a transformation of the human condition:

> As soon as there will exist for everyone *a margin of real freedom beyond the production of life, Marxism will have lived out its span; a philosophy of freedom will take its place. But we have no means, no intellectual instrument, no concrete experience which allows us to conceive of this freedom or of this philosophy.*[11]

The Significance of Existentialism

Critics of existentialism, who preferred a more analytic and scientific approach to things, complained that existentialism was simply an emotional reaction to the dark side of human existence and did not offer anything of cognitive value. As one analytic philosopher said to me, "Everyone is an existentialist at 3 A.M. on a sleepless night." Nevertheless, existentialism, as a way of approaching the human condition, was enormously influential and found adherents in any field that touched on distinctively human concerns, such as art, literature, psychology, theology. Although existentialism as a movement is not as strong today as when Sartre was in his prime, the existentialist spirit will always be alive. It is a spirit of revolt against the pretensions of reason, against the dehumanizing conditions of modern life, and against the attempts of the sciences to reduce persons to simply one more type of object among others in nature.

Questions for Understanding

1. In the context of this chapter, what is naturalism and why does Husserl reject it?

2. What does Husserl mean by "phenomenology"?

3. In what sense is Husserl's phenomenology a rationalism and in what sense is it a radical form of empiricism?

4. According to Husserl, what is the natural standpoint?

5. What does Husserl mean by "bracketing" or epoche? How does it differ from Descartes's method of doubt? Why does Husserl think it is important to do this?

6. What is Husserl's view of consciousness? What does he mean by "intentionality"?

7. What is the life-world, according to Husserl? What is its relation to the scientific account of the world?

8. How did philosophers such as Heidegger and Sartre modify Husserl's philosophy to transform it into an existential phenomenology?

9. In Heidegger's philosophy, what is meant by "ontology"?

10. What is the distinction Heidegger makes between beings and Being? According to him, how did Western thought lose sight of Being?

11. What does the German word Dasein mean? Why does Heidegger use it to refer to human existence? Why does Heidegger think the study of ontology should begin with an analysis of our existence?

12. How does Heidegger's notion of Being-in-the-world differ from Descartes's approach to human existence?

13. What unique meaning does Heidegger give to the notion of "world."

14. What is the difference Heidegger observes between an object being "present-at-hand" and "ready-at-hand"?

15. Why does Heidegger say that knowing is not our most basic relationship to the world? What does he think is our more fundamental way of relating to the world?

16. What do the following expressions mean in Heidegger's philosophy: "facticity," "thrownness," "Being-ahead-of-itself," "fallenness," "anxiety," "Being-towards-death," "conscience"?

17. According to Heidegger, what constitutes the difference between authentic and inauthentic existence?

18. How does Heidegger define "truth" in his later work?

19. What is the problem of language according to Heidegger? What is the remedy?

20. According to Heidegger, what problems for our relationship to the world have been caused by technology? What is the solution?

21. According to Sartre, what are the two kinds of reality? How does he describe each of them?

22. What are the two arguments Sartre uses to defend his atheism?

23. What does Sartre mean by saying "existence precedes essence"? Why does it imply that there is no human nature?

24. What does Sartre mean by "facticity" and "transcendence"? How do these concepts illuminate his slogan "I-am-what-I-am-not and I-am-not-what-I-am"?

25. What does Sartre mean by "bad faith"? How does it contrast with his notion of "authenticity"?

26. What are the implications of Sartre's philosophy for our relationship to others?

27. Why does Sartre say that human existence is "a useless passion"? In the light of this, why does Sartre consider himself to be an optimist?

28. What is the significance of Sartre's turn toward Marxism? Is it consistent with his earlier philosophy?

Questions for Reflection

1. Make an attempt to try out Husserl's method of bracketing. Stand back from being naively involved with the world and try to be attentive to the acts of consciousness in terms of which the world is given to you or constituted by you. What do you find when you take this perspective?

2. Do you think Husserl's point is plausible, that consciousness cannot be treated as just another natural object within the world?

3. In what ways is Heidegger's view of experience different than that of the British empiricists?

4. Do you agree with Heidegger's claim that poetry is more revelatory than other, more objective forms of speech?

5. Argue for or against Sartre's claim that if God existed, then humans would not be free.

6. Do you think Sartre is correct in claiming that "existence precedes essence"? What are some of the implications of embracing this principle for one's life?

7. List some features of your life that Sartre would describe as your "facticity." Now, for each one, list some of the choices you have for deciding the meaning of that fact.

Notes

1. Quoted in Herbert Spiegelberg, *The Phenomenological Movement*, 2d ed. (The Hague, Netherlands: Nijhoff, 1965), 1:82.

2. Throughout this chapter, the works of Edmund Husserl are referenced by means of their page numbers, using the following abbreviations:

   CM   *Cartesian Meditations*, trans. Dorion Cairns (The Hague, Netherlands: Nijhoff, 1960).

   I   *Ideas: General Introduction to Pure Phenomenology*, trans. W. R. Boyce Gibson (New York: Collier Books, 1962).

   PCEM "Philosophy and the Crisis of European Man," in *Phenomenology and the Crisis of Philosophy*, trans. Quentin Lauer (New York: Harper & Row, 1965).

3. William Barrett, *What Is Existentialism?* (New York: Grove Press, 1964), 82.

4. Quoted in Spiegelberg, *The Phenomenological Movement*, 1:284.

5. Ibid.

6. Martin Heidegger, "The Way Back into the Ground of Metaphysics," in *Existentialism from Dostoevsky to Sartre*, trans. and ed. Walter Kaufmann (New York: New American Library, 1956), 207.

7. The works of Martin Heidegger are referenced in terms of the pages of their English editions using the following abbreviations:

BT   *Being and Time*, trans. John Macquarrie and Edward Robinson (London: SCM Press, 1962).

ET   "On the Essence of Truth," trans. R. F. C. Hull and Alan Crick, in Martin Heidegger, *Existence and Being*, ed. Werner Brock (Chicago: Regnery, 1949).

HEP   "Hölderlin and the Essence of Poetry," trans. Douglas Scott, in Martin Heidegger, *Existence and Being*.

IM   *Introduction to Metaphysics*, trans. Ralph Manheim (Garden City, NY: Anchor Books, Doubleday, 1959).

LH   "Letter on Humanism," trans. Edgar Lohner, in *Philosophy in the Twentieth Century*, Vol. 3: *Contemporary European Thought*, ed. William Barrett and Henry D. Aiken (New York: Harper & Row, 1962).

QCT   "The Question Concerning Technology," in Martin Heidegger, *The Question Concerning Technology and Other Essays*, trans. William Lovitt (New York: Harper & Row, 1977).

WM   "What Is Metaphysics?" trans. R. F. C. Hull and Alan Crick, in Martin Heidegger, *Existence and Being*.

8. Quoted in J. L. Mehta, *Martin Heidegger: The Way and the Vision* (Honolulu: University Press of Hawaii, 1976), 336.

9. Quotations from Jean-Paul Sartre's works are referenced by their page numbers, using the following abbreviations:

BN   *Being and Nothingness*, trans. Hazel Barnes (New York: Washington Square Press, 1956).

EH   "Existentialism Is a Humanism," trans. Philip Mairet, in *Existentialism from Dostoevsky to Sartre*, ed. Walter Kaufmann (New York: Meridian Books, New American Library, 1956).

EP   *Existential Psychoanalysis*, trans. Hazel E. Barnes (New York: Philosophical Library, 1953).

10. "What's Jean-Paul Sartre Thinking Lately? An Interview by Pierre Bénichou," trans. Patricia Southgate, *Esquire*, December 1972, 286.

11. Jean-Paul Sartre, *Search for a Method*, trans. Hazel E. Barnes (New York: Vintage Books, Random House, 1963), 34.

34

Recent Issues in Philosophy

WHERE IS PHILOSOPHY NOW, AND WHERE IS IT going? If the history of philosophy has taught us anything, it is that it would be risky to answer this question in too much detail. Thirty years ago, when I was an undergraduate philosophy major, no one could have anticipated some of the issues philosophers are writing about today. Likewise, it is hard to predict which philosophers in our own time will have the most lasting influence in the decades and centuries to come. Philosophers who were unappreciated by their contemporaries often get rediscovered hundreds of years later.

Perhaps Jean-Paul Sartre was right—the past is never finished but is continually receiving its meaning in terms of the present moment. Furthermore, Sartre, as well as the pragmatists and process philosophers, emphasized that the future is always open. From our stance within the present, we are continually deciding what the future will become. The most I will try to do in this final chapter, therefore, is to say a few words about what new issues and movements are currently creating philosophical commotion, as well as briefly mentioning a few

names to guide the reader who wants to study philosophy's present in more detail.

Rethinking Empiricism

One significant development in the latter part of the twentieth century has been a radical reassessment of the fundamental assumptions of modern empiricism. Although this is not a recent turn of events, it has influenced the philosophical environment that produced many of our current philosophical movements. From Francis Bacon on, the empiricists claimed to have provided the philosophical foundations of science. Subsequently, as scientists developed their methods and theories through the centuries, they accepted the empiricists' story of what scientists were doing. When classical empiricism came into question, it required a rethinking of what scientific knowledge is all about. Furthermore, many philosophers who still remained within the empiricist tradition had to radically revise the nature of empiricism.

W. V. O. QUINE

One of the most influential philosophers leading the charge against traditional empiricism has been Willard Van Orman Quine (1908–2000).* His classic essay "Two Dogmas of Empiricism" (1953) shook the foundations of empiricism.[1] The first "dogma" of empiricism he attacks is the traditional distinction between **analytic** and **synthetic** statements.† The assumption that we can make this sharp distinction has been a fundamental pillar of modern empiricism, from John Locke to the logical empiricists. Quine, however, makes the startling statement that the distinction between analytic and synthetic statements is "an unempirical dogma of empiricists, a metaphysical article of faith." He makes his case by systematically chipping away at every attempt to formulate the difference between analytic and synthetic statements.

One traditional way to define "analyticity" is to say that a statement is analytic if it can be reduced to a logical truth based on the logical law of identity, "A is A." Take, for example, the statement "All bachelors are unmarried." We presume that the analytic nature of this statement can be demonstrated if we turn it into a logical truth by substituting one synonym for another. Since "unmarried man" is a synonym for "bachelor," we can translate the original sentence into the logical truth "All unmarried men are unmarried."

The problem here, Quine argues, is that this definition of analytic statements assumes we can explain what we mean when we say one word is *synonymous* with another. To show that this is problematic, he first considers the suggestion that

the synonymy of "bachelor" and "unmarried male" might be explained by saying that this is how we define these terms or that people normally use these words interchangeably. Quine replies that this reference to people's linguistic behavior is a sociological observation and does not help explain why the analytic-synthetic distinction is thought to be a *logical* one.

Second, in a series of complex arguments I will not reproduce here, he argues that all attempts to define analytic statements end up defining "analyticity" in terms of "synonymy" and defining "synonymy" in terms of "analyticity." Hence, without a defining criteria that is clear and noncircular, empiricism cannot maintain a logical distinction between analytic and synthetic statements.

The second "dogma" of empiricism Quine attacks is that of "reductionism." This is the belief that a statement is meaningful if and only if it can be translated completely into statements about immediate experience. This assumption is contained in the logical positivist's **verifiability principle**. Even in its weakest forms, reductionism supposes that an individual statement can be confirmed or disconfirmed in isolation from other statements. This assumption lies at the foundation of analytic philosophy, for only if it is possible to consider our beliefs one by one can we subject them to piecemeal analysis.

In opposing reductionism, Quine argues that "our statements about the external world face the tribunal of sense experience not individually but only as a corporate body." In other words, whether we consider an individual statement to be proven or disproven depends on our entire belief system, including background assumptions about what experiences should be accepted or disregarded, how we should interpret them, and what we see their implications to be.‡ Furthermore, Quine says the two dogmas are really the same. Lurking in the analytic-synthetic distinction is the notion that the

---

*W. V. O. Quine was an important American philosopher who taught for many decades at Harvard University. He made many contributions to the theory of logic and its application to epistemology and metaphysics, which created considerable turmoil within the philosophical community. His work was influenced by both the analytic and pragmatic traditions.

†To review, analytic truths are those whose truth is based on the meanings of the terms, such as "All mothers are parents." A synthetic statement is one whose predicate adds information that cannot be deduced by analyzing the subject term, such as "All mothers are under 20 feet tall."

‡This thesis is a development of the position of the great French historian and philosopher of science, Pierre Duhem. Hence, it is sometimes referred to as the "Duhem-Quine thesis."

truth of synthetic statements depends on experience, while analytic statements are logically different because they are true no matter what we find in experience.

In contrast to the traditional empiricist's distinction, Quine says that "any statement can be held true come what may" and that "no statement is immune to revision." This means that whether or not we treat a statement as analytic or synthetic will depend on (1) the degree to which we are inclined to embrace it no matter what counterevidence arises, as opposed to (2) our willingness to revise it if it conflicts with new experiences. Furthermore, this choice is a practical one and not one dictated by logic.

Quine says the totality of our knowledge, ranging from our commonsense beliefs to the laws of logic, is "a man-made fabric which impinges upon experience only along the edges." In other words, the beliefs on the periphery of our belief system are the ones we would abandon most willingly if experience conflicted with them. This is because we can discard the beliefs on the edge without making major changes to the rest of our beliefs. Other beliefs, particularly the laws of science, mathematics, and logic, are deeply embedded in the interior of our belief systems. It is improbable that an everyday experience would cast them in doubt. Furthermore, because they have so many connections to the rest of our beliefs, we would be inclined to doubt our observations rather than abandon these central beliefs.

Despite the centrality of our scientific, mathematical, and logical beliefs, Quine believes there could be situations when even one of these would have to be modified, to preserve the coherence of the rest of our beliefs. For example, the logical principle known as the "law of excluded middle" states: either *P* or *Not-P* is true—there is no third possibility. Because of this logical law, we consider the statement "Either John is married or he is not married" to be true no matter what the facts about John may be. However, experimental results in an area of physics known as *quantum mechanics* have led some scientists to doubt the law of ex-

cluded middle. Others, who think it would be disastrous to abandon this principle, reinterpret the evidence to preserve the logical law. Quine says that the history of science shows us that even the most central assumptions of our belief systems are open to revision. For example, Ptolemy's assumptions were replaced by Kepler, Newton's by Einstein, and Aristotle's assumptions were overthrown by Darwin.*

To summarize, Quine has changed the hard-and-fast logical distinction of the empiricists between analytic and synthetic statements into a distinction made on the basis of pragmatic considerations. He has also challenged the notion that there can be any direct empirical verification or falsification of a single statement. Quine says the radical effects of abandoning these two dogmas include that of "blurring the supposed boundary between speculative metaphysics and natural science." The modern physicist's belief in physical objects and the ancient Greek's belief in Homer's gods are simply two beliefs that find their place within different sorts of belief systems. "In point of epistemological footing the physical objects and the gods differ only in degree and not in kind," Quine says. However, he retreats from total relativism and embraces pragmatism because he thinks we can argue for the practical superiority of one belief and its supporting assumptions over another belief. As Quine says,

The myth of physical objects is epistemologically superior to most in that it has proved more efficacious than other myths as a device for working a manageable structure into the flux of experience.

*Thomas Kuhn, a philosopher and historian of science, applies Quine's notion that a proposition is accepted or rejected in terms of how it fits in with our entire network of beliefs to explain the process of scientific inquiry. Kuhn shows the way scientists interpret their experience to maintain their current theories and documents the fact that scientific revolutions are not produced by the discovery of new data, but by large-scale displacements of the reigning scientific paradigm. This is developed in his book, *The Structure of Scientific Revolutions*, 2d ed., enlarged (Chicago: University of Chicago Press, 1970).

Rethinking Philosophy: Postmodernism

A relatively recent event in philosophy has been the rise of **postmodernism**. Postmodernists are a loose-knit group of thinkers united around the belief that they are the pallbearers of the modern tradition that originated in the Enlightenment. The tradition of modernism they reject includes the following beliefs: (1) there is one true picture of reality, (2) it is possible to obtain universal, objective knowledge, (3) science is a superior form of knowledge, (4) the history of modern thought has been a cumulative progression of increasingly better theories about reality, and (5) the autonomous, knowing subject is the source of all ideas.

Postmodernists join with Nietzsche and Heidegger in unmasking the pretensions of reason and the illusions of metaphysics. According to these thinkers, the dream of finding a central theme or set of categories for understanding reality is now over. There are no essences or certitudes on which we can pin our hopes. We must now face our stark, uncharted waking experience for the first time. We are the products of history, and history is nothing but an aimless play of shifting social forces. What is left for us to do is to analyze or "deconstruct" the dream of reason, to see how it arose and why it seemed so real, or else to revel in the endless play of interpretations and perspectives, realizing that it is a game without a final goal. For these reasons, postmodernists frequently allude to the death of epistemology, the death of metaphysics, and even the death of philosophy, at least as it has traditionally been understood. The most frequently discussed postmodernists in current philosophy are Michel Foucault, Jacques Derrida, and Richard Rorty.

MICHEL FOUCAULT

Frequently spoken of as the most important French thinker since Sartre, Michel Foucault (1926–1984) has been one of the central figures in postmodernism.* The works of Foucault's first period are *Madness and Civilization*, *The Birth of the Clinic: An Archaeology of Medical Perception*, *The Order of Things: An Archaeology of the Human Sciences*, and *The Archaeology of Knowledge*, all originally published in the 1960s. The word "archaeology" in most of the titles indicates how he conceived his task at that time. He was digging down beneath the surface of our social-intellectual traditions to uncover the strata of various historical eras. The "strata" he examines are called *epistemes*.† An *episteme* is the dominant conceptual framework of a given historical period. It makes no sense to ask which one is "true," for any notion of *truth* is the product of a particular *episteme*. As Foucault expresses it, " 'Truth' is to be understood as a system of ordered procedures for the production, regulation, distribution, circulation and operation of statements."[2] Embracing a form of relativism, Foucault believes the notion of one, universal truth is no longer viable, since it belongs to the *episteme* of an earlier age.

An *episteme* consists of a number of discursive practices (or structured linguistic patterns). The discursive practices Foucault is interested in are those that have been awarded the status of truth by society and that, in turn, effectively control that society. Hence, he looks at the normative discourses of medicine, psychiatry, law, and morality for his data. The dominant discursive practices of an era define what it makes sense to say, what is excluded from discourse, what questions are meaningful, and how behaviors are to be described. They create a social reality in their own image by indicating (implicitly or explicitly) how the world should be divided up according to such categories as

---

*Throughout his academic career, Michel Foucault lectured in universities around the world, including a number of American universities. At the time of his death he held a distinguished chair of the history and systems of thought at France's most prestigious institution, the Collège de France.
†*Episteme* is the Greek word for "knowledge." However, Foucault pluralizes the term, indicating that he believes there is a plurality of "knowledges."

true–false, madness–sanity, rational–irrational, moral–immoral, or normal–perverse.

Foucault rejects the referential view of language, which is the theory that the meaning of a word is the object to which it refers. Instead, he claims that words receive their meaning from their role within the whole network of discourse and practices. Employing what appears to be a sort of linguistic Kantianism, Foucault points out that words do not refer to objects as much as they constitute them. Although it is obvious that words cannot literally create a tree, we know things (including a tree) *as* this or that sort of thing—that is, in terms of some description or other.*

Reversing the Enlightenment assumption that philosophers' ideas create society, Foucault maintains that an *episteme* is a system of external social structures that determine our ideas. Hence, the Enlightenment *episteme* created the Enlightenment intellectuals, the intellectuals did not create their age. Even though Foucault speaks of "rules of production" that govern the discursive practices of a society, these rules have not been consciously invented and are never explicitly formulated by their participants. Each historical period is an unconscious play of forces that Foucault seeks to understand by "decoding" their patterns. The notion that human institutions and history exhibit rationality and continuity is attacked as an illusion. Instead, history is a purposeless series of ruptures, gaps, transformations, and displacements, as socially created realities come and go without order or reason.

After the May 1968 student uprisings in the Paris universities, Foucault came to a greater appreciation of the role of power structures. Instead of discourse being primary in the constitution of social reality, he now saw it as merely one outcome of an ever-expanding institutionalized social power. In this stage of his work, the term "genealogy" looms large. It is a term Nietzsche used when he discussed how the "will to power" expressed itself in covert ways. Foucault frequently uses the phrase "power/knowledge" to indicate that the two always go together. He says we must realize

> that power and knowledge directly imply one another; that there is no power relation without the correlative constitution of a field of knowledge, nor any knowledge that does not presuppose and constitute at the same time power relations.[3]

For Foucault, intellectual history is nothing more than a display of the way in which the notion of "truth" has been used to mask the will to power operating beneath the surface. In the following statement, notice how he wraps the notion of "truth" in political phrases: "Each society has its own régime of truth, its 'general politics' of truth: that is, the type of discourse which it accepts and makes function as true."[4]

This stage of Foucault's research is best exemplified in his 1975 work, *Discipline and Punish: The Birth of the Prison*. This study discusses the way in which the historically evolving architecture, policies, and practices of prisons in the nineteenth century exemplified the mechanisms of power and control. Although the concern for "technologies of control" may seem a necessary feature of a prison system, Foucault cites historical documents to show how the same mechanisms and ideology were applied to the organization of armies, schools, hospitals, and factories. In all these institutions, power and control were exercised under the guise of scientific, enlightened, humanitarian social reform. Through its "régimes of truth," society imposes its historically relative ideals on individuals, whether they are criminals, students, patients, or workers.

Consistently, Foucault recognized that his relativistic view implied that his own work was not an objective march toward universal truth. He applied to himself his claim that discourse is not the product of an autonomous subject but reflects the *episteme* of the time. Speaking about his book *The Order of Things*, he said,

---

*To roughly illustrate Foucault's point, think of words such as *credit*, *wife*, *sin*, *success*. Their meanings are not made clear by pointing to a certain object or action. Instead, to understand what is being described, you have to understand the complex network of words and practices that create the worlds of economics, social institutions, religion, and social ideals.

my book is a pure and simple "fiction": . . . it is not I who invented it; it is the relation of our epoch and its epistemological configuration to a whole mass of utterances. So, although the subject is in effect present in the totality of the book, it is an anonymous "someone" who speaks today in everything which is said.[5]

JACQUES DERRIDA

Another of the leading French postmodernists is Jacques Derrida (1930–).* The influence of Derrida's writings is matched only by the magnitude of their difficulty. The main project of his work is to deflate the pretensions of reason that are manifested throughout the history of thought. According to Derrida, the entire history of philosophy is a series of variations on "the myth of presence." In other words, every philosophy starts by assuming some central presence that is the axis around which the whole system revolves. This center may be Plato's Forms, Aristotle's substance, the medievals' God, Descartes's self, Newton's material particles, Kant's moral law, and so forth. In each system, this central reality (whatever it may be) is thought to be the rock-solid certitude that serves as the key for unlocking all the secrets of reality. As Derrida says,

The function of this center was not only to orient, balance, and organize the structure . . . but above all to make sure that the organizing principle would limit what we might call the play of the structure.[6]

By "play" Derrida means an openness to unexplored possibilities and novel approaches. In seeking to anchor thought and language in a "center," the philosopher limits and freezes our modes of interpretation, seeking security in a foundation that will not fail us. Derrida's strategy is not to refute these claims, but to unmask them by exposing the underlying motives and illusions that animate them all. He calls for an approach "which is no longer turned toward the origin, affirms play," and that abandons the dream of "full presence, the reassuring foundation, the origin and the end of play."[7] Derrida calls this process "deconstruction" and its result is a "decentering" of our systems of thought.

With Nietzsche and Foucault, Derrida rejects "logocentrism" or the notion that language refers to an order of meaning and truth, an order that is based in a reality that exists independently of our historically relative perspectives. However, if there is no certainty, no possibility of finding *the* center, no meanings or universals external to the language we invent, then everything is interpretation. The logical conclusion of this position is that all we ever achieve are reinterpretations of interpretations. As Derrida states it,

Reading . . . cannot legitimately transgress the text toward something other than it, toward the referent (a reality that is metaphysical, historical, psychobiographical, etc.) or toward a signifier outside the text whose content could take place, could have taken place outside of language, that is to say, in the sense that we give here to that word, outside of writing in general. . . . There is nothing outside of the text.[8]

Assuming that language cannot refer beyond itself, Derrida concludes that the meaning of a term is a function of the place it occupies within a system of linguistic concepts.† More specifically, terms receive their meanings from the role they play in differentiating one category of things from another.‡ For example, nature does not present us

---

*Jacques Derrida was first a student and later a critic of both Husserl and Heidegger. He taught philosophy at the École Normale Supérieure in France from 1965 to 1984. From 1960 to 1964, he taught at the Sorbonne in Paris. Since the early 1970s he has divided much of his time between Paris and the United States, where he has lectured at such universities as Johns Hopkins, Yale, Cornell, and the University of California at Irvine.

†Some have supported Derrida's point by noting that a dictionary explains a word by associating it or contrasting it with other words.
‡Derrida's thesis is a radical interpretation of a position known as "structuralism," which was based on the thought of linguist Ferdinand de Saussure and anthropologist Claude Lévi-Strauss.

with any absolute divisions corresponding to the terms "warm" or "hot," any more than it does for the contrasting terms of masculine–feminine or normal–abnormal. Instead, Derrida says, all such terms receive their meanings from the distinctions that are created within language. From the premise that language has no absolute, external point of reference, Derrida concludes that language is arbitrary, imposing no limits on the play of meanings and interpretations readers may find in a text.* Deconstructionists seek to reveal the incoherencies within texts, for from the conflict of multiple interpretations new possibilities of interpretation are generated.

To provide a concrete summary of the preceding points, Derrida creates a French pun with the word *différance*. This has the double meaning of "differ" and "defer." Because words do not have a fixed, positive meaning, but meaning emerges from the way they *differ*, then we have to continually *defer* any final interpretation or assignment of meaning. To undermine the seriousness of language and to underscore the element of "play," Derrida sprinkles his writings with puns, plays on words, unlikely metaphors, amusing allusions, and phonic and typographical tricks.†

Derrida realizes that even his own language is infected with metaphysical pretensions. The words "essence," "existence," "experience," "consciousness," "subject," and "object" carry with them the baggage of thousands of years of philosophical speculation and inescapably reflect the metaphysics of presence. Finding it impossible to critique philosophy without employing the traditional terms of philosophy, Derrida uses them, as he says, "under erasure." Thus, when he writes a word such as *thing*, he literally crosses it out, indicating that in using it he is not taking it seriously.

This brief glimpse of Derrida's thought is enough to give the flavor of his iconoclastic undermining of all traditional notions of truth, logic, rationality, objectivity, language, and interpretation. His deconstructionism has had its major impact in the field of literature where, in the last few decades of the twentieth century, it has become one of the most important movements within literary theory.

RICHARD RORTY

Within American philosophy, Richard Rorty (1931–) has been the most influential advocate of postmodernism.‡ Rorty started out as a doctrinaire analytic philosopher but eventually became disillusioned, concluding that analytic philosophy was far from the revolutionary philosophy it aspired to be. Although analytic philosophers were innovative in their use of linguistic methods, he said, they were still pursuing the age-old project of finding the universal foundations of knowledge that animated the Descartes-Locke-Kant tradition. Questioning the validity of this project, Rorty scandalized his analytic colleagues by rejecting this tradition and turning to Dewey's pragmatism instead. As Rorty's pragmatism became increasingly radical, he continued to cause a stir by developing his nontraditional vision of philosophy from the ideas of the unlikely combination of Dewey, Wittgenstein, and Heidegger. Consequently, Rorty has been a leading force in building bridges between Anglo-American philosophy and European Continental thought.

In his book *Philosophy and the Mirror of Nature*, Rorty attacks traditional epistemology and

---

*Critics often point out that deconstructionists inconsistently object when they believe the "true" meaning of their own texts have been wrongly interpreted. See Derrida's essay "Signature, Event, Context" in *Glyph* 1 (1977), 172–197, and John Searle's response "Reiterating the Differences: A Reply to Derrida" in the same issue, 198–208. In Derrida's retort, "Limited, Inc. abc" in *Glyph* 2 (1977), 162–254, Derrida complains that Searle misunderstood his position.

†The element of "play" in Derrida's view of language (referring to both the lack of restraint and the lack of seriousness) has been the target of criticism. Some Marxists and feminists accuse him of an escapism that lacks any serious political agenda. Similarly, conservatives and traditionalists accuse him of **nihilism**.

‡Richard Rorty spent most of his philosophical career as a faculty member in the philosophy department at Princeton. Beginning in 1983, he held the position of professor of humanities at the University of Virginia. After retiring there, he became a professor of comparative literature at Stanford University in 1998.

its attempt to set out the conditions that enable us to grasp "how things really are."[9] As the title of his book suggests, Rorty contends that traditional philosophy views the mind as a mirror that "reflects" the external world. Since the surface of the mirror was thought to be hazy or uneven, traditional philosophers tried to produce more accurate representations by "inspecting, repairing, and polishing the mirror" (PMN 12). Drawing on Dewey's insights, Rorty opposes traditional philosophy with four theses: the mind does not mirror nature, statements are simply tools for accomplishing certain tasks, an idea is true if it works, and there are no final ends in either philosophy or life.

The radical nature of Rorty's philosophy is captured by his call to abandon the project of epistemology. Epistemology is based on the notion that we can arrive at ideas or statements that will give us the one, true picture of reality. However, drawing on the insights of Quine and the philosopher of science T. S. Kuhn, Rorty argues that our beliefs and statements are always components of large-scale systems of practices that are chosen for practical reasons. If, as Dewey said, beliefs and statements are tools, then their effectiveness for our tasks is the issue and not their correspondence to reality. Referring to Wittgenstein and Heidegger, Rorty says that

> they do not think that when we say something we must necessarily be expressing a view about a subject. We might just be saying something—participating in a conversation rather than contributing to an inquiry. Perhaps saying things is not always saying how things are. (PMN 371)

What is the purpose of philosophical discourse if it is not that of "saying how things are"? Rorty's answer is that philosophy is "edifying discourse." The purpose of edifying philosophy is "finding new, better, more interesting, more fruitful ways of speaking" and "to keep the conversation going rather than to find objective truth" (PMN 360, 377). Rorty agrees with Jean-Paul Sartre that human beings are not fixed like objects, but we are always on the way, continually remaking ourselves:

> To see keeping a conversation going as a sufficient aim of philosophy, to see wisdom as consisting in the ability to sustain a conversation, is to see human beings as generators of new descriptions rather than beings one hopes to be able to describe accurately. (PMN 378)

If the mind does not mirror reality and our statements do not correspond to what is out there, is there any place at all for the notion of "truth"? In his essay "Solidarity or Objectivity?" Rorty repeats William James's statement that truth is "what it is good for *us* to believe" (SO 22).[10] But this notion of truth means it can never be conceived as some sort of final destination, for it is continually being reinvented. Rorty suggests we replace the epistemologist's static goal of "objectivity" with the pragmatist's goal of "intersubjective agreement" or "solidarity." The problem is, how can we agree if there is no objective reality about which we can agree? From Rorty's standpoint, the only possible answer is that our lives overlap, we engage in common projects, and we have similar needs and sentiments. Out of these common bonds, we create cohesive communities and a sense of solidarity. Hence, "truth" and "rationality" are inescapably social notions, for they cannot be discussed apart from "descriptions of the familiar procedures of justification that a given society—*ours*—uses in one or another area of inquiry" (SO 23).* Rorty says some are repelled by this view because it is hard for them to admit that we exist in a "lonely provincialism" and that "we are just the historical moment that we are" (SO 30). Nevertheless, even if we abandon the belief that there can be a final philosophy or an objective, universal picture of the world, we can still strive to break down the barriers between communities.

> For pragmatists, the desire for objectivity is not the desire to escape the limitations of one's community, but simply the desire for as much intersubjective

---

*Rorty's position has similarities to that of the later Wittgenstein (Chapter 32), who claimed our beliefs and ways of speaking are not grounded in logic but in our "form of life." "What people accept as a justification—is shewn by how they think and live," Wittgenstein said.

agreement as possible, the desire to extend the reference of "us" as far as we can. (SO 23)

Rethinking Philosophy: Feminism

Feminism is another contemporary movement that is seeking to rethink philosophy.* Since this is a movement and not a doctrine-laden school of thought, there are many conceptions among its adherents as to what constitutes feminist philosophy. Generally, feminist philosophers stress the role of gender in shaping the patterns of thought, society, and history. Furthermore, feminists focus on the ways in which our male-dominated historical traditions have excluded women from the intellectual and political realms. Consequently, feminists make it their goal not only to describe the world but also to change it, producing a society that recognizes women and men as both different and equal.

It is obvious that the history of philosophy, like that of most of our disciplines, has been shaped by men. This does not mean that there have not been women philosophers. In fact, we can find women philosophers all the way back to ancient Greece.† It does mean, however, that opportunities for women to have their voices heard have been limited. A work on the history of philosophy, such as this one, necessarily focuses on those thinkers in the past who have been most *influential*. A book exclusively devoted to those philosophers whose ideas have been the most sound or the most deserving of an audience would include women and men who are not included in standard histories, while others

would be dropped from their position of historical prominence.

A few male philosophers throughout history have criticized the exclusion of women. Plato in his *Republic* and John Stuart Mill in *The Subjection of Women* both argued that women of superior intellect and abilities should take their place with their male peers in providing intellectual and political leadership. Too often, however, Aristotle's attitude has prevailed. He asserted that only the free adult male is qualified to rule society, for only he is invested by nature with full rational capacity.[11] Furthermore, some feminists argue that when philosophers such as Kant discuss the political rights and equality of all "men," they often are not talking about human beings in general, but specifically about *males*.[12] For such reasons, feminists tend to agree with thinkers such as Marx, Nietzsche, and Foucault that "objective thought" often disguises underlying interests and power structures.

In addition to developing theories about the role of gender and power in the history of ideas, feminist philosophers focus attention on topics of particular concern to women, such as issues concerning equality, rights, sex roles, the family, and social structures. For this reason, the feminists have done a great deal of work in ethics and social philosophy.

Feminists are divided into two categories. The first category consists of (what are variously called) "equity," "liberal," or "first wave" feminists. The equity feminists want to retain the current social structures and the intellectual tradition of the Enlightenment. Their concern is that women be given full intellectual and political participation in society. Thus, they want to open up society, correct the distortions in our traditions, and modify our intellectual disciplines. The second group of feminists is called "gender," "radical," or "second wave" feminists. Gender feminists claim that the fundamental structures, assumptions, methods, and discourse of our Western heritage reflect the fact that it has been controlled by men. Using their own term, the gender feminists' approach is much more "subversive," for instead of making piecemeal corrections to the Western tradition, they

---

*In addition to the many books and anthologies that are now available, *Hypatia: A Journal of Feminist Philosophy* provides many examples of what this movement is about. (Hypatia was a fifth-century female leader of the Neoplatonist movement who was condemned to death as a heretic and died a brutal death at the hands of Christian fanatics.)

†For a comprehensive survey of women in the history of philosophy, see *A History of Women Philosophers*, ed. Mary Ellen Waithe, 4 vols. (Dordrecht, Netherlands: Kluwer Academic, 1987–1994). This series covers women philosophers from ancient Greece through the twentieth century.

Simone de Beauvoir (1908–1986) is best known for her novels and essays which made her one of France's most celebrated twentieth-century writers. Her book The Second Sex *became an influential document in the feminist movement and contained the often quoted words, "one is not born a woman but becomes one." She was the lifelong companion of existentialist Jean-Paul Sartre.*

want to bring the validity of that whole tradition into question and to devise alternatives.

The notion of "gender" is, itself, one of the most controversial topics within the feminist movement. A distinction is frequently made between sex and gender. Sex is a biological category that refers to the obvious physical differences between males and females. Gender, however, is a social-psychological category. It includes (but is not limited to) the notions of masculine-feminine, social roles, sexuality, and the apparent psychological differences between men and women. Some feminists are *essentialists*, claiming that there is a distinct and essential female nature. Some essentialists are biological determinists who see female nature as rooted in women's unique biology. Looser versions of essentialism claim that the

properties constituting the female gender are rather stable, although created through the unique and common features of female experience. Feminists who are *nonessentialists* or *nominalists* deny that gender characteristics are fixed in any way at all, viewing them as purely social constructs that are open to change and redefinition. Rejecting both extreme essentialism and nominalism, Simone de Beauvoir expresses a mediating position in her famous quote "One is not born, but rather becomes, a woman."[13] Briefly, her view is that gender characteristics are not biologically determined, but they can be either socially imposed or subjectively chosen. The role gender plays in feminist thought can be illustrated by a brief and selective look at ways feminists are attempting to remap the terrains of epistemology and ethics.

FEMINIST APPROACHES TO EPISTEMOLOGY

According to gender feminists, traditional theories of knowledge have been based on the following assumptions:

1. There is one, universal, human nature. Hence, epistemology is the attempt to describe the fundamental cognitive structures of the generic human being.

2. The particular identity of a knower (including gender, race, class, and social-political-historical circumstances) is irrelevant to the production and assessment of that person's knowledge claims.

3. It is possible to obtain knowledge that is purely objective, value-free, and politically neutral.

In contrast to these assumptions, gender feminists claim that (1) there is no universal human nature, (2) knowledge is always related to the standpoint of a particular knower, and (3) knowledge claims reflect the dominant values and political structures of a society. Feminists claim that the picture of generic humanity has actually made men's experiences and interests the paradigm. Other points of view and characteristics, particularly those of women, that deviate from the standard picture have been excluded or marginalized for being too subjective, idiosyncratic, or unconventional. Traditional epistemologists seek for universal standards of rationality; feminists ask, "Standard and rational for whom?" This concern is expressed in the title of Sandra Harding's book *Whose Science? Whose Knowledge?*[14] Similarly, in criticizing a recent book on rationality that enthrones traditional notions of reason, Lorraine Code asserts, "Critics must ask for whom this epistemology exists; whose interests it serves; and whose it neglects or suppresses in the process."[15]

Most feminist writers contend that women's experiences and ways of thinking differ from those that have been the basis of traditional (male) epistemologies. Just as the standards used to evaluate oranges do not apply to apples, grapes, and lemons, so there cannot be one paradigm for epistemology. Feminists appeal to empirical research on children, which has provided interesting data on gender-specific ways of knowing. Boys tend to organize the world in terms of independent, manipulable, discrete units. Girls, in contrast, perceive the world in terms of functional, relational characteristics and interdependent connections. If there are these sorts of differences, then there cannot be one, generic theory of knowledge.

A major topic within feminist epistemology is the nature of rationality and its relation to the emotions. The majority position in Western tradition, feminists charge, has defined rationality in a way that devalued the emotions. Addressing this issue in an essay titled "The Man of Reason," Genevieve Lloyd discusses this traditional ideal of rationality.[16] She has an easy task demonstrating that the standard equations throughout history have been "male = rational" and "female = nonrational." Descartes's dualism aggravated the problem by creating the following divisions: intellect versus the emotions, reason versus imagination, mind versus the body. The consequence of Descartes's divisions was that the emotions, the imagination, and the sensuous dimension were assigned to women as their special area of responsibility, while excluding them from the realm of reason.

According to Lloyd's analysis, "If women's minds are less rational than men's, it is because the limits of reason have been set in a way that excludes qualities that are then assigned to women."[17] Furthermore, this ideal of rationality has political consequences. "Exclusion from reason has meant exclusion from power."[18] In rejecting our traditional definition of rationality, Lloyd also rejects the romantics' solution, for they accepted the preceding polarities such as intellect versus emotions and then went on to exclusively embrace the second half of each dichotomy. Instead, she calls for a broader notion of reason that seeks for the unity beneath the divisions, which have been the basis of illegitimate sexual stereotypes.

Taking a different approach from Lloyd, Alison Jaggar is willing to accept that women have a richer emotional life than men, but argues that this makes women better knowers.[19] While recognizing that emotions such as love and hate can undermine critical reflection, she still insists that the emotions may be helpful and even necessary to the construction of knowledge. Referring to work in the epistemology of science, Jaggar argues that all observation is selective. As part of this selection process, our values, motivations, and interests direct our cognitive pursuits, shape what we know, and help determine its significance. Yet these subjective factors that influence cognition are heavily imbued with emotional dimensions.* Jaggar argues that the emotions of marginalized people (such as women) make them epistemologically privileged. For example, the pain and anger women feel in response to subtle sexual harassment or injustice allows them to perceive features of the prevailing social structures that are invisible to men.

FEMINIST APPROACHES TO ETHICS

Feminists apply the same sorts of analyses in ethics that they do in epistemology. Traditionally,

---

*Jaggar suggests, for example, that Jane Goodall's important scientific contributions to our understanding of chimpanzee behavior was made possible only by her love and empathy for these animals.

ethical theory has been presented as though the topic were objective and neutral. As a matter of fact, feminist critics charge, the theories have contained pervasive gender biases. In 1982, Harvard psychologist Carol Gilligan published *In a Different Voice: Psychological Theory and Women's Development*.[20] This book ended up being one of the most influential books in feminist ethics.* Gilligan noted that empirical research on the development of moral reasoning was carried out primarily by males and on mostly male subjects. The result was that psychological theories about this topic took male reasoning as the norm.

According to Gilligan's research, males and females solve ethical dilemmas with different sets of criteria. Males tend to employ a "judicial" model, which emphasizes equality, justice, rights, impartiality, objectivity, universal principles, and logic. In contrast, females tend to approach ethics in a more person-centered way, stressing care, compassion, trust, mercy, forgiveness, preventing harm, and feelings. Gilligan concludes that these two separate ethical perspectives are products of the different ways that males and females are socialized. The problem is that traditional theories of moral development characterize the judicial (male) approach as the highest stage and characterize more relational (female) approaches as less mature stages of development.† However, Gilligan says these two approaches cannot be ranked on the same scale, for they are different ways of achieving moral maturity. Furthermore, she says each approach has its strengths and weaknesses,

suggesting the need for a more adequate ethical perspective that includes both dimensions.

Other feminists start with the uniqueness of the female approach to ethics and go on from there to argue for its superiority over traditional (male) morality.‡ However, many are not sure that this is a good strategy. Feminist critics say that narrowing feminist ethics to the "ethics of caring" reinforces gender stereotypes and supports the traditional dogma that women are best suited to be mothers and nurses, rather than lawyers and executives. Furthermore, critics charge, downgrading the principles of impartiality, autonomy, and justice found in traditional moral theories undermines women's drive for equality.

To summarize, feminists have raised important questions, such as, How do power structures and social conditions shape and limit the development of ideas? To what extent are our personal identities formed by biological factors, to what extent are they constructed by social forces, and to what extent do we freely choose them? To what degree is knowledge relative to the situation of the knower? In our personal lives and in our theories, how do we find a balance between reason and emotion or justice and caring? Although these sorts of questions arose out of women's attempts to rethink history and their own experience and identities, the impact of these questions goes far beyond issues that are exclusively concerned with women.

Philosophy in a Global Village

The feminists' attempt to rethink our philosophical tradition has been paralleled by a new interest in non-Western philosophical traditions. Just as

---

*At least since Kant, many traditional philosophers have tended to say that empirical psychology has no relevance to issues concerning standards and foundations in epistemology and ethics. Thus, they would see Gilligan's book on psychology as irrelevant to philosophy. Many feminists, however, see disciplinary boundaries as artificial structures that are used to fragment human experience and maintain control over the sorts of questions that may be raised. They claim that our psychological structures, gender, values, politics, social patterns, relationships of power, knowledge, and conceptions of reality are all intertwined in making our experience the way it is.

†Gilligan illustrates her point by analyzing the work of Lawrence Kohlberg, one of the leading researchers in the area of moral development.

‡See, for example, Annette Baier, *Postures of the Mind: Essays on Mind and Morals* (Minneapolis: University of Minnesota Press, 1985), Nel Noddings, *Caring: A Feminist Approach to Ethics and Moral Education* (Berkeley: University of California Press, 1984); Sara Ruddick, *Maternal Thinking: Toward a Politics of Peace* (Boston: Beacon Press, 1989); and Margaret Walker, "Moral Understandings: Alternative 'Epistemology' for a Feminist Ethics," *Hypatia: A Journal of Feminist Philosophy* 4, no. 2 (Summer 1989).

feminists sought to make room within philosophy for the "different voice" represented by women's experiences, so has there been a growing concern to open up Western philosophy to include the perspectives of other cultures. More and more, multicultural approaches are being explored in order to broaden our outlook on traditional philosophical questions. Because of space limitations, this book has covered only Western philosophy. However, becoming aware of the hidden assumptions solidified in Western history can be a broadening rather than a limiting experience if it makes us more discerning in our dialogue with other traditions.

New Issues in Philosophy of Mind

The development of computer technology, particularly artificial intelligence research, has raised new questions and suggested new methods and directions within the area of philosophy of mind. In fact, a new interdisciplinary field has emerged called *cognitive science*, which is a hybrid of the disciplines of artificial intelligence, philosophy, psychology, neuroscience, and linguistics. A basic feature of this new approach is the "computational model of the mind," which assumes that the analogy between computers and human cognition will be a fruitful one. This is an attempt to fulfill La Mettrie's vision that he set out in his 1747 work, *Man the Machine*. The philosophers working in this field hope that an increased understanding of how to make computers intelligent will give us a better understanding of human cognition, and a better understanding of human cognition will help us make computers more intelligent.

Although many researchers in this area think that the psychology of information processing will answer our philosophical questions about our mental life, other philosophers insist that we must get down to an even more fundamental level to explore the biological basis of thought. If we understand the details of how the brain works, they say, we will resolve the mysteries of human cognition. Two important philosophers in this movement are Patricia Churchland, with her aptly titled book *Neurophilosophy* (1986), and her

husband, Paul Churchland, who wrote the influential book *Matter and Consciousness* (1984). If their approach is correct, an adequate scientific understanding of the brain will eliminate the need for such terms as "mind," "self," "beliefs," "thoughts," "desires," or "intentions." Instead, all future talk about human cognition will be cast in terms of brain states. If this happens, then the traditional discipline of philosophy of mind that uses these epistemological terms will be cast aside as "folk psychology," just as medical science has unseated many theories of folk medicine. As it stands now, the neurological approach to philosophical psychology is a research program that is still in its beginning stages. The critics of this approach have revived Edmund Husserl's arguments against naturalism, claiming we will never be able to consistently develop a theory that does away with the knowing subject who did the theorizing in the first place.

New Issues in Ethics

Another development that has come to the forefront of philosophy in recent decades is *applied ethics*. Unlike the previous movements mentioned in this chapter, applied ethics is not a particular philosophy or point of view. Instead, it is a new application of ethical theory to practical ethical problems, particularly as they are found in the various professions. The best-known example of this new topic is the field of medical ethics. The issues that make the headlines (and the law courts) are, typically, abortion, euthanasia, physician-assisted suicides, surrogate motherhood, and genetic engineering. However, there are many, more subtle ethical issues in medicine dealing with such topics as autonomy–paternalism, the physician–patient relationship, consent, disclosure, and issues concerning privacy or confidentiality. Although some of these issues were unheard of fifty years ago, the relevance of the history of philosophy is indicated by the fact that such names as Immanuel Kant and John Stuart Mill continually occur in contemporary discussions of current problems. In addition to medical ethics, there has also been a growing demand for philosophers to clarify the ethical dimensions of professions such as business, accounting, journalism, and engineering, as well as the issues arising out of our environmental concerns.

A Parting Word

With all this emphasis in these last six chapters on the new movements in philosophy, it should not be thought that the traditional positions have been abandoned. Plenty of thinkers still believe that Plato, Aristotle, Augustine, Aquinas, or one or more of the moderns from Descartes to Hegel got at least part of the picture right. For example, I have a colleague in law and one in mathematics who are Hegelians. I also know physicists who think that metaphysical idealism makes a lot of sense. Philosophy is a unique discipline in that its theories have more enduring value than those of any other field. There is still much to be learned from positions that are centuries old.

I can think of no better way to end this book than by returning to a quote from Martin Heidegger. He addresses the accusation that "you can't do anything with philosophy." Heidegger acknowledges that this claim is true. Certainly (to elaborate on his remarks), philosophy will not get us to the farthest planets, it will not lead to a cure for any fatal disease, nor will it help us make a killing on the stock market. However, Heidegger cautions that this is not the last word on philosophy. "Granted that *we* cannot do anything with philosophy, might not philosophy, if we concern ourselves with it, do something *with us*?"[21] I hope that you have found this to be the outcome of reading this book.

Questions for Understanding

1. What two "dogmas of empiricism" does Quine attack? What arguments does he use in his attack?

2. What is meant by "modernism"? How has it been attacked by postmodernism?

3. What does *episteme* mean? In his epistemology, why does Foucault replace it with the plural term *epistemes*?

4. According to Foucault, what is the relationship between power and knowledge?

5. What does Derrida mean by the following terms: *the myth of presence*, *deconstruction*, and *logocentrism*?

6. What is Derrida's account of the meaning of a word?

7. What four theses does Rorty assert in his critique of traditional philosophy?

8. According to Rorty, what is the purpose of philosophical discourse?

9. Rorty replaces the notion of "objectivity" in traditional epistemology with what goal?

10. What are the differences between "first wave" feminists and "second wave" feminists?

11. What is the distinction feminists make between sex and gender?

12. What is the difference between feminists who are essentialists and those who are nonessentialists?

13. According to gender feminists, what are the three assumptions of traditional theories of knowledge and why do they reject them?

14. What is Genevieve Lloyd's thesis about rationality?

15. What does Alison Jaggar say about the role of the emotions in knowledge?

16. What does Carol Gilligan say about the role of gender in the development of moral reasoning?

17. What is cognitive science?

18. What is meant by the "computational model of the mind"?

19. Why do philosophers such as Patricia and Paul Churchland think that notions such as "mind" or "belief" should be eliminated? What notions will they use to replace them?

20. Why has applied ethics become such an important topic recently?

Questions for Reflection

1. According to Quine, how are modern physics and Greek mythology epistemologically similar? If they are similar in this way, why does he prefer modern physics as a way of understanding the world? Is he rational in this preference?

2. To what degree do you agree or disagree with Foucault that power defines what will be accepted as knowledge? Think of some examples in the past or the present that he could use to illustrate this point.

3. If everyone accepted Rorty's claim that solidarity and not objectivity is the goal of thought, how would this change the activity of philosophy? How might society be different? What problems would be solved by this point of view? What problems might be created?

4. If female thinkers had predominated throughout the history of philosophy, would it have developed differently? How so?

5. Is our outlook on the world or our philosophy affected by our gender? How so? What are the implications of your answer for the doing of philosophy?

6. Is there, ideally, one true philosophy or are there necessarily only many philosophies? If there is no possibility of any particular perspective being the correct one, what is the value of doing philosophy? How would Rorty or a feminist respond?

7. What are some of the issues on which the feminists disagree with each other? In each case, which feminists do you think have the most plausible view?

8. Do you think research on the brain will solve our epistemological questions? Why or why not? What philosophical questions (if any) do you think will not be illuminated, much less solved, by further scientific research?

Notes

1. Willard Van Orman Quine, "Two Dogmas of Empiricism," in *From a Logical Point of View*, rev. ed. (New York: Harper Torchbooks, Harper & Row, 1961).

2. Michel Foucault, *Power/Knowledge: Selected Interviews and Other Writings, 1972–1977*, ed. Colin Gordon, trans. Colin Gordon, Leo Marshall, John Mepham, and Kate Soper (New York: Pantheon Books, 1980), 133.

3. Michel Foucault, *Discipline and Punish: The Birth of the Prison*, trans. Alan Sheridan (New York: Vintage Books, Random House, 1977), 27.

4. Foucault, "Truth and Power," in *Power/Knowledge*, 131.

5. Quoted in Pamela Major-Poetzl, *Michel Foucault's Archaeology of Western Culture* (Chapel Hill: University of California Press, 1983), 19.

6. Jacques Derrida, "Structure, Sign, and Play in the Discourse of the Human Sciences," chapter in his *Writing and Difference*, trans. Alan Bass (Chicago: University of Chicago Press, 1978), 278.

7. Ibid., 292.

8. Jacques Derrida, *Of Grammatology*, trans. Gayatri Chakravorty Spivak (Baltimore: Johns Hopkins University Press, 1976), 158.

9. Richard Rorty, *Philosophy and the Mirror of Nature* (Princeton, NJ: Princeton University Press, 1979). This work is cited in the text using the abbreviation PMN.

10. Richard Rorty, "Solidarity or Objectivity," chapter in his *Objectivity, Relativism, and Truth*, Philosophical Papers, vol. 1 (Cambridge, England: Cambridge University Press, 1991). This essay is cited in the text using the abbreviation SO.

11. Aristotle, *Politics*, bk. 1.

12. Susan Mendus, "Kant: An Honest But Narrow-Minded Bourgeois?" in *Women in Western Political Philosophy: Kant to Nietzsche*, ed. Ellen Kennedy and Susan Mendus (New York: St. Martin's Press, 1987).

13. Simone de Beauvoir, *The Second Sex*, trans. H. M. Parshley (New York: Knopf, 1975), 267.

14. Sandra Harding, *Whose Science? Whose Knowledge?* (Ithaca, NY: Cornell University Press, 1991).

15. Lorraine Code, "Taking Subjectivity into Account," in Linda Alcoff and Elizabeth Potter, eds., *Feminist Epistemologies* (New York: Routledge, 1993), 23.

16. Genevieve Lloyd, "The Man of Reason," in *Women, Knowledge, and Reality: Explorations in Feminist Philosophy*, ed. Ann Garry and Marilyn Pearsall (Boston: Unwin Hyman, 1989), 111–128. Originally published in *Metaphilosophy* 10, no. 1 (January 1979): 18–37. See also, the book-length treatment, Genevieve Lloyd, *The Man of Reason: "Male" and "Female" in Western Philosophy* (Minneapolis: University of Minnesota Press, 1984).

17. Ibid., 124.

18. Ibid., 127.

19. Alison M. Jaggar, "Love and Knowledge: Emotion in Feminist Epistemology," in *Women, Knowledge, and Reality: Explorations in Feminist Philosophy*, ed. Ann Garry and Marilyn Pearsall (Boston: Unwin Hyman, 1989), 129–155. Previously published in *Inquiry: An Interdisciplinary Journal of Philosophy* (June 1989) and in *Gender/Body/Knowledge: Feminist Reconstructions of Being and Knowing*, ed. Alison M. Jaggar and Susan R. Bordo (New Brunswick, NJ: Rutgers University Press, 1989).

20. Carol Gilligan, *In a Different Voice: Psychological Theory and Women's Development* (Cambridge, MA: Harvard University Press, 1982).

21. Martin Heidegger, *An Introduction to Metaphysics*, trans. Ralph Manheim (Garden City, NY: Anchor Books, Doubleday, 1959), 10.

This Glossary contains all the terms set out in bold in the preceding chapters. Terms set out in bold within the definitions are defined elsewhere in the glossary. The chapter in which the term is introduced as well as those in which it plays a central role are indicated in parentheses.

Aesthetics (or esthetics)—An area of philosophy that pursues questions concerning art, including the nature and role of art, the standards for evaluating art, and the nature of beauty. (Introduction chapter)

Agnosticism—With respect to a particular issue, the claim that nothing can be known, one way or another, because the evidence is thought to be insufficient to provide us with any knowledge. Hence, the agnostic argues that we must suspend judgment on the issue. Typically, agnosticism refers to the position that the existence of God can neither be affirmed nor denied. (Chap. 21)

Altruism—The claim that people either are or ought to be motivated to serve the interests of others. The opposite of **egoism**. (Chap. 24)

Analytic judgment—A knowledge claim expressed by an **analytic statement**. (Chap. 22)

Analytic philosophy—A twentieth-century movement in philosophy, particularly strong in America and Britain, that approaches philosophical problems primarily through an analysis of language. Also called *linguistic philosophy*. (Chap. 32)

Analytic statement—A statement in which the predicate is contained within the subject (its truth is based on the meaning and relationship of its terms) and its denial results in a logical contradiction, e.g., "All mothers are parents." Contrasted with synthetic statements. (Chaps. 22, 32)

Antinomy—A pair of seemingly reasonable conclusions that flatly contradict each other and hence cannot both be true. Kant used antinomies to argue that reason contradicts itself when it reaches beyond its proper limits in attempting to answer traditional metaphysical questions about the nature of reality. (Chap. 22)

A posteriori—A type of knowledge, statement, or concept whose content and truth are derived from experience. For example, "Water freezes at 32°F" is an *a posteriori* truth. Contrasted with **a priori**. (Chaps. 13, 22)

Appearance—The way in which something presents itself to the senses which is different from how it is in reality. For example, a straight stick in water appears to be bent, even though it really is not. (Chaps. 2, 3, 6, 22, 23)

A priori—A type of knowledge, statement, or concept whose content and truth can be known prior to or independently of experience. For example, some philosophers believe that "two plus two equals four" and "every event has a cause" are *a priori* truths which cannot be proven by experience. Contrasted with **a posteriori.** (Chaps. 13, 22)

Argument—An attempt to establish the truth of a statement (the conclusion) by showing that it follows from, or is supported by, the truth of one or more other statements (the premises). (Introduction chapter, Chap. 5)

Atomism—A metaphysical position originating with the ancient Greeks that claims that reality is made up of numerous, indivisible particles of matter moving in a void. (Chap. 2)

Autonomy—Being one's own authority or rule giver, as opposed to being subject to external authority. In Kant's ethics this is an essential condition for rational morality. (Chap. 22)

Categorical imperative—According to Kant, a command that is binding on all rational persons at all times, which generates universal moral laws. It commands us to always act in such a way that we could rationally wish that everyone followed the principle governing that action. Contrasted with hypothetical imperatives, in which the command applies only under certain conditions. (Chap. 22)

Cogent argument—An **inductive argument** that is (a) inductively strong and (b) has all true premises. (Introduction chapter)

Cognition—Knowledge or the act of knowing.

Cognitive meaning—The informative content of a statement that asserts a claim that may be either true or false. The cognitive meaning of a statement is sometimes contrasted with its emotive meaning, or the emotional attitude it expresses or evokes. (Chap. 32)

Coherence theory of truth—The theory that a true assertion or belief is one that coheres with our entire system of interconnected and mutually supporting beliefs. (Chap. 24)

Compatibilism—The theory that human beings are *both* determined and free as long as their actions proceed from their own, inner choices and are not compelled by an external cause. (Chap. 17)

Conceptualism—The claim that **universals** are mental concepts obtained by abstracting the common qualities appearing in similar particular objects. See **Nominalism** and **Realism**. (Chap. 10)

Consequentialism—See **Teleological ethics**.

Contingent—A contingent event is one that is not logically necessary, for whether it occurs or not is dependent on other events. Similarly, a contingent statement is one whose truth is not logically necessary. It may be denied without asserting a contradiction. (Chaps. 12, 13, 16, 17)

Correspondence theory of truth—The theory that a true assertion or belief is one that corresponds with the fact or state of affairs in reality to which it refers. (Chaps. 27, 33)

Cosmological argument—An argument for the existence of God based on the claim that the universe requires a cause for its existence. (Chap. 11)

Deduction—The form of reasoning we use when we attempt to argue from the truth of one proposition or set of propositions to a conclusion that necessarily follows from those propositions. (Introduction chapter)

Deductively valid—See **Valid**.

Deism—A religious outlook, based on reason, that acknowledges the existence of God and his creation of the world, but denies that God intervenes in the world either in the form of miracles or revelation. Deists argue that the divinely ordered natural laws and reason make both nature and humanity self-sufficient. (Chap. 19)

Deontological ethics—From the Greek word *deon*, meaning "duty" or "obligation." Deontological ethics defines the moral rightness or wrongness of an act in terms of the intrinsic value of the act. According to this theory, our duty to perform an action (or to refrain from doing it) is based on the nature of the act itself and not on its consequences. Kant was a leading proponent of this theory. Contrasted with **teleological ethics**. (Chap. 22)

Determinism—The metaphysical position that claims every event (including human actions) follows necessarily from previous events. (Chaps. 14, 17, 30)

Dialectic—(1) For Socrates, a conversational method for progressing toward the truth, by continually examining proposed answers to a question, repeatedly replacing inadequate answers with more refined and adequate ones. (2) For Plato, it was the philosophical method of rising above particulars and hypotheses to achieve the highest form of knowledge. (3) For Hegel, it is a historical process in which both thought and reality develop as oppositions and tensions are resolved at a higher stage. (4) Marx adopted Hegel's historical dialectic, but changed it into the conflict and development of material forces. (Chaps. 3, 4, 24, 25)

Dogmatism—Asserting a position without providing adequate reasons for its truth.

Dualism—A theory that asserts that there are two irreducible realities, such as mind and body, spirit and matter, or good and evil. (Chaps. 2, 4, 15)

Egoism—(1) Psychological egoism is a descriptive theory that claims people always pursue what they perceive to be their own best interests. (2) Ethical egoism is a prescriptive theory that claims people *ought* to always act according to their own best interests. The opposite of **altruism**. (3) In both of the preceding types of egoism, egoistic **hedonism** identifies pleasure with one's best interests. (Chaps. 6, 14, 27, 28)

Empirical—Related to sense experience.

Empiricism—The theory that knowledge is obtained solely from sense experience. (Chaps. 2, 13, 19, 20, 21, 28, 32)

Epicureanism—A version of **hedonism**, based on the philosophy of Epicurus (341–271 B.C.), which claims that (1) only pleasure is intrinsically good and (2) all pleasures are not to be desired equally, the more prudent and sedate pleasures being the ones that lead to true happiness. (Chap. 6)

Epistemology—An area of philosophy that pursues questions concerning truth and knowledge. (Introduction chapter)

Essence—The defining characteristic of something. That property or set of properties without which it would not be the sort of thing that it is. (Chaps. 5, 11)

Ethical egoism—See **Egoism**.

Ethical hedonism—See **Hedonism**.

Ethics—An area of philosophy that reasons about morality, particularly the meaning and justification of claims concerning right or wrong actions, obligation, moral rules, rights, virtue, the good life, and the possibility of objective morality. (Introduction chapter)

Existentialism—A nineteenth- and twentieth-century philosophy that focuses on the nature and meaning of human existence as understood from the subjective standpoint of the subject. Repudiating the notion of a fixed human nature, existentialists claim that we are continually creating the self. They stress the priority of subjective choosing over objective reasoning, concrete experience over intellectual abstractions, individuality over mass culture, human freedom over determinism, and authentic living over inauthenticity. (Chaps. 23, 26, 27, 29, 33)

Feminism—A movement within philosophy and other disciplines that (1) stresses the role of gender in shaping the patterns of thought, society, and history, (2) focuses on the ways in which women have been assigned roles throughout history that excluded them from the intellectual and political realms, and (3) strives to produce a society that recognizes women and men as both different and equal. (Chap. 34)

Forms—According to Plato, the Forms are the ultimate realities and objects of genuine knowledge. Forms are nonphysical, eternal, known only through reason, and impart intelligibility and reality to things in the physical world that imitate them. For example, Plato believes all circular things (rings, hoops, wreathes) are imperfect representations of the Form of Circularity. (Chap. 4)

Hedonism—The position that claims pleasure is the only thing that has intrinsic value. (1) Psychological hedonism claims that it is a psychological fact that people always strive to pursue pleasure and avoid pain. (2) Ethical hedonism claims that pleasure is what people *ought* to pursue. (Chaps. 2, 6, 14, 28)

Historicism—The theory that everything human is affected by the processes of history, such that any idea cannot be understood apart from its historical context and is valid only for a particular time, place, and community. (Chaps. 23, 24)

Idea—(1) In general, any object of thought. (2) For Plato, Ideas were another term for the **Forms** (e.g., the Idea of Justice, the Idea of Circularity). (3) For Descartes and Locke an idea was any mental content, which could include sensations (redness, sweetness, heat) or the mind's mental states (doubting, imagining, believing). (4) For Berkeley, ideas and the minds that contained them were the whole of reality. (5) For Hume, an idea was a copy of an original sensation (called an *impression*) that was recalled in memory or the imagination. (Chaps. 4, 15, 19, 20, 22)

Idealism—The theory that reality is ultimately mental or of the nature of a mind. Idealism characterizes the philosophies of Leibniz, Berkeley, and Hegel. Contrasted with **materialism** and contemporary forms of **realism**. (Chaps. 17, 20, 23, 24)

Indeterminism—The theory that some events in the world (particularly human choices) are not the necessary result of previous causes, because these events are either random or the products of free will. (Chap. 30)

Induction—The form of reasoning we use when we argue from what is true of one set of facts to what is probably true of further facts of the same kind. An inductive argument either concludes something about a new case, based on what was true of similar cases, or it arrives at a generalization concerning all cases similar to those that have been observed. (Introduction chapter, Chap. 21)

Inductively strong argument—A successful inductive argument in which the premises, if true, would make the conclusion highly probable. (Introduction chapter)

Innate ideas or knowledge—Mental contents that are inborn or part of the natural content of the human mind and not derived from experience. Their existence is defended by most ratio-

nalists and attacked by empiricists. (Chaps. 3, 4, 15, 17, 19)

Intellectualism—The theory that the intellect is prior to or superior to the will. Accordingly, it is claimed that the intellect or reason perceives that certain ends or goals are desirable and then directs the will to achieve them. Theological intellectualism claims that God's intellect first knows that certain actions are either intrinsically good or evil and then he wills that they should be done or avoided. The opposite of **voluntarism**. (Chap. 10)

Intuition—(1) Knowledge that is directly and immediately known by the mind, rather than being the product of reasoning or inference; or (2) the object of such knowledge. According to Kant, humans can have only sensory intuitions. (Chap. 22, 31)

Linguistic philosophy—See **Analytic philosophy**.

Logical atomism—The philosophy of Russell and the early Wittgenstein, which claimed that the structure of language and reality are the same, since language is reducible to elementary units corresponding to the fundamental units that compose the world of facts. (Chap. 32)

Logical positivism—A twentieth-century version of **empiricism** and a version of **analytic philosophy**, which states that (1) logical and mathematical statements are logically necessary statements (**tautologies**) that do not provide information about the world and (2) factual statements are meaningful only if they are capable of being verified in sense experience (**verifiability principle**). (Chap. 32)

Logos—A particularly rich Greek term that has a large number of related meanings: speech, discourse, word, explanation, reason, order. It is the source of many English words such as "logic," "logo," "biology," "psychology." Heraclitus believed that *logos* was the rational principle that permeated all things. The Stoics identified it with God, Providence, Nature, or Fate. Christian writers identified it with God or Christ. (Chaps. 2, 6, 7)

Marxism—The philosophy based on the writings of Karl Marx, which asserts that (1) reality is material, (2) history follows a dialectical pattern controlled by economic forces, (3) each era of history is characterized by conflict between opposing economic classes, (4) history is a **dialectic** in which each economic stage produces its own contradictions, giving way to its successor, and (5) the present stage of capitalism will be overcome by socialism, leading to the final stage of pure communism in which class conflict will be abolished. (Chap. 25)

Materialism—The metaphysical position that claims matter is the only reality. Also called *material monism*. (Chaps. 2, 14, 25)

Material monism—See **Materialism**.

Metaphysical dualism—See **Dualism**.

Metaphysics—An area of philosophy that pursues questions about the nature of reality. (Introduction chapter)

Monism—Any metaphysical position that asserts that there is only one kind of reality. **Materialism** claims that matter is the only reality, while **idealism** claims that it is mental. (Chap. 2)

Monotheism—The belief that there is only one God.

Moral relativism—See **Relativism**.

Naive realism—The belief that the properties we perceive objects to have are the properties that they really do have in the external world. (Chap. 20)

Naturalism—The metaphysical position that claims that physical nature encompasses everything that is real and that all of reality can be completely explained by the natural sciences. (Chap. 33)

Naturalistic fallacy—The fallacy of attempting to derive ethical claims (what we ought to do) from factual claims (what is the case). (Chap. 32)

Natural law—In ethics, the claim that there is an objective moral law, transcending human conventions, which may be discerned by examining human nature. (Chaps. 3, 6, 10, 11)

Natural theology—A discipline within philosophy that attempts to prove conclusions about God based on our natural reason and experience without appealing to revelation. (Chap. 11)

Nihilism—From the Latin word for nothing; the belief that there is no knowledge or truth and, particularly, that nothing has any genuine value, meaning, or purpose. (Chap. 27)

Nominalism—The claim that there are no real, independently existing **universals** and that uni-

versal terms refer only to collections of particular things. See **Conceptualism**, **Realism**. (Chaps. 10, 12, 14, 20)

Noumena—Things as they really are in themselves, as opposed to how they appear in experience. Kant claimed that the noumena were unknowable. They are the opposite of **appearances** or **phenomena**. (Chaps. 22, 23)

Occasionalism—The claim that there is no causal relationship between mental events and physical events, but that certain mental events always seem to occur simultaneously with certain physical events only because the occurrence of one is the occasion on which God produces the other. (Chap. 15)

Ockham's razor—The principle that our explanations should always be as simple as possible, avoiding the postulation of unnecessary entities. Named after William of Ockham (c. 1270–1350), whose formulation of this principle was very influential, particularly in scientific methodology. (Chap. 12)

Ontological argument—An argument for the existence of God based on the concept of God's perfection and unsurpassable greatness. The argument was defended by Anselm, Descartes, Spinoza, and Leibniz and attacked by Kant, among others. (Chaps. 10, 15, 16, 22)

Ontology—The study of the generic features of being, as opposed to the study of the particular things that exist. Ontology is concerned with questions such as "What is most fundamentally real?" "What does it mean to exist?" and "What is the structure of reality?" Some writers virtually identify ontology and **metaphysics**, while others view it as a subdivision of metaphysics. Other philosophers, such as Heidegger and Sartre, distinguish their ontology from metaphysics in order to avoid the latter's association with questions about God, substance, and the origin of the universe. (Chap. 33)

Panentheism—The belief that God's being includes that of the world but is not limited to it. (Chap. 31)

Panpsychism—A form of **idealism** that maintains that all of reality consists of multiple centers of experience, such as minds or souls, who have various degrees of awareness. Leibniz called them "monads," and Whitehead referred to them as "actual occasions." (Chaps. 17, 31)

Pantheism—The belief that God and the world are identical. (Chap. 16)

Parallelism—The claim that there is no direct causal relationship between mental and physical events, but that the two series run parallel to each other. Essentially the same as Leibniz's **pre-established harmony** doctrine. (Chap. 15)

Phenomena—Things as they appear within experience, in contrast to how they are in reality. Kant said that this is all that we could know about the world. They are the opposite of **noumena**. (Chaps. 22, 23)

Phenomenalism—The doctrine that all statements about material objects can be completely analyzed into statements about sense data without making reference to any reality external to sensation. This position is the contrary of **representative realism**. (Chap. 20)

Phenomenology—The attempt to describe the structure and contents of consciousness in a way that is free of presuppositions and that does not go beyond what appears to consciousness. Versions were set out by Hegel, Husserl, and Heidegger. (Chaps. 24, 33)

Pluralism—The metaphysical position that claims that there are many kinds of reality. (Chap. 2)

Positivism—The view that all knowledge claims must be limited to observable facts, that only science provides genuine knowledge, and that the role of philosophy is to apply the findings of the sciences to problems of human conduct and social organization. Positivism rejects all metaphysical claims and any inquiry not reducible to scientific method. Advocated by Auguste Comte and John Stuart Mill. The movement was a predecessor of **logical positivism**. (Chap. 28)

Postmodernism—A movement that arose in the late twentieth century, that was influenced by Nietzsche and Heidegger and that embraces **relativism** and **historicism**. Postmodernists seek to unmask what they consider to be the pretensions of reason and the illusions of metaphysics. They repudiate the Enlightenment ideal of seeking for objective, rational truth and they replace the no-tion of one, true picture of reality with that of multiple, ongoing interpretations. Postmodernism has been particularly influential in literary studies. (Chap. 34)

Pragmatism—A philosophy that stresses the intimate relationship between thought and action. Pragmatists claim, for example, that the meaning of a concept is identical to the practical effects of the object of our conception. Likewise, a true belief is defined as one that will effectively guide action in the long run. (Chap. 30)

Pre-established harmony—The doctrine that events in the world, particularly the activities of the mind and body, do not causally interact, but have been arranged by God from the beginning of time to work in unison like two independent clocks that keep the same time. Leibniz was its most important proponent. (Chap. 17)

Primary qualities—Those qualities of an object that may be represented mathematically such as size, shape, number, quantity, motion, and location. According to Galileo and the early modern philosophers, such as Descartes and Locke, primary qualities represent the world as it really is. Contrasted with **secondary qualities**. (Chaps. 13, 15, 19)

Psychological egoism—See **Egoism**.

Psychological hedonism—See **Hedonism**.

Rationalism—The theory that at least some knowledge is obtained by the mind independently of experience. (Chaps. 2, 4, 13, 15, 16, 17)

Realism—(1) In its contemporary usage, the thesis that reality exists independently of our consciousness of it, in contrast to **idealism**. (2) In ancient and medieval thought: (a) Platonic or extreme realism refers to the claim that **universals** have an objective, independent existence apart from the minds that know them or the individuals that exemplify them; (b) moderate realism claims that universals are abstracted by the mind from objective features of individuals, but that they do not have any reality apart from minds or individuals. (This is sometimes called Aristotelian realism or equated with **conceptualism**.) All medieval versions of realism are in opposition to **nominalism**. (Chap. 10, 32)

Relativism—(1) In epistemology, the claim that there is no absolute knowledge, because different individuals, cultures, or historical periods have different opinions on the truth and all opinions are equally valid. (2) Likewise, in ethics, the claim that there are no objective moral truths, for all moral judgments are said to be relative to the knowing subject and equally correct. (Chaps. 3, 4)

Representative realism—The epistemological claim that the mind is directly acquainted only with its own ideas, but that these ideas are caused by and represent objects external to the mind. (Chap. 19)

Scholasticism—The dominant philosophy of the medieval period in which logic was used to demonstrate the harmony of philosophy and the authoritative writings of the religious tradition. (Chap. 10)

Secondary qualities—According to the early modern philosophers, these are the subjective sensations (colors, tastes, odors, sounds, temperature) produced within us by the **primary qualities** of an object. (Chaps. 13, 15, 19)

Sense data—A term used to refer to the particular, individual impressions received in sensation, such as particular colors, tastes, sounds, odors, and textures. Reference to sense data need not presuppose anything about their cause. (Chap. 32)

Skepticism—The claim that it is impossible to know anything to be absolutely true. (Chaps. 2, 3, 6, 21)

Social contract theory—The theory that the justification of government is based on an explicit or implicit agreement made by individuals among themselves or with a sovereign power (Hobbes, Locke, and Rousseau). (Chaps. 3, 14, 19)

Solipsism—The view that nothing can be known apart from my self and the contents of my conscious experience, usually leading to the conclusion that "only I exist." Finding solipsism to be implausible, philosophers such as Descartes were motivated to find demonstrations of the external world or other minds. (Chaps. 15, 20)

Sophists—A group of educators in fifth-century Athens who taught the skills of rhetoric and argumentation, usually to prepare people for political careers. Most of the Sophists were advocates of **skepticism** and **relativism**. (Chap. 3)

Sound argument—A deductive argument that is (1) **valid** and (2) has all true premises. (Introduction chapter)

Stoicism—The view that we will find happiness only if we resign ourselves to accept whatever may happen in life. Historically, this view was based on the belief that the universe is fulfilling the benevolent purposes of divine providence and that every event is inevitable. (Chap. 6)

Substance—A fundamental and independently existing reality that supports or underlies the various qualities or properties we perceive. Various philosophers who believe in substances disagree over how many kinds there are and what sorts of things qualify as substances. The concept was particularly important in the philosophies of the Pre-Socratics, Aristotle, Descartes, Spinoza, Leibniz, and Locke. (Chaps. 2, 5, 15, 16, 17, 19, 21, 22)

Synthetic judgment—A knowledge claim expressed by a **synthetic statement**. (Chap. 22)

Synthetic statement—A statement in which the predicate adds information to the subject that is not logically contained within it and in which its denial (even if false) does not result in a logical contradiction, e.g., "All mothers are under fifty feet tall" is a synthetic statement. Contrasted with **analytic statements**. (Chap. 22)

Tautology—A statement that is true because of its logical form; e.g., "X is identical to X." (Chap. 32)

Teleological argument—An argument for the existence of God based on the evidence of purpose and design in the world; e.g., Aquinas's fifth argument for God. (Chap. 11)

Teleological ethics—Any ethical theory that defines moral rightness or wrongness in terms of the desirability or undesirability of an action's consequences. Contrasted with **deontological ethics**. (Chaps. 11, 22, 28)

Teleological explanation—An explanation of an event or thing in terms of the end, goal, or purpose it tends to achieve. (Chaps. 4, 13)

Teleology (or teleological)—From the Greek word *telos*, meaning "purpose" or "end." A teleological metaphysics claims that nature exhibits purpose; i.e., events in the world are directed to the fulfillment of some goal. (Chaps. 4, 5, 11)

Theism—The belief that there is one God, who transcends the world.

Things-in-themselves—According to Kant, the contents of reality as they are, independent of the mind's apprehension of them. Identical to the **noumena**. (Chap. 22)

Transcendental—Refers to conditions within the knower which makes knowledge or action possible. Kant's critical philosophy tried to set out the transcendental conditions that enable us to be knowers and agents. (Chap. 22)

Universal—(1) Any general term or concept that refers to a number of particular things that are members of the same group; e.g., "human" is a universal that applies to each member of the human race. Since the time of Plato, there has been a controversy as to whether universals exist in reality, or whether they are mere concepts or words. See **Conceptualism**, **Nominalism**, and **Realism**. (Chap. 4, 10) (2) As an adjective, it designates that which applies to all persons, at all times, in all circumstances, e.g., universal truths, universal moral rules. (Chap. 4, 22)

Utilitarianism—A theory of ethics and a political philosophy built around the claim that a good action is one that creates the greatest amount of good for the greatest number over any other alternative action. (Chap. 28)

Valid argument—A successful deductive argument whose form is such that if the premises are true, the conclusion necessarily must be true. (Introduction chapter)

Verifiability principle—The criterion of meaning developed by the **logical positivists** stating that (1) a factual statement has **cognitive meaning** only if sense experience can provide evidence of its truth and (2) the experiences that would demonstrate its truth are identical to its meaning. (Chap. 32, 34)

Voluntarism—The theory that the will is prior to or superior to the intellect or reason. Accordingly, reason is viewed as merely an instrument for achieving the ends or goals that the will voluntarily chooses. Theological voluntarism claims that God declares an action to be morally good or evil solely on the basis of his free choice, for he is not compelled to do so because of any intrinsic property in the action itself. The opposite of **intellectualism**. (Chap. 10, 12)

INDEX